FALLEN ANGELS

FALLEN ANGELS

The Lives and Untimely Deaths of Fourteen Hollywood Beauties

KIRK CRIVELLO

Citadel Press
Secaucus, New Jersey

Published by Citadel Press
A division of Lyle Stuart Inc.
120 Enterprise Ave., Secaucus, N.J. 07094
In Canada: Musson Book Company
A division of General Publishing Co. Limited
Don Mills, Ontario

Queries regarding rights and permission should be
addressed to: Lyle Stuart, 120 Enterprise Avenue,
Secaucus, N.J. 07094

Manufactured in the United States of America

Library of Congress Cataloging-in-Publication Data

Crivello, Kirk.
        Fallen Angels : the lives and untimely deaths of fourteen
    Hollywood beauties / Kirk Crivello.
            p.   cm.
        ISBN 0-8065-1096-X : $18.95
        1. Motion picture actors and actresses--United States--Biography.
    2. Actresses--United States--Biography. 3. Motion picture industry--
    California--Los Angeles--Employees--Case studies. 4. Violent
    deaths--Case studies. 5. Hollywood (Los Angeles, Calif.)--
    Biography. I. Title. II. Title: Untimely deaths of fourteen
    Hollywood beauties.
    PN1998.2.C75   1988
    791.43'028'0922--dc 19
        [B]   88-25733
                                                                  CIP

Dedicated to
KENNETH MACDONALD
And to the Memory of
JORGE SAMANIEGO

ACKNOWLEDGMENTS

I am deeply grateful to the many who have assisted and contributed valuable reminiscences. Many thanks to each of you: Mara Corday Long, George Russell, Sheilah Wells, the late Milton Lewis, Richard Quine, Fran Jeffries, Rory Calhoun, Natalie Kelley Grasko, June Lang, Judith Woodbury, David Chierichetti, Mamie Van Doren, Mariska Hargitay, Raymond Strait, Marguerite Chapman, Lawrence J. Quirk, Beverly Thompson, William Travilla, Allan "Whitey" Snyder, Kathleen O'Malley, Richard Lamparski, Beverly Linet, Ken Murray, the late Jody Lawrance, May Mann, Mary Castle, Henry Koster, Betty Jane Howarth, George Eells, Hal Gefsky, the late Claire James, Samson DeBrier, Bebe Goddard, Ronald Tonkins, Charles K. Stumpf, James Brent Dunsford, Teresa Seeger, Larry Kleno, Don Bain, Lou Valentino, Betty Henry, Gloria Davis, James Robert Parish, Andrew J. Fenady, Frank Edwards, Judy Karl Anderson, James Haspiel, Mary Winters, Sabin Gray, Leonard Maltin, Donna O'Connor, Kay Marvis Marx, Evelyn Moriarty, Mary Miller, JoAnne Sherlock, Gene Ringgold, Gavin Lambert, Carol Young, Richard Hudson, John Roberts, Buck Rainey, Roy K. Windham, Greg Schreiner, Lee Graham, Steven Ochoa, Sugar Geise, Devron Conrad, Tina Scala, Jacqueline Virla, Ralph Benner, Michael Szymanski, Dore Freeman, Robert Cotney, Sandy Davis, Lois Laurel Hawes, Tony Hawes, Jayne Quinn, Bill Chapman, Douglas J. Hart's Back Lot, Ray Gain, Eddie Colbert, Yani Begakis, Clair Peterson, Arthur C. Peterson, Darlene Hammond, Rick Carl, Jay Joringson, Movie Star News (Paula Klaw), and Eddie Brandt's Saturday Matinee.

To Don Lee Miller, who has worked closely with me since the project's inception. A special thanks to John Cocchi, Doug McClelland and Jim Meyer for their invaluable assistance and encouragement. I owe a special debt of gratitude to Sam Gill of the Department of Special Collections, Academy of Motion Pictures, for allowing me access to the personal scrapbooks of Gail Russell. To Leith Adams for his generosity in giving me access to the Warner Bros. archives at the

University of Southern California. I also wish to acknowledge information gleaned from the many books and periodicals consulted during the preparation of the manuscript.

Unlimited help was furnished by the staffs of the following organizations: The Academy of Motion Picture Arts and Sciences, Beverly Hills; West Hollywood Library; Lincoln Center Library of the Performing Arts, New York City; The British Film Institute, London; and UCLA Theatre Arts Library, Westwood Village, Calif. Special thanks to the following studios for the use of photographs: Universal Pictures, Warner Brothers, Columbia Pictures, Metro-Goldwyn-Mayer, RKO Radio Pictures, Twentieth Century-Fox, Paramount Pictures, Republic Pictures Corporation and United Artists Corporation.

CONTENTS

Contents

Helen Walker
Dorothy Abbott
Joan Tabor
Carol Thurston
Suzanne Dalbert
Pier Angeli
Bella Darvi
Peggie Castle
Judith Rawlins
Barbara Colby
Georgia Davis
Allison Hayes

Maggie McNamara
Claudia Jennings
Vicki Morgan
Dorothy Stratten
Jenny Maxwell
Brenda Benet
Dominique Dunne
Sunny Johnson
Carol Wayne
Samantha Smith
Elizabeth Hartman
Heather O'Rourke

INTRODUCTION

Tragedy and beauty, that paradoxical combination, are no strangers to Hollywood. Both the movie industry and its environment have their legends. Death, particularly at one's prime, has been "standard operating procedure" in the movie colony since drug-addicted Olive Thomas's mysterious death by poison in Paris (1920) made headlines around the world. The violet-eyed actress, whom artist Harrison Fisher called "The Most Beautiful Woman in the World," was only 25. Hollywood has always been viewed cynically by educated members of society because it indiscriminately glorifies our mass fantasies and myths.

The star is often someone who believes the fantasies of the star system more intensely than anyone else and therefore becomes a very willing participant in the perpetuation of the myth. The situation is not something that is forced upon them, it is something they crave, also allowing an outlet for their inate narcissism. They seldom anticipate the problems that achieving their goals will unavoidably create. In a town where it is difficult to exercise a sense of perspective, where the publicity machine is at the same time its backbone and its most vulgarizing feature, it's not hard to lose control of one's self and career. An old story that has become all too familiar.

They had, it seems, everything to live for—beauty, fame, wealth and limitless opportunities. Everything going for them. And nothing. Born with natural beauty, many were unable to handle the public spotlight thrust upon them through no wish of their own, while a few sported overdeveloped egos or a case of galloping ambition. Most of them became rebellious, troubled, unsatisfied, always seeking that which they did not possess. At the point when they did possess it, they were to learn it wasn't what they wanted after all. Their facades cracked, leaving them splintered like glass in drugs, alcohol, scandal, misguided passion, suicide and even murder.

There are differences, of course. The complex Marilyn Monroe died at the height of her charismatic magnetism of alcohol-abetted emotional confusion. While Carole Landis called it quits because of a desolated romance and the deep fears of fading youth and diminishing stardom. Some, like the frail Susan Peters, died of that despair of the spirit which the newspapers often refer to as "a broken heart." The drowning accident of Natalie Wood stunned the movie colony and shocked an entire nation. Jayne Mansfield's decline was mirrored in and by her last film efforts. Life beat pathetic Barbara Payton up pretty badly, yet she carried with her a reckless bravery. The delicate Barbara Bates died of self-inflicted wounds that took several years to accumulate. The screen's "Joan of Arc," Jean Seberg won a fair reputation for her tragically self-destructive behavior. Gia Scala was so gifted and beautiful—and yet so messed up. Inger Stevens was self-taught in the school of hard knocks. Marie McDonald, known as "The Body," was like an alluringly vulnerable prop that never overcame her self-willed creation. Sad-eyed Gail Russell paid the hard costs of alcoholism and ruined romantic faith. The murder of Sharon Tate was the perfect example of the American Dream gone sour. These victims of doom share a closeness and an immediacy of observation.

There could be enough written on so many ill-fated actresses to make a book twice this length. The sometimes dark and sad lives of Jean Harlow, Carole Lombard, Lupe Velez, Frances Farmer, Linda Darnell, Dorothy Dandridge, Judy Garland, and Maria Montez have been documented by others. The heartbreaking, compassionate study of lesser personalities are compiled within the final chapter, providing, a powerful, intriguing glimpse into the frequent high cost of early fame. They, too, suffered through a life of triumph and tragedy and deserve an exploration of their brief moment of glory. The list seems endless.

With few exceptions (Marilyn Monroe, Jayne Mansfield, Natalie Wood, Jean Seberg), the aim of this book is: to present a

collection of actresses whose paralleled stories have been somewhat overlooked by other film historians, to detail their film accomplishments, and to ponder their eventual downfall. They
too have paid a high price. Their lives were all to be wrecked by
Hollywood, driven to despair by the obliterating glare of fame
and, for some, the fear that this glare was vanishing. Certainly,
there were, indeed, other aspects to their problems; in almost
every case, Hollywood, the industry, bore the brunt of the
blame, with its glossy facade of celluloid adulation that helped
to destroy each of these victimized heroines.

FALLEN ANGELS

GAIL RUSSELL

The dreamy, sapphire blue eyes of Gail Russell took on a deep and brooding sadness. By the early 1950s, the roller coaster film career of the raven-haired "Hedy Lamarr of Santa Monica" had just about burned itself out. The media coverage was partially to blame for Gail's problems just as it was crucial to her publicized rise to overnight Hollywood stardom. The velvety-voiced, vulnerable actress seemed so magical, and serious about her work. Somewhere underneath the mask was an incredible dark fear. "I was possessed with an agonizing kind of self-consciousness where I felt my insides tightening into a knot, where my face and hands grew clammy, where I couldn't open my mouth, where I felt impelled to turn and run if I had to meet new people," she once said. The press began portraying her as a "hard luck actress" bent on self-destruction. When her acting jobs became scarce, Gail returned to her first love, painting. But by then, booze became the center of her being, an easy escape for her terrifying shyness and she eventually lost touch. It was purely a case of being trapped in a profession that had conflicting demands and being unable to compete.

Gail Russell was born in Chicago, Illinois, on September 23, 1924 (or 1921), to Gladys and George Harrison Russell. Her brother George (five years older), became a musician and played with a trio, The Three Bachelors. Much of Gail's childhood was spent on her uncle's farm in Michigan. It was yet another version of the old Hollywood myth—the mother who had wanted to be an actress and couldn't pursue it, then wanting her daughter to have the fame she was denied. Her mother, Gladys, was from a small town in Pike County, Illinois, one of seven children. She was an orphan at nine. When, as a teenager, she moved to Chicago, she found work selling California fruit in a market near the old Essanay Studios. It wasn't long before she was offered a screen test. In fear of taking time off from her job, she declined the offer. When Gladys met George Russell in Peoria, he was playing clarinet in an orchestra, but soon after they married he became an auto insurance salesman.

At five, Gail started sketching. At seven, she was drawing cartoons. At ten, she wanted oil paints and began to work in that medium. "It was a happy childhood and musical," Gail told Hedda Hopper. "My father played just about everything— piano, the clarinet, banjo and guitar. We lived in a tiny South Side, Hyde Park apartment complex. I played bass drum, my brother, a guitar, and Dad, the violin." In another interview, Gail would remember, "Dad used to tell me that I could be anything, anything I wanted to be, but I thought he was saying that because he loved me."

Plagued throughout her life with an agonizing kind of self-consciousness, she spent most of her after-school hours in her room, sketching and painting. Gail once recalled those years, "Until I was twelve, I was so shy you couldn't get me to open my mouth! When my parents had guests, I would run, get under the piano and hide there. Whenever I had to recite lessons or speak pieces in school, I behaved like an imbecile. Or I didn't show up." Sometimes she used to roller skate over to the Picadilly Theatre to see her idol, Ginger Rogers, in a musical. In fact, Gail had four large scrapbooks full of articles and pictures of the star.

It was Gail, then twelve, who helped to make the decision to move to California instead of to Florida. The family first settled in Glendale where Gail attended Wilson Junior High. Her first ambition was to be a commercial artist, not an actress. Then the family decided to move back to Chicago for a short time. But they soon returned to California and settled in Santa Monica, then moved to Van Nuys, where Mr. Russell was employed by Lockheed Aircraft, and brother George went into the Army. Gail told *Movie Stars Parade* magazine: "On my first day at Van Nuys High School, being the shy type, I was quite bewildered by all the new faces, all the activity. At the first roll call, the name Russell was announced, and a firm young voice answered, 'Here!' Timidly, I echoed, 'Here.' The Russell who owned the other voice turned out to be Jane. I can remember how she looked that day—healthy, wholesome—even then wearing her future husband Bob Waterfield's sweater—which, incidentally, reached almost to her knees! She was so different from me, extroverted, confident, friendly. She took me in tow, taught me the ropes, and helped me so much—in ways she never knew. I wouldn't have missed her friendship for the world." Jane Russell was born in 1921 and graduated from Van Nuys High School in 1939, three years before Gail joined Paramount Pictures. In a *Screenland* magazine interview, Gail would confess her real age: ". . . But if I am to be autobiographical, I must begin at the beginning, mustn't I? Well, I was born in Chicago, on September 21, 1921. I tell my real age now." When brother George Russell was asked if September 23, 1924, was the correct date of birth, he said, "It sounds right." At any event, Gail's tombstone marker reads simply 1924-1961.

Paramount Pictures publicity forces would claim that in March, 1942, studio executive William Meiklejohn gave two teenage boys, Charles Chase and Charlie Bates, a ride to Balboa Beach. They began to rave about a classmate of theirs at University High School, known on the campus as "The Hedy Lamarr of Santa Monica." Meiklejohn sent a memo to Milton Lewis (head of new talent at Paramount) to contact Gail through the school, and arrange an appointment with her and her mother. Meanwhile, Gail was attending Santa Monica Tech, and was studying commercial art. Contrary to Paramount publicity over the years that she graduated from University High or Santa Monica High, Gail once said she never completed high school. Shortly before his death in 1986, a frail Milton Lewis remembered there was some difficulty in locating her. A phone message was placed on Gail's desk at Santa Monica Tech: "Please call Milton Lewis at Paramount Studios regarding screen test. HO 2411, Ex. 642. Please call as soon as possible. L.G." Gail thought the note was a schoolmate playing a practical joke. She balked at going to the Paramount interview and was seemingly unimpressed. "Mother," she admitted, "practically dragged me there. I had just applied for a job with Bullock's-Wilshire department store," Gail's mother, knowing of her daughter introverted nature, said, "It is difficult even for me to understand how it is possible for Gail to be an actress."

The late Milton Lewis became sentimental when he spoke about that initial meeting. "A lovely girl who didn't belong in the movie industry. I believe she would have had a happy life had she become a commercial artist instead of a movie actress. I never doubted that the studio wouldn't okay a contract. Gail had that very special star-like quality mixed with artistic sensitivity. I knew it the minute she walked into my office. About three days later, Gail responded well to direction in her test (a scene from MGM's *Love Finds Andy Hardy*) for my assistant, Bill Russell. She was radiant to look at, with a touch of mystery about her. William Meiklejohn was tremendously impressed." On July 17, 1942, Gail was signed to a seven-year contract which provided for annual raises or revisions and a starting salary of $50 a week. Following the advice of Paramount, she obtained the services of Myron Selznick, the high-powered agent brother of David O. Selznick.

Paramount was enthusiastic about Gail's movie potential, and assigned her to her first film, *Henry Aldrich Gets Glamour* (1943). She was the high school vamp who steals Jimmy Lydon away from his steady girl, Diana Lynn. The *Henry Aldrich* series was a training ground for many young Paramount players, much as the *Andy Hardy* series was at Metro-Goldwyn-Mayer. Gail said, "The first time I ever danced with a boy in my life was with William Blees in a scene we did for *Henry Aldrich Gets Glamour*, my first picture. That was the first time I ever wore high heels, too. I'd never been to a dance before. When someone would ask me, I'd lock myself in my room with a book and eat graham crackers."

Gail once discussed *Henry Aldrich Gets Glamour*, "The first day I sat on the sidelines, trembling. I was so scared," she said. "I'd never done any acting, except for my screen test. Thanks to my drama coach, Bill Russell, I was able to get through it." The *Hollywood Reporter* stated: "A flash that will count is registered by Gail Russell as the town belle most impressed by Henry's Hollywood conquest. You'll be hearing from Gail Russell."

Gail and Diana Lynn spent every Wednesday evening entertaining servicemen at the Hollywood Canteen. One evening,

Gail met her look-alike Hedy Lamarr there. Said the Metro-Goldwyn-Mayer star as they shook hands, "Miss Russell, you should be in the movies." Flustered, an awesome Gail replied, "So should you." Gail asked for an autograph and added it to her scrapbook. Paramount encouraged the budding starlet to date young players, among them Jimmy Lydon, Freddie Bartholomew and Bill Edwards. Studio voice coaches taught her to use her voice to a deeper and impressively sexier level. Though scheduled for various 1942-43 productions, Gail did not appear in *Henry Aldrich Haunts a House, Let's Face It* or *Tornado*. She was being considered for the Jean Heather role in Bing Crosby's movie about the priesthood, *Going My Way*, then entitled *The Padre*.

Instead, Gail was cast in the bizarrely ornate film of the stage hit *Lady in the Dark* (1944) that failed to live up to its potential. Gail was Ginger Rogers' rival who entices Rand Brooks away from her. As a musical, it isn't much, but as a tour-de-force of visual style, the film is startling, outrageous and artistic. Ginger Rogers was still Gail's favorite movie actress. In 1941, Gail and her mother attended the Santa Anita races and saw the actress in a box. On the set, when they met, Rogers was amused that Gail could describe in detail the dress she had worn that day. In David Chierichetti's biography of Mitchell Leisen, the director described his recollections of working with Gail: "Ginger insisted we use Gail Russell as Barbara, the girl who steals Liza's boyfriend right after she sang "My Ship." The poor girl was gorgeous, but she had hysterics every time the camera started to turn. She only had a couple of lines, but it took us almost two days to get them shot. Ginger felt so sorry for her that she tried to work with her and help her as much as she could. She was really a neurotic character and I'm not surprised she became an alcoholic."

Ginger Rogers taught Gail the Charleston for the dance scene. "After that, we used to talk about art, between scenes on the set," said Gail. "And about music. And books. I drew cartoons of Ginger and she put them in the mirror in her dressing room. Ginger was, so to speak, the turning point in relaxing me." Ginger took such an interest in the complex young actress that she told Paramount production chief Buddy DeSylva that the girl was worthy of important assignments.

When Ginger moved across the Paramount lot to RKO Studios to film *Tender Comrade*, Gail was invited to share Ginger's on-the-set 32nd birthday party with co-stars Robert Ryan, Ruth Hussey, Kim Hunter and director Edward Dmytryk.

From the pages of Gail's scrapbook, Ginger Rogers wrote on stationery, engraved GRB (she had just married Jack Briggs): "My dear Gail: How's my favorite pupil? You're the right kind of pupil to have as I don't have to do anything about it but address you as such—anyway, we can pretend can't we? I just loved the drawing you enclosed in your note. You are a darn clever girl and if you aren't careful you're going to have so many accomplishments you aren't going to know which one to enjoy. As for that laugh, you are definitely going to get one—my nose is sunburned and I have so many freckles I look like a bowl of cornflakes. You tell those people at Paramount they had better treat you right or I shall conjure up some thunder, they'll never forget. Tell them they should give you a pretty dressing room as they should start spoiling you right away. After you've worked too hard, it then becomes difficult to appreciate spoiling. Be good—and bless you. Affectionately, Ginger."

Drama coach William Russell worked with Gail for six months perfecting a British accent for the role as the haunted heroine in *The Uninvited* (1944). Through the combined efforts of Bill Russell, leading man Ray Milland, and the director, Lewis Allen, studio executive Buddy DeSylva was persuaded to take a calculated risk and cast Gail in the role of Stella. Paramount had been coaching seventeen-year-old Gwen Carter under a test option for the role until she suddenly eloped with Donald O'Connor and abandoned her career.

Dorothy Macardle's popular novel, *Uneasy Freehold*, was about two very real ghosts who haunt an old, mist-shrouded mansion set high on the edge of rugged cliffs on the Cornish Coast of England. Gail was the granddaughter of Donald Crisp, who owns Windward House, the deserted house that Milland and Ruth Hussey want to purchase. Cornelia Otis Skinner played her mother's deranged, mysterious confidant. "Introducing the exciting beauty of Paramount's new star, Gail Russell whose first love is shadowed by the spectres of the past," the ads read. *The Uninvited* firmly established Gail as a movie star and brought on immediate pressures. The handsomely mounted film has been called the *Casablanca* of Hollywood's ghost genre. *Variety* confided: "As the girl involved in this eerie drama, which has been told so simply and yet so forcefully, Gail Russell displays dramatic talents which assure her place in the star firmament. She has youth, beauty, loveliness of a kind the screen is crying for, and she possesses the presence of a veteran actress." The New York *Post* said: "Any man who would not fight a couple of ghosts for Gail Russell, and thank her for the privilege, is missing something." Composer Victor Young's noteworthy score, including the classic, "Stella By Starlight," is forever associated with Gail.

Gail's highly publicized "paralyzed with fright" state while filming *The Uninvited* climaxed in a nervous breakdown by the time the film was completed. The studio hushed it up, and arranged for a three-week stay at the Camel Back Inn in Phoenix, Arizona, accompanied by girlfriend Carmelita Lopez. A Scandinavian-Mexican blond beauty, Carmelita did some minor parts at Paramount and eventually married studio executive Mel Epstein. Early in Gail's career, whenever squabbles occurred in the Russell household, she would move in with the Lopez family. Mr. Lopez was an assistant cameraman at Twentieth Century-Fox.

Paramount sent Gail on her first trip to New York for magazine interviews, fashion and photo layouts. Once again, Hollywood had successfully launched a legend.

The studio next placed Gail as Cornelia Otis Skinner, with Diana Lynn as Emily Kimbrough, in *Our Hearts Were Young and Gay* (1944). The comedy was based on Skinner and Kimbrough's autobiography of their girlhood friendship and 1920s European frolics. It lacked some of the knowing charm of the book, but it's flapper-era look is still appealing. The irresistible charm of the young stars enchanted audiences and reviewers alike. Diana Lynn had encouraged Gail to go after the role. Gail wrote in a by-lined article in the *Saturday Evening Post* (May 27, 1950): "Diana Lynn practically pushed me into the role of Cornelia Otis Skinner . . . she decided that I must play Cornelia."

From her New York apartment, Cornelia Otis Skinner wrote Gail on August 10, 1944, "Dear Gail: Thanks so much for letting me see a copy of the story that's to be published by Movieland magazine. It's most interesting and I like it very much. I attended a private showing of *Our Hearts Were Young and Gay* and I think it's excellent and you're charming in it. I'm sorry I did not see you when you were in New York, but when you come back again do get in touch with me. See you again. Affectionately, Cornelia."

All of a sudden Gail Russell was a star. But the truth of the matter was she was a frightened girl who needed courage to face up to being famous. A quick drink now and then gave her courage to face the cameras and all the attention. Gail's sets were closed to all visitors. Directors had to rant and rave over countless rehearsals, countless retakes. In time, the drinking would increase in her dressing room between takes. The studio was very understanding toward Gail's problem—that is, until in later years it became uncontrollable and interfered with her work.

Paramount cast her in *The Unseen* (1945), which obviously was intended to be another *The Uninvited*. This time Joel McCrea was a widower who appoints Gail to look after his two children in a mysterious house after their last two governesses were murdered. It was a first-rate suspense yarn based on Ethel Lina While's novel, *Her Heart In Her Throat*. Gail next joined Alan Ladd in *Salty O'Rourke* (1945). Ladd's a smooth tough-guy aiming to clean up a pugnacious jockey, Stanley Clements, who has a crush on schoolteacher Gail. In this racetrack script, Ladd kept his status as the studio's top ranking box-office star.

In Paramount's star-clustered *Duffy's Tavern* (1945), Gail joined Helen Walker and Jean Heather, accompanying Bing Crosby in a satirical rendition of "Swinging on a Star." Numerous Paramount players made guest appearances in this comedy about bar preservation, based on the popular radio show. Gail's ex-drama coach, William Russell, directed her and Diana Lynn in *Our Hearts Were Growing Up* (1946), a moderately amusing sequel to *Our Hearts Were Young and Gay*, with James Brown and Bill Edwards repeating their original roles as the girls' beaus. Gail and Diana are attending a big Princeton football weekend and end up with bootleggers, Brian Donlevy and William Demarest, as their most unwilling chaperones. By the time of this film, the actresses were such close friends that they insisted upon using the same dressing room.

In 1945, Gail met 23-year-old Guy Madison in the offices of coach Lester Luther. The future teen heartthrob was just beginning his career, and Gail was already a star. She wasn't all that impressed by the husky blond sailor. A few months later, they met again at a dinner party at the home of Henry Willson. This time it was a different story—Gail finally met someone she genuinely cared about, not a studio-arranged escort. The chemistry was right between them, and Gail fell in love with Guy Madison. Willson was the legendary talent scout for David O. Selznick, and his ballyhooed engagement to Diana Lynn was in actuality an "arrangement of convenience" staged by the Paramount and Selznick publicity offices. He was a homosexual who had a phenomenal knack for discovering extraordinary looking young talent with no previous acting experience and molding them into stars. Sara Davidson wrote in *Rock Hudson, His Story*: "Henry Willson was a notorious homosexual. He had an entourage of young men who accompanied him to nightclubs and came to his house in Stone Canyon for swimming parties. Willson was not attractive. He was short, with a soft chin and flaccid body, a prominent nose and receding frizzy hair. . . . But Willson was brilliant at spotting talent and launching careers."

Gail dropped out of *The Virginian*, the third remake of the Owen Wister tale about the age-old Western struggle between ranchers and rustlers. Paramount then assigned Barbara Britton to play opposite Joel McCrea and Brian Donlevy. It proved to be the studio's least successful remake of Wister's resilient classic. United Artists borrowed Gail for *The Bachelor's Daughters* (1946) instead. She was one of four salesgirls (with Claire Trevor, Ann Dvorak and Jane Wyatt) who fake a wealthy background in order to snare well-heeled husbands. It was another variation of the *Moon Over Miami* plot and its many remakes. Gail next moved over to Republic as John Wayne's Quaker girlfriend who converts the gunfighter criminal to a peaceable life in the expensively-mounted Western *The Angel and the Badman* (1947). The *Los Angeles Reader* wrote: "One of the strongest aspects of James Edward Grant's script and realization is his conception of the Quaker girl; no stereotype, she rejects the idea of violence but expresses a disarmingly healthy attitude toward sex. Wayne and the hauntingly beautiful Russell have a wonderful rapport, and the most interesting sequences are intimate ones."

A melange of murder and espionage from Chungking to Calcutta had a wicked Gail as the arch villainess who remains unrevealed until the last few reels of *Calcutta* (1947). It found Alan Ladd avenging his co-pilot buddy William Bendix's murder. Gail was terrific, playing against type as the cold-blooded killer and brains of a giant international jewel smuggling ring. Wrote Alain Silver and Elizabeth Ward in *Film Noir*: "Paramount alternated Veronica Lake and Gail Russell as romantic 'damsels in distress' in Ladd's films, but in a shrewd bit of reverse casting, Russell is allowed to play the femme fatale in *Calcutta*, and a nasty one at that. Russell's exotic features, warm manner, and soft voice invariably gave her a connotation of innocence and vulnerability, which were capitalized on in most of her films. By contrast, when Ladd rips a pendant from her neck or slaps her around, it makes him appear all the more impervious to women. Their interaction holds this film together and demonstrates the misogynistic strain of hard-boiled fiction."

Gail began spending a lot of time with *Calcutta* director John Farrow (the husband of Maureen O'Sullivan and father of Mia Farrow). Reportedly, Farrow had been through countless on-set romances in the past, usually ending when the film was completed. The egomaniacal Farrow was notorious in the film industry for having a cruel and sadistic streak in dealing with actors who failed to stand up to him. His macho appeal and put-downs intrigued Gail. Actress Beverly Thompson recalled that Gail, John Farrow, Byron Barr and herself would sometime make a foursome and head for Lucey's, a bar and restaurant near Paramount. It was a popular hangout which drew a regular clientele from both Paramount and RKO players. Beverly remembers Gail would drink in moderation until Farrow would start critically analyzing her work. "Then she would have a few more vodkas," she said. Gail also enjoyed the company of homosexual or bisexual men. She was frequently seen on the Sunset Strip in the company of Billy DeWolfe, John Dall or Johnny Mitchell.

In Paramount's tribute to the Variety Club of America, *Variety Girl* (1947), a galaxy of studio stars was spotlighted, including starstruck hopefuls Mary Hatcher and Olga San Juan, who try to make it in Movieland. Gail's contribution to the all-stops-out extravaganza was in the circus production number on a merry-go-round alongside Gary Cooper. Gail inherited Joan Caulfield's role in the mystery thriller *Night Has a Thousand Eyes* (1948). Edward G. Robinson portrayed a clairvoyant who vainly tries to convince the police that Gail, his daughter whom he had earlier relinquished, will "die under the stars" on a certain day and hour. This is the definitive Russell display, and for a second time she bloomed under John Farrow's loving guidance. Gail never looked so gorgeous as in this absorbing mystery, superbly photographed by John F. Seitz in sleek, slick style. Singer Nat "King" Cole's popular recording of Victor Young's title tune contributed generously to the film's success.

Republic reunited Gail and John Wayne in *Wake of the Red Witch* (1948). Gail was the French commissaire's niece who perishes tragically of an incurable tropical disease mid-way through the sailing adventure but is spiritually reunited with her lover, sea captain Wayne, on the ghostly *Red Witch* after he dies while diving to bring up a sunken treasure in gold. The public heartily endorsed the colossal Garland Roark novel, which became an all-time Republic Pictures grosser. In *Moonrise* (1948), Gail provided one of her best dramatic efforts as the schoolteacher love of troubled Dane Clark. Seemingly condemned to repeat the sins of his father, Clark stumbles into murder, falls into love and hides in the moody backwood swamps. It had the look of the dreamy German impressionist style of the 1930s, overcoming its middling budget. The mythical, often stunning, *Moonrise* was the last in a package of three films that Frank Borzage directed at Republic Pictures.

In February, 1949, Gail and Guy Madison took a one-month holiday, visiting her hometown, Chicago, so that Madison could meet her many relatives. They then proceeded to Florida and sailed on a cruise to Havana, Cuba. There were no Paramount projects awaiting Gail upon her return from Caribbean waters, so Columbia Studios borrowed her for *Song of India* (1949) with Sabu. It was a generally amateurish venture and cast Gail as an East Indian princess on a tiger hunt, but the tight budget was painfully obvious. The cheap-jack production played mainly the lower half of double-bill engagements. The actress returned on Paramount ground with John Payne in *El Paso* (1949), a lame Cinecolor Western produced by the Pine-Thomas unit. Payne comes West to marry his sweetheart, Gail, and clean up a corrupt Texas town in the post-Civil War period. Gail was then coupled with Dennis O'Keefe in United Artists' *The Great Dan Patch* (1949). O'Keefe was unhappily married to snobbish Ruth Warrick and in love with his horse trainer's daughter, Gail. It was evident that her box-office appeal was diminishing.

With a fanfare of publicity, a radiant Gail and Guy Madison were married in Santa Barbara on August 31, 1949, at the posh Biltmore Hotel. Paramount secretary Mary Lou Van Ness was her maid of honor. Gail wore the white gabardine suit designed by Edith Head for the just completed film *Captain China*. The wedding was held in the hotel's lush outdoor courtyard. The couple were married under a white gazebo decorated with yellow roses (Gail's favorite flower). The wedding reception was held on another part of the hotel grounds overlooking the Pacific Ocean. Guests included Mr. and Mrs. Jim Davis and Mr. and Mrs. Howard Hill. Gail's parents and brother did not attend the ceremony. As the wedding festivities came to a close, a beaming Gail told Mary Lou Van Ness, "This is the happiest day of my life." The couple honeymooned in Yosemite National Park.

"I want to make movies with deep heart appeal, to be more than the girl in male stars' action pictures," said Gail. "I'd be delirious if I could become an actress like Olivia de Havilland. My stand-in Aloha Wray was originally hers. Wonder if that signifies anything for my future?" Gail became the perfect wife. She learned to hunt and fish and accompanied Madison on excursions into the High Sierras. Gail did a series of Technicolor tests in a long red wig for the Bing Crosby opus, *A Connecticut Yankee*, which perhaps might have saved her sagging career. The studio assigned Rhonda Fleming the plum role as Lady Alisande.

Captain China (1949) was temporarily withdrawn from theaters by Paramount when several critics pointed out its many similarities to a Columbia film, *Cargo to Capetown*, already in general release. In the rip-roaring adventure, Gail was fought over by John Payne and Jeffrey Lynn. It contained a sensationally effective typhoon sequence which was the real star of this sea yarn. In a 1973 interview, John Payne, who co-starred with Gail in two films, mentioned her as one of his all-time favorite leading ladies.

Gail's final job under her Paramount pact was *The Lawless* (1950), a story of mob violence. She was cast as a Mexican-American reporter who tries to help a Latino immigrant, Lalo Rios, wrongly accused of raping Gloria Winters in a small California town. *Time* magazine observed, "Pretty actress Gail Russell is so good that filmgoers may feel they are seeing her for the first time." Her reviews for *The Lawless* were undoubtedly the best she had ever received during her seven years in films. It was directed by Joseph Losey, who would be blacklisted during the McCarthy era. Doug McClelland wrote in *StarSpeak* what Joseph Losey had to say about working with Gail: "Gail Russell died of alcoholism because she was deathly frightened of acting, but she had in her the makings of a great star. I think she had the most beautiful eyes I have ever seen, the most moving eyes. And she was immensely sensitive. Paramount had her under contract—like a horse. On *The Lawless*, I had absolute instructions from them not to let her have a drink. The first time I shot with her I had a long night-tracking shot. She couldn't remember a single line and it was three or four pages of important dialogue. And she grabbed me—her hands were icy cold, she was absolutely rigid—and she said, 'Look, I don't want to be an actress. I'm not an actress. I can't act. I never had a director who gave me a scene this long before. I can't do it.' And I said, 'Oh, yes you can, and you *are* an actress.' 'No, I'm not, I've never kidded myself. I hate it, I'm frightened of it. Get me a drink and I'll be all right.' So I said, 'You know, I've been told not to get you a drink.' She said, 'Get me a drink!' I got her a drink and she did the scene."

Paramount put her on suspension for refusing *Flaming Feather* with Sterling Hayden and then quietly let her contract expire. Gail was slipping into dark moods of melancholy silence while rumors persisted about her drinking problems.

Projects like *Loan Shark* with George Raft and the Balanese slave girl in Republic's *Fair Wind to Java* opposite Fred MacMurray went astray.

In Universal's *Air Cadet* (1951), Gail looked thin and drawn and sported an unbecomingly short hair style as Stephen McNally's estranged wife. Madison was busy on his teleseries, "Wild Bill Hickok," and was unable to visit her. She was depressed and weary most of the time. The long hours of lonely drinking had sapped Gail's stamina and it began to show in her work. On location at a jet pilot school at William Field, Arizona, she would return to her motel room after a long day of shooting and drink herself into a stupor. Gail shied away from her Universal co-workers, who included Richard Long, Rock Hudson, Robert Arthur and Peggie Castle. *Air Cadet* was the first film to depict the training of jet fighter pilots who received their baptism of fire in Korea.

Gail and Madison separated and she tersely said, "We were unable to work things out." They reconciled after a bit, but from then on it was obviously a case of two people struggling to make the best of a union which already had been strained to the breaking point. In October, 1953, John Wayne's wife Esperanza named Gail as correspondent in her divorce suit against the actor. In Wayne's testimony, he insisted upon the innocence of his relations with Gail. In John Wayne's biography, *Shooting Star*, Maurice Zolotow quoted Wayne: ' "That poor kid went to work for us on loanout from Paramount. We paid Paramount a lot of money but Gail only got her contract player's salary. She was workin' for practically nothin'. She did a great job in our picture (*Angel and the Badman*) and we tried to get her some of the loanout money but those pricks over at Paramount wouldn't give her any. So Jimmy Grant (the director/screenwriter) and I, we chipped in five hundred dollars apiece and gave it to her. It was for a down payment on a car. It was open and aboveboard. Sure I did take Gail home from that party—but her mother and her brother were there.' "

The ordeal of the court hearings was too much for Gail, and she entered a Seattle, Washington, sanitarium for intensive psychotherapy treatment. Madison busied himself with a grueling schedule of tours and rodeos in connection with his "Wild Bill Hickok" TV series. The drinking began to land Gail in serious trouble without the powers of a major studio to shield her from the press. In November, 1953, she was arrested for drunken driving and bailed out by Madison. "My husband has been a tower of strength throughout my crisis," said Gail. The following year, they divorced. Hardly anyone was too surprised. Madison told reporters, "I'm heartsick about our separation. I'm still devoted to Gail. I had the chance to experience a strong, honest emotion. I still believe we'll be back together." Madison married actress Sheilah Connolly in 1954 and had two daughters. They divorced in 1963.

John Wayne, who had considerable impact on her life, offered her a co-starring role with Randolph Scott in his Batjac Company's *Seven Men From Now* (1956) a Warner Bros. release. Although she looked matronly, her compassion and sincerity were still there in this CinemaScope Western. Her old friend from Paramount, Bing Crosby, tried to resuscitate her spirit and wanted her for *High Society* at Metro-Goldwyn-Mayer, in the role Celeste Holm eventually played. In Universal's courtroom drama, *The Tattered Dress* (1957), she had a strong, meaty role. *The Los Angeles Times* noted: "Gail Russell returns very lustrously as the woman under Jack Carson's domination who principally testifies against Jeff Chandler." In a highly dramatic scene, Gail kills her lover Carson on the courthouse steps. Her comeback swiftly waned.

The same year (1957), Gail formed a deep relationship with singer Dorothy Shay, billed as the sophisticated "Park Avenue Hillbilly." Gail was immediately drawn to the experienced, worldly woman whose tenderness and understanding was a great help to the troubled actress. Shay encouraged her to go out more to openings or do some shopping. "They shared a special intimate friendship. Dorothy really tried to help her, but poor Gail was so consumed by emotional problems, just wouldn't or couldn't help herself," said a mutual friend of both women. Gail and Dorothy were included in the circle of Rock Hudson, Ross Hunter, Margaret Lindsay and Mary McCarty. The "learning experience" with Dorothy Shay lasted close to two years. Following a long retirement, Shay returned to show business as a character actress, appearing as a regular on the ABC-TV series, "Starsky and Hutch." She died of a stroke in October, 1978, in Santa Monica.

In the summer of 1957, the worst came. A disheveled Gail was arrested again, when her convertible smashed through the window of Jan's Coffee Shop, pinning the night janitor under the wheels. A Los Angeles judge asked Gail, "How many drinks did you have?" She replied, "A few, maybe two. Maybe four." Then, her trembling hands covered her face as she sobbed, "I don't know how many. It's no one's business but my own." She was given a 30-day suspended jail sentence, fined $420 and put on three years probation. Gail's drinking had worsened and her moods altered drastically. The bitter truth was that she had not conquered her alcoholism and never would.

At Republic, Gail starred in the low-budget *No Place to Land* (1958) with John Ireland and Mari Blanchard, a triangle that lands nowhere. In *The Silent Call* (1961), Gail and David McLean were the parents of a boy, Roger Mobley, in a true story of a Nevada family who move West and discover that their dog, which they had abandoned, has followed them.

In 1960, Gail appeared on the daytime television series, "Here's Hollywood," exhibiting her oil paintings and talking about plans to resume her career. She did an episode of "The Rebel," entitled "Noblesse Oblige," with Nick Adams and Robert Vaughn. Producer Andrew J. Fenady had been a big fan of Gail's in his youth and hired her for two days, to shoot on the Paramount lot. Fenady recalls that when Gail walked into his office to read for the part of Cassandra, she said, "You know, Mr. Fenady, this used to be Charlie's office." "Charlie who?" asked Fenady. "Charlie Brackett, he produced *The Uninvited*." Thrilled to be "home" again, Gail visited Edith Head, who arranged for her to wear a gown that Margaret Sullavan had worn in *So Red the Rose*. Old friends Nellie Manly did her hair and Wally Westmore her make-up. "Although Gail had some problems with her lines," Fenady said, "we finished the show on time and Gail Russell was absolutely radiant." Gail's Paramount mentor, director William Russell, persuaded Raymond Burr to use her on "Perry Mason"—but on the first day of filming, Gail didn't show up. She was replaced by Martha Vickers.

Just when Gail felt everything in her life had disintegrated and deteriorated, an offer came to appear on the syndicated TV series "Manhunt." In her last interview, given on the set of "Manhunt," Gail explained: "I guess there are still doubts about me but you have to take the bitter with the better in this business. My morale is high. All you need is a little sunshine and a pat on the back now and then. I have peace of mind for the first time in my life, and I'm happier than ever before."

With no more offers of work, Gail went back to drinking. On August 27, 1961, the girl who never really wanted to be an actress was found dead in her Brentwood apartment. The litter of empty vodka bottles in her apartment (1436 S. Bentley Ave.) gave mute testimony that the dark-haired beauty had long since lost her battle with alcoholism. Dressed in pajama bottoms and a print blouse, Gail's body was found sprawled on the living room floor beside a couch, dead of alcohol abuse and related liver disease. A neighbor had seen her four days earlier when Gail came to her apartment and begged for a drink. She then locked herself in the apartment that same day and never came out. Other neighbors talked to her through the window but she refused to come out. These same neighbors became worried when they noticed that the lights had been burning in the apartment for three days and they notified the police. The police estimated that Gail died "some time between August 24th and August 26th."

"I know Gail had a sincere desire to stop drinking," said a neighbor, "but she couldn't. It's a tragic thing. She didn't seem to have any friends except the neighbors who tried to look after her and a man from Alcoholics Anonymous who would visit. I knew her drinking had caused serious liver problems." She continued, "She would go through periods where she wouldn't drink, and then the bad periods when she couldn't stop. The pressures to take a drink must have been enormous."

Private funeral services were held at the Westwood Village Chapel, followed by burial at the Valhalla Memorial Park in North Hollywood. Among those attending were Alan Ladd and his wife Sue Carol, James Lydon, Diana Lynn, William Russell, Mona Freeman and Milton Lewis. Through years of stardom and times of sorrow, Diana Lynn and Gail had clung to their friendship. "Gail felt her life and career were going nowhere," said Diana Lynn in an interview. "She was drowning her sorrows these last few years." Diana would suffer a fatal stroke ten years later, at only 45. Guy Madison has remained absolutely private regarding Gail.

In 1982, a play based on Gail's life was presented by an Arizona college theatrical group, including a retrospective program of six of her most important films. Her brother, George Russell, kept all of her oil paintings, which were exhibited at the Redondo Beach Center for Women, a charitable organization formed to give aid to women suffering from acute alcoholism and related problems.

Shortly before Gail Russell died, she commented about the turmoil of her movie star years. "Everything happened so fast. I was a sad character. I was sad because of myself. I didn't have any self-confidence. I didn't believe I had any talent. I didn't know how to have fun. I was afraid. I don't exactly know of what—of life, I guess."

SHARON TATE

The term "heartbreakingly beautiful" could have been coined for Sharon Tate. With her huge, almond-shaped gray eyes, high cheekbones, up-tilted nose and Mona Lisa smile, it's really no surprise that she started winning beauty contests from the early age of six months. Sharon Tate was a portrait of the Hollywood goddess—flawlessly beautiful and successful. Her reality soon became a nightmare, and everything she had taken for granted—security, a husband's love, impending motherhood and an important film career—would lead to events so gruesome they would be termed "the most brutal and bizarre murders of the decade." The world was stunned by the violent slayings. "She had hopes and dreams and was a thoughtful member of society until a crazy man decided for no reason that she shouldn't be around any more," said Sharon's mother.

Sharon Marie Tate was born on January 24, 1943, in Dallas, Texas. Both her parents, Doris Gwen and Paul Tate, were natives of Houston. Her father was a lieutenant colonel in Army Intelligence, and Sharon, with her two younger sisters, Patricia and Deborah, saw a good deal of the United States as the family was shifted from Army post to Army post. When she was six months old, Sharon won her first beauty contest, "Miss Tiny Tot of Dallas." Mrs. Tate had sent in photos of the refreshingly natural child to contest officials. As a teen-ager, Sharon won a number of beauty contests, claiming the titles of "Miss Richland, Washington," at sixteen and "Miss Autorama" at seventeen, and at the Vicenza American High School in Verona, Italy, she was a cheerleader and baton twirler, and was chosen "Homecoming Queen" and "Queen of the Senior Prom."

In 1961, Sharon met Twentieth Century-Fox actors Richard
Beymer and Susan Strasberg, who were on location in Verona,
filming *Hemingway's Adventures of a Young Man* (1962). She was
working in the crowd scenes, and Beymer encouraged the
lovely teen to try her luck in Hollywood. Through a choreographer friend, Sharon landed a bit on "The Pat Boone Show," a
TV series being filmed in Italy. She can also be glimpsed in *Ba-
rabbas* (1962), a film about ancient Rome, with Jack Palance and
Anthony Quinn. It's possible that during this period, she did
extra work in other Italian-based productions, although they
never appeared in any of her biographies. "I always had Hollywood in my mind," Sharon would say. "I was so happy when
my father was transferred from Italy back to San Francisco,
which is within such easy distance of Hollywood."

The Tate family moved back to the United States in February
1963, settling in San Pedro, just south of Los Angeles. Sharon
contacted Hal Gefsky, Richard Beymer's agent, on her first day
in California. Today, Gefsky's quiet-spoken charm and gentleness of character remain intact. He has never forgotten the impression Sharon Tate made on him during that first meeting.
"She was incredibly beautiful—I'd never seen anyone like her,
before or since. She just took your breath away." Since Beymer
was out of town, Gefsky escorted the newcomer to P.J.'s, a
popular cabaret theater then, for dinner and the Krofft Bros.
Puppet Show. "The owner, Paul Raffles couldn't take his eyes
off her," Hal Gefsky remembers. "I told him she was an Italian
actress and couldn't speak a word of English. Sharon spoke
several languages and was most fluent in Italian. She was
staying with a family in Nichols Canyon at the time."

Just five days later, Sharon moved into the Hollywood Studio Club. When an aggressive roommate made some lesbian
advances, she requested a change to another room. Sharon
then took a large double room with actress Mary Winters, overlooking the club's garden patio. "When I think of Sharon, I remember all the happy memories," Mary Winters says today.
"So loving, vulnerable and very disciplined when it came to
her career. She was very family oriented; we'd often drive to
Palos Verdes Estates to have dinner with them. She was especially close to her mother, Doris. Sharon evoked a kind of
warmth. Everybody felt very protective towards her. I guess

we lived at the Hollywood Studio Club for about six months, then Sharon took an apartment on Fuller Street in the building that Richard Beymer's mother, Eunice, managed."

Sharon's first job was dressing up in an Irish costume for Lipper Productions and handing out Kelly-Kalani Wine in Los Angeles restaurants at $25 a day for ten days. She also appeared in two television commercials for Chevrolet Automobiles and Santa Fe Cigars. There is one thing during this period that all her close friends agree on. Sharon was the most beautiful girl in the world! "Everywhere I took her she caused a sensation," Gefsky said. "I would take her into a restaurant and the owner would pay for her meal. She collected more business cards than anyone I've ever known."

Gefsky took Sharon to meet Herbert Browar, an assistant to Al Simon of Filmways, Inc. They were casting three unknown actresses as the daughters of Bea Benaderet in CBS-TV's "Whistle Stop." Browar took one look at her and rushed her into the office of Martin Ransohoff, the president of Filmways, Ransohoff, recognizing the physical potential of the young actress, decided not to use her in the series but, instead, groom her for motion pictures. "Whistle Stop" would become the popular "Petticoat Junction" and the original three daughters would be played by Jeannine Riley, Linda Kaye Henning and Pat Woodell.

Marty Ransohoff told writer Jim Bowers in a *Saturday Evening Post* interview (1967): "I have this dream where I'll discover a girl who's a nobody and turn her into a star everybody wants. I'll do it like Louis B. Mayer at Metro-Goldwyn-Mayer used to, only better. But once she's successful, then I'll lose interest. That's how my dream goes."

"When I was put under contract, I thought, 'Oh, how nice, but'—I was just a piece of merchandise. No one cared about *me*, Sharon," she explained. Her drama coach Charles Conrad remembers, "Such a beautiful girl, you would have thought she would have all the confidence in the world. But she had none."

Sharon would continue to maintain a close platonic relationship with Richard Beymer, while she began spending a considerable amount of time with a French actor, Philippe Forquet, who pursued her avidly. It became common practice for her to

remain friendly with former admirers. Forquet was in Holly-
wood to play opposite Sandra Dee in *Take Her, She's Mine* at
Twentieth Century-Fox. The alliance with Forquet often resulted in frequent battles. Reportedly, she was hospitalized
due to a beating during the period they were seeing each other.
It was a heated romance and ended when Sharon became romantically involved with the men's hairstylist Jay Sebring.
They met on Thanksgiving Day, 1964, at the home of Elmer
Valentine, who operated The Whisky A Go Go and later The
Roxy nightspots. Jay Sebring had recently opened his own es-
tablishment, Sebring International. Through his acquaintance-
ship with Steve McQueen, Sebring's clientele soon included
Paul Newman, James Garner, Frank Sinatra, Henry Fonda, Pe-
ter Lawford and George Peppard. Sebring, who was born
Thomas Kummer, in Detroit, Michigan, had once been a barber
in the Navy and was recently divorced from model Cami
Sebring. Sharon and Sebring became very friendly with Steve
McQueen and his wife, Neile Adams, spending a week with
them in Hawaii.

Petite, blonde Sheilah Wells had just been signed by Universal Studios when she met Sharon Tate. In the serenity of
Sheilah's spacious Hancock Park home, she recalled their first
meeting. "We were introduced by my agent as well as hers,
Hal Gefsky, at a bakery coffee shop, Puppi's, on the Sunset
Strip," she said. "It was instant friendship. We discovered that
we lived next door to each other and within a week decided to
try and find an apartment together. Sharon ended up moving
into my one-bedroom place (1148 N. Clark St.) with her little
white poodle, Love. It was sort of crazy, since I also had an af-
ghan hound, Shadrack, which she became very attached to and
carried his picture in her billfold." It was Sharon who introduced Sheilah Wells to her future husband, the late actor Fred
Beir.

Occasionally, Sharon did small parts on Filmways/MGM television series, such as "The Man From U.N.C.L.E.," "The
Beverly Hillbillies" and "Petticoat Junction," usually disguised
under a black wig and mostly in the background. On "The
Beverly Hillbillies," she portrayed Janet Trego, a bank secretary. Marty Ransohoff assigned her minor roles in his Metro-
Goldwyn-Mayer features, *The Wheeler Dealers* (1963), *The Ameri-*

canization of Emily (1964) and *The Sandpiper* (1965). On *Sandpiper*'s location at Big Sur (near Carmel, Calif.), Sharon became friendly with the girl who photo-doubled Elizabeth Taylor in the beach sequences. Her name was Raquel Welch. Mary Winters remembers that returning to Hollywood, Sharon was involved in a near fatal car crash. "She turned her car over four and a half times, but somehow managed to escape with only a quarter-inch scar under her left eye and one beside the eye. Her new Triumph automobile was totaled."

Metro-Goldwyn-Mayer announced Sharon would co-star with Mike Henry, the ex-Los Angeles Rams linebacker, in *Tarzan and the Valley of Gold*. Just prior to sailing to Acapulco to begin filming in January, 1965, Ransohoff had mixed reactions about the casting and decided against the loan-out. Sharon dropped out and Nancy Kovack stepped in. She then tested for *The Cincinnati Kid* with Steve McQueen but director Norman Jewison made a strong stand for Tuesday Weld. Ransohoff sent Sharon off to New York to study with Lee Strasberg at the Actors Studio. "She was only with me a few weeks," Strasberg once said. "But I remember her and that Mona Lisa smile."

It was Jay Sebring and his pal Steve McQueen who persuaded Sharon to change agents and sign with the prestigious William Morris Agency. She went to see Hal Gefsky and explained the situation. Gefsky remembers, "She wanted to sign again with me first, so that I would be protected by all her future earnings. It was a very honorable thing to do, but then that's the kind of girl she was."

One night, alone in the home of Jay Sebring, Sharon fell asleep. The strange Bavarian-style house had a haunted quality. It once belonged to Jean Harlow and her husband, Paul Bern, who shot himself to death on Labor Day, 1932. It had secret passageways leading from the bedroom to a side door on the first level. Sharon awoke to see the vision of a little man standing at her bedside. She was certain it was the figure of Paul Bern. Terrified, Sharon fled the room and ran downstairs only to come upon the incredibly frightening sight of a figure, throat slashed, tied with white cord to the stair railing. She quickly fled and returned to her own apartment.

In September, 1965, Sharon went to London to begin her first major role in *Thirteen*, the story of a devil-worshipping cult which engages in human sacrifice. She was Odile, a fragile French country girl possessed of witch-like powers which influenced the local marquis, David Niven, and his wife, Deborah Kerr. Kim Novak had injured her back just ten days before the film's completion and had to be replaced by Kerr. It was finally released as *Eye of the Devil* (1967). Sharon "portrayed a chillingly beautiful but expressionless girl engaged in witchcraft," said *The New York Times*. While in production, Ransohoff introduced Sharon to director Roman Polanski at a cocktail party at the Dorchester Hotel. "We shook hands, made polite conversation, and exchanged phone numbers before going our separate ways. I remember thinking her an exceptionally good-looking girl, but London was full of good-looking girls," Polanski would say in his autobiography, *Roman*. Producer Marty Ransohoff was then in the pre-production phase of the youthful-looking director's next film assignment, *The Fearless Vampire Killers*. Polanski had a reputation as a disturbed and complex talent.

In 1966, Roman Polanski, indulging his preoccupation with the occult and the supernatural, was planning his horror spoof, *The Fearless Vampire Killers* (a.k.a. *Pardon Me, But Your Teeth Are in My Neck*). It was specifically aimed at the growing interest in occultism. Polanski had decided on Jill St. John as the feminine lead. Ransohoff, eager to launch Sharon in an important role, persuaded Polanski to hold up on a decision until he could test Sharon. "Although Sharon's sun-kissed, milk-fed Southern looks hardly fitted the role of a Jewish innkeeper's daughter, I wanted to accommodate my producer (Ransohoff) if possible," Polanski said in his autobiography. Polanski soon forgot all about Jill St. John and cast Sharon as the star of the macabre carryings-on to be filmed in England. The director found Sharon to be "A rare combination—bright, interesting, and attractive." It wasn't long before Sharon fell in love with Roman Polanski. It was the beginning of a succession of ironies that were to be sealed in the ultimate tragedy.

The astute Polanski not only directed the Hammer-styled *The Fearless Vampire Killers* (1967), but also played the assistant to the mad professor, Jack MacGowran, who comes to Transylvania to obliterate a family of Slovonic Vampires. Sharon was a vampire lass kept captive by the bloodthirsty throng. Ransohoff cut twenty minutes prior to the initial release, and the director-perfectionist was livid. Polanski demanded that his name be removed from the credits, which was impossible since he created, wrote, directed, and starred in it.

In a letter to Sheilah Wells, written while *Fearless Vampire Killers* was in production, Sharon wrote: "Dear Sheilah: Golly it's been so long, I've almost forgotton how to write—things are going great over here. I've never enjoyed working so much as on this picture. Roman Polanski is the director and he is an absolute genius, in every sense of the word. I asked Jay (Sebring) how you were doing and he said fine, are you happy first of all and how is Ron (Roth). I was very sad about breaking up with Jay but it just wasn't fair for him, plus I knew it wasn't the right romance. I didn't want to hurt him and I tried to keep it going. I just couldn't fool myself, so I thought it wiser to tell him, I hope he's okay and has himself a sweet girlfriend. Please write and tell me all about yourself and how you're doing, I miss you, you should come over. All my love, Sharon." Polanski would say upon his first meeting with Sebring in London, "We developed an immediate rapport, almost as if we'd known each other for years, and he quickly became a regular member of our circle."

Sharon returned from England with her new mentor, Polanski, and they rented a luxurious Santa Monica house, built by silent screen queen Norma Talmadge and later shared by Cary Grant and Randolph Scott. The beach house (1038 Palisades Beach Road) on "Millionaires Row" was then owned by Brian Aherne. Reflecting on this period of their lives, Polanski wrote: "Despite all my problems, Sharon and I were having fun becoming part of the Hollywood scene. It was always party time in Beverly Hills and Bel Air, and we could have gone out every night of the week. As a popular young couple rising in the film world, we were showered with hospitality by Hollywood residents ranging from the old-established, like Danny Kaye, Otto Preminger, and Ruth Gordon and her husband, Garson Kanin, to the younger and more hip, like Mike Nichols or John and Michelle Phillips of the Mamas and the Papas."

Sharon's next film for Metro-Goldwyn-Mayer/Filmways was *Don't Make Waves* (1967), a spoof on life in Malibu Beach, in which she was a surfboard-riding, sky-diving foil for Tony

Curtis. It didn't make any waves, or money either. Her scenes in a brief bikini caused a small furor, while Italian import Claudia Cardinale had the female lead. In *TV Movies*, Leonard Maltin writes: "The one gem out of nine million bad Tony Curtis comedy vehicles; satire on Southern California has good direction (Alexander Mackendrick), funny performance by Sharon Tate." Commenting on Sharon's beauty, Polanski said: "I'm trying to get her to be a little meaner. She's too nice and she doesn't believe in her beauty. Once when I was very poor in Poland I had got some beautiful shoes, and I immediately became ashamed of them. All my friends had plain, ordinary shoes, and I was embarrassed to walk in front of them. That's how Sharon feels about her beauty. She's embarrassed by it."

Roman Polanski began work immediately on Paramount's *Rosemary's Baby*. The Ira Levin story of witchcraft and diabolism starred Mia Farrow, John Cassavetes and Ruth Gordon. Film cultists consider this Polanski's greatest film achievement. It continued the absorbing and perceptive reign of horror he crafted in film after film. While Polanski was shooting in New York City's famed Dakota Apartments, where most of the story took place, Sharon jetted in for three days. During the brief visit, she posed for an *Esquire* magazine layout and, with Polanski, attended Sheilah Well's Broadway debut in *Star Spangled Girl* opposite Tony Perkins at the Plymouth Theatre. Sheilah took over for Connie Stevens, who opened the play.

When asked by columnist Norma Lee Browning about doing another film with Roman Polanski, "I'd be thrilled to death to do a Polanski film," said Sharon. "But he has to ask me. I wouldn't ever dream of asking him for a part." In photos taken by the director, Sharon appeared semi-nude in the March, 1967 issue of *Playboy*. They were taken on the set of *The Fearless Vampire Killers*, accompanying an article, "This Is the Year That Sharon Tate Happens." In October, 1967, Sharon accompanied Polanski to San Francisco to accept an award for *Knife in the Water* at the San Francisco Film Festival.

Author Jacqueline Susann's pleasantly trashy *Valley of the Dolls* was on *The New York Times* best-seller list for 23 weeks. Raquel Welch, Ann-Margaret and Candice Bergen were the first choices for the Susann novel. When the Mark Robson helmed *Valley of the Dolls* (1967) opened for the Christmas rush, it starred Patty Duke as singer Neely O'Hara, Barbara Parkins as Anne Welles, the television cosmetics pitchwoman, and Sharon as Jennifer North, the soft-core, doomed sex symbol who loses her breast to cancer and kills herself. Judy Garland's signing for the stage star, Helen Lawson, generated a great amount of ballyhoo.

Just three days into Garland's filming of *Valley of the Dolls*, Twentieth Century-Fox decided to dump the unreliable star. Susan Hayward stepped in and walked away with the best notices. The Susann sudser was the biggest non-roadshow money-making attraction in the history of Twentieth Century-Fox. The reviews were brutal and the material seems tame by today's standards. Sharon's final screen moments have enormous dramatic impact, considering she would be dead within two years. Haunting closeups linger over her lovely face in the suicide scene. Sharon's portrait of the doomed Jennifer North is both impressive and moving.

"Ten years ago, *Valley of the Dolls* stars Parkins, Duke and Tate would more likely have been playing hat-check girls than movie queens; they are totally lacking in style, authority or charm," snarled *The Saturday Review*. "Sharon Tate emerges as the film's most sympathetic character, who takes an overdose of sleeping pills when breast cancer threatens to rob her of her only means of livelihood. William Daniels' photographic caress of her faultless face and enormous absorbent eyes is stunning," gasped *The Hollywood Reporter*.

On January 20, 1968, four days before her 25th birthday, Sharon married Roman Polanski, 34, in a civil ceremony at the Chelsea Registry Office in London. "Sharon and I are very, very happy," Polanski proclaimed after the ceremony. To which Sharon added, "I'm so happy you can't believe it." Attending the wedding reception were Leslie Caron, Warren Beatty, Richard Harris, Christine Kaufmann, Jacqueline Susann and her husband, Irving Mansfield, Terence Stamp and Michael Caine. Sharon's co-star in *Valley of the Dolls*, Barbara Parkins, was maid of honor. The newly marrieds went skiing in the Swiss Alps on their honeymoon. In a 1971 *Playboy* interview, Polanski said: "At the beginning of our relationship, I was afraid of getting too deeply involved and losing my freedom. But she was extremely understanding, tactful and clever.

Being around me, she still made me feel absolutely free. She did not make demands, and she made it clear that she was not going to engulf me. I remember once her words, 'I am not one of those ladies who swallow a man.' . . . After a while, I realized that she would like to get married. She never asked me, never said a word about it. So finally I said, 'I'm sure you would like to get married,' and she said she would. So I said, 'We'll get married then,' and we did. By that time I wasn't nervous about it at all."

For Columbia Pictures, Sharon joined Dean Martin, Elke Sommer and Nancy Kwan in *The Wrecking Crew* (1969). This was the fourth of Donald Hamilton's Matt Helm special agent series in which Sharon was Martin's sole ally, a bungling and spectacled agent posing as his Danish tourist guide involved with international gold hijackers. As *The Hollywood Reporter* noted: "In a role which paraphrases Stella Stevens in *The Silencers*, Sharon Tate reveals a pleasant affinity to scatterbrain comedy and comes as close to walking away with this picture as she did in a radically different role in *Valley of the Dolls*." Columbia had hired Bruce Lee, then a leading martial arts instructor and consultant, to teach Sharon the art of kung fu for particular scenes.

In 1968, soon after returning from the Cannes Film Festival, Sharon managed to buy her way out of her exclusive contract with producer Martin Ransohoff. Her image of Ransohoff had changed from that of a kindly benefactor to a cunning exploiter. She would have to turn over 25 percent of her earnings for the next four years to Ransohoff's Filmways company. In a poll of movie exhibitors taken by the trade journal *Motion Picture Herald*, Sharon was named first runner-up to Lynn Redgrave as the top "Star of Tomorrow."

The Polanskis were part of the glittery new Hollywood life, frequently at the trendy Factory, Daisey and Candy Store nightclubs. Their friends were the rich and young stars who dabbled in soft drugs, Indian mysticism and seances. "I love the new generation," Sharon told one interviewer. "They're fascinating and they're fun. I think the hippies are great, they just want to be left alone and they want everything to be nice and peaceful. That's my philosophy, to live and let live. But I'm not just a hippy. I'm not just an anything."

For a short time, Sharon and Polanski took a bungalow at the Chateau Marmont, a longtime fashionable Hollywood address. Then they moved into a rented home in February, 1969; the grounds were beautifully landscaped and the house remote and serene. It was on a narrow street that abruptly winds upward from Benedict Canyon Road and comes to a cul-de-sac at the high gate of 10050 Cielo Drive. Just a week later, Sharon and Roman took off for Europe.

Sharon was to film *Twelve Plus One* (1970), from the old Russian novel. The Italian-French co-production told the fable about the legatee whose fortune is in one of the thirteen chairs he's already sold. One of the pleasures of *Twelve Plus One* is that Sharon is enchanting in what proved to be her final role, with Orson Welles, Vittorio Gassman and Vittorio de Sica. However, the nude footage of Sharon gave the comedy an unpleasant element of tasteless exploitation at the time of its European release.

To Sharon's bitter disappointment, Polanski remained in London for story conferences on *The Day of the Dolphin* and was unable to accompany her back to California in July, 1969. She was eight months pregnant when she sailed on the *QE 2*. In his autobiography, Polanski says he had a morbid feeling about that last goodbye. "Something about this parting made it different from other, more casual leave-takings, and both of us had tears in our eyes. 'Okay, go now,' Sharon said abruptly. We walked down the companionway to the main exit. She hugged me tightly, pressing her belly against me in a way she'd never done before, as if to remind me of the baby. As I held and kissed her, a grotesque thought flashed through my mind: you'll never see her again. If nothing had happened, I might have no recollection of this premonition; as it is, the memory remains indelible."

In Hollywood, Sharon was spending most of her days at the house on Cielo Drive quietly, making preparations for the expected baby by redecorating the nursery. Everything now centered around the baby. Sheilah Wells recalls their many afternoons together: "Sharon was taking every precaution to have a healthy baby and wouldn't do anything to jeopardize the child. She wanted to be a mother more than anything in the world."

Sharon was excited about plans to star for Just Jacckin for his next project, *The Story of O,* dealing with erotic sex and sadism. An announcement from Allied Artists was planned after the birth of her baby. Corrine Clery subbed for Sharon in Jacckin's first in a series of soft-porn French films. Sharon had also read the Thomas Hardy 1891 novel, *Tess of the D'Urbervilles,* and persuaded Polanski to do it for her. She was to have played the title role in the sentimental love story, Tess. Polanski's astonishingly faithful rendition of the Hardy novel would ultimately star Nastassia Kinski, with whom he became romantically involved in 1980.

On August 7, 1969, actor Robert Lipton and Connie Kreski took Sharon to a screening of a "Marcus Welby, MD" episode at Universal Studios, which featured Lipton. "She was so pregnant that I'm sure it tired her just sitting through an hour episode," he remembered. "The next night, I talked to her again on the phone. She asked that we come up to the house but I said we were going to an Orson Welles film. Knowing that Sharon just finished a film with Welles, once again I invited her to come along. She said she was too tired but asked that we come up after the screening. I figured if she was that tired, the last thing she wanted was company late at night—so we didn't go."

Joanna Pettet and Barbara Lewis stopped by that Friday (August 8th) for a leisurely lunch. It was a relaxing afternoon, the women would say later, talking mostly about the expected baby, and Roman's return in time for his birthday, on August 18th. Sharon had been planning a birthday party for Polanski, who was going to be 36. *Photoplay* columnist Steve Brandt and Cass Elliott would say later they declined invitations to stop by on the evening of August 8th. Subsequently many friends, including Steve McQueen, would claim to have been invited, and, at the last minute, changed their minds. Jacqueline Susann would remember that Sharon called her at the Beverly Hills Hotel and invited her to a party that incredible night. Instead, she opted for a quiet dinner with chum Rex Reed.

Sheilah Wells recalls the night of August 8th very vividly: "I was having a small dinner party, Sharon, Alex Cord and Joanna Pettet, Stella Stevens and Skip Ward." Then, Sheilah continued, "I called Sharon around seven o'clock and told her not to park in the driveway because the neighbors in back were complaining about the noise. She said she was too tired, that Jay Sebring had called, and they just might drive down to Dolores's Drive-in for their special hamburgers, which Sharon loved. I tried to persuade her to come afterwards and spend the night. It was a very hot summer night—but she said she wanted to wash her hair and get to bed early. That was the last time we ever spoke," she said.

On Saturday morning, August 9th, the housekeeper, Winifred Chapman, arrived for her daily work at the secluded, sprawling house at the end of 10050 Cielo Drive, high above Bel Air. But what she found inside the rustic red-and-beige estate that morning could hardly have been more bizarre and gruesome had it appeared in one of Polanski's own nightmarish films. Chapman entered the residence by the service porch entrance and found a living room with blood everywhere. The first chilling sight was the mutilated bodies of Sharon Tate and Jay Sebring, brutally knifed on the living room floor in front of the long couch. A white nylon cord ran around Sharon's neck, over a ceiling beam, then to the neck of Jay Sebring, 35, who had been shot and stabbed numerous times, his head shrounded in a towel-like hood.

Outside, on the sun-drenched lawn of the house, the horror-stricken Winifred Chapman discovered the bodies of Abigail Folger, 25, daughter of the chairman of the board of the A.J. Folger Coffee company, and Wojtek Frykowski, 32, a boyhood friend of Polanski from Poland, both horribly slashed and smeared with blood. While the Polanskis were in Europe, the couple had moved in and were staying on with Sharon until Roman returned from London. On the front door was smeared "Pig" in blood. Nearby, the body of Steven Parent, 18, who didn't even know the other victims; also gashed and drenched in gore, he sat slumped on the seat of a stalled white Rambler automobile, near the gate. Parent had been visiting the 19-year-old caretaker of the property, William Garretson, who lived in the guest house to the back of the main house. Garretson was in the cottage during the entire massacre, but police subsequently determined that he had been unaware of what was happening at the main house because the loud rock music on his stereo prevented him from hearing the screams.

The scene was one of the most grisly in the gaudy annals of

Hollywood. There were no indications of ransacking or robbery. The house once had been occupied by Cary Grant and
former wife Dyan Cannon, and more recently by Candice
Bergen and Terry Melcher, son of Doris Day. The house was
owned by personal managers Rudi Altobelli and Stuart Cohen,
who were away in Europe.

Roman Polanski, still in England, learned the news from his
business manager, William Tennant, who was called off the
tennis court to identify the bodies. After being told of his wife's
death, a bewildered Polanski with tears in his eyes, said in
London, "She was so good—what kind of country? What kind
of people?" The police found drugs in and around the prem-
ises, including hashish, MDA, a hypnotic drug, cocaine and
marijuana. Polanski immediately flew back to Los Angeles and
held a press conference, chiefly to deny rumors that the murders were drug-oriented. Rumors of orgies and kinky sex had
trailed Jay Sebring for years. A police report released after his
death, stated: "He was considered a ladies' man and took numerous women to his residence in the Hollywood Hills. He
would tie the women up with a small sashcord and, if they
agreed, would slap them, after which they would have sexual
relations."

The chapel atop the flower-dotted slopes at the Holy Cross
Memorial Park in Culver City was crowded with more than two
hundred persons. As the crowd outside grew, it become increasingly unruly. The arrangements were handled by producer Robert Evans' Paramount offices. Polanski and Mrs. Tate
clung together emotionally while Mr. Tate and Sharon's two
sisters managed to maintain their composure. "She was a fine
person," eulogized a tearful Father O'Reilly, whose Catholic
Church Sharon often attended, "and we were in no small measure devoted to her. . . . Goodbye Sharon, and may the angels
welcome you to heaven, and the martyrs guide your way," he
said before the flower-closed casket of Sharon and her unborn
son, Paul Richard Polanski.

The canyon massacre looked drug-related, perhaps the outcome of a deal that went haywire. Then, on December 1, 1969,
the police announced to the news media that murder com-
plaints had been issued for what would eventually be known
as the "Manson Family"—Charles Manson, Patricia

Krenwinkel, Tex Watson, Susan Atkins and Linda Kasabian. They first lived in a hippie commune on the Spahn Ranch, a onetime Western movie location site, some thirty miles from Los Angeles. Their cult leader, Charles Manson, preached love and sent them out to commit murder, with a ferocity that some detectives had never seen before. The Manson worshipers boasted of some thirty-five murders (including the LaBianca murders). The true number may never be known. Manson and his devoted followers later moved to the remote Barker Ranch, in Death Valley, before being taken into custody.

The man who put the "Manson Family" behind bars, Vincent Bugliosi, then a deputy district attorney for Los Angeles, published his own exhaustive account of their satanic whim in *Helter Skelter: The True Story of the Manson Murders* (1974), with collaborator Curt Gentry.

The motives for the murderous holocaust remain sketchy, the most popular theory being that Manson, through the acquaintance of the late Dennis Wilson, drummer of the Beach Boys, was introduced to Terry Melcher, while Melcher was still living at Cielo Drive to discuss some songs Manson had written. Melcher, then a record producer, was unimpressed by the material. Manson's orders to "the family" on that August night were to kill whoever was in the house. The house on Benedict Canyon represented a "symbol of rejection" and Manson's dreams of a recording contract turned into cold-blooded contempt. There was never any evidence that the black-clad intruders knew Sharon or the other occupants on Cielo Drive that horrid evening.

Two of Sharon's most prominent films, *Valley of the Dolls* and *The Fearless Vampire Killers* were quickly hauled out, now billing her name above the title, in an effort to capitalize on the sensational publicity.

Charles Manson, responsible for the devastating horror story, is serving nine life sentences for the grisly murders in the California State Prison at San Quentin. His programmed puppets remain incarcerated in other California prisons. After a period of inactivity, Roman Polanski resumed his brilliant, if erratic, director's career with an adaptation of Shakespeare's *Macbeth*, followed by *Chinatown, Tess, Pirates* and *Frantic*. On the Paris stage, Polanski starred as Wolfgang Mozart in

Amadeus (1982) and played Gregor Samsa, the man who turned into an insect, in a stage version of Franz Kafka's *Metamorphosis* (1988). He has accepted with difficulty the idea that there is life after Hollywood. A complicated statutory rape incident with a thirteen-year-old girl in 1977 has made him a fugitive in Paris, but hasn't curtailed his show business activities throughout Europe. He cannot take up residence in any country which has an extradiction treaty with the United States. Asked about his intentions toward returning to the U.S., Polanski answered, "I will say what I said before: 'I want to clear up my legal problems for my peace of mind, not to live there.' I am not going to try to make a publicity stunt out of my return. It is not only my future but the future of other people that is involved."

Sharon Tate's family were also victims—but they're not dead. Today, Mrs. Doris Tate keeps herself busy, emerging from her grief, and devoting much time to the organization Parents of Murdered Children (POMC) and Citizens For Truth. The feisty, strong-minded mother of Sharon successfully gathered 350,000 signatures for a statewide petition urging California officials to deny parole to the "Manson Family" murderers. Mrs. Tate doesn't believe the notion that Sharon's killers were under the spell of Manson when they killed her daughter. "Prisoners should serve the sentences they were given, and you know they were sentenced to death originally," she said. "My daughter was sentenced to death without cause, and I was sentenced to life in prison without any possibility of parole. Sharon was begging for her life, her baby's life. She was being held down and stabbed to death. Who can force you to kill like that?" And she adds mournfully, "When I got to the point where I couldn't stand it, I flipped open the Bible. Through my religion I learned you go directly to your God. That's where the answers come from."

Partly as a result of Mrs. Tate's testimony, Sharon's murderers are still in prison. "People remember the case, and the petitions and my testimony had an effect," Mrs. Tate said. "But I didn't do it just for me. I did it for all the parents." A clever businesswoman, Mrs. Tate operates three very successful beauty salons and is also active in real estate. Sharon's retired father Paul Tate is now a private investigator. The family still reside on the Palos Verdes peninsula.

In Sharon Tate's very last interview which took place just two weeks before her death, European journalist Enrico di Pompeo asked if she believed in fate. "Certainly," she said. "My whole life has been decided by fate. I think something more powerful than we are decides our fate for us. I know one thing—I've never planned anything that ever happened to me." Obviously, Sharon didn't plan the horrible, ghastly fate that befell her on that hot summer night of August 9, 1969.

BARBARA PAYTON

Flamboyant Barbara Payton's name has filtered down through the years as somewhat of an embarrassment. This reputation is somewhat ill-deserved, because one of her most important performances, in *Kiss Tomorrow Goodbye*, was far above average. "In 1950 I was sitting on top of the world. My peculiar acting talents were worth $10,000 a week, and I was in constant demand. I know it sounds unbelievable, but it's true that Gregory Peck, Guy Madison, Howard Hughes and other big names were dating me. Almost everything I did made headlines," said Barbara. She was beset by self-doubt and perhaps a small amount of masochism. Therein lies her poignant tragedy. Barbara never achieved the heights of some of her celebrated contemporaries like Marilyn Monroe or even Jayne Mansfield, but then she never had their driving ambition to become a star. Her unconventional life-style, public brawls and longtime bout with booze contributed to her obvious mental collapse. Barbara Payton's share of personal ugliness gradually assumed soap opera overtones.

Barbara Redfield was born on November 16, 1927, in Cloquet, Minnesota. Cloquet, called Tree City, U.S.A., because of all the pine trees, is a town of about 12,000, some 20 miles west of Duluth. It's a unionized, blue-collar mill town where blond hair and blue eyes predominate. The only other well-known Cloquet native is Jessica Lange. When she was eleven, Barbara's grandfather's timberlands were burned out by a forest fire and the family decided to move to Odessa, Texas, an oil town on the west Texas prairie. Her father, E. Lee Redfield, was in the construction business. The Redfields were of Norwegian-German stock and Barbara had a younger brother, Frank Redfield. "I wanted to be a movie star more than anything in the world," she once said. "We were poor and whenever possible I'd escape to the local movie house, the Chief Theater. I know it's hard to believe, but I was once an introverted child and Hollywood was my big fantasy."

Barbara attended Baylor Junior High and completed her education at Odessa High School. By her early teens, she developed into a beautiful, leggy blonde, continually sought after for dates. There was an elopement with her high school sweetheart, William Hodge, in her junior year. Barbara's parents had the marriage quickly annulled. In 1943, James Cagney came to Odessa to appear in person at a war bond rally, and a starry-eyed Barbara managed to get tickets to see her favorite actor. She later went backstage to ask for an autograph. The absolutely awestruck teenager never dreamed that one day she would be his leading lady.

On February 10, 1945, Barbara, 17, married handsome John Payton, an air force pilot in Monroe, Louisiana. They honeymooned in Hollywood, where the young bride secured an RKO Studios screen test. Preparing for the test with drama coach Lillian Albertson, Barbara discovered that a baby was on the way. When she informed Charles W. Koerner, the head of production at RKO, he suggested she return to Texas, have her baby and return the following year. The pregnancy, however, ended in a miscarriage. Later, in 1947, Barbara gave birth to a son, John Lee Payton, her only child.

In the spring of 1948, the marriage to John Payton had long run its course and was over. Barbara's youthful dream of becoming a film star took hold once again. So, with her mother and infant son in tow, she whisked away to Hollywood. Barbara knew how to get attention and she began making the rounds of the studios. RKO Studios were no longer interested. Eventually, William Goetz, Universal-International's production chief, had her placed under contract at $100 a week. Her studio biography stated she had been a model and later operated her own modeling school until director-actor Abner Biberman discovered her in a Don Loper fashion show, staged at Slapsy Maxie's nightclub. For her screen test, she selected the comically ignorant chorine (Billie Dawn) character from *Born Yesterday*.

Barbara was placed in Universal-International's stock-player training program, joining Tony Curtis, Piper Laurie, Rock Hudson, Peggie Castle, Donna Martell, Peggy Dow, James Best, Ann Pearce and Lucille Barkley. Her initial Universal entry was as a nightclub photographer in a Robert Montgomery and Ann Blyth comedy, *Once More My Darling* (1949). In the musical Western genre, Universal had begun a strange series of odd-length featurettes in 1948. In *Silver Butte* (1949), starring Tex Williams, a popular Western-&-Country bandleader, Barbara had the feminine lead. The 27-minute short is sometimes listed as *Silver Bullet*. The studio paired the leads again in *The Pecos Pistol* (1949). After fifteen Western musical shorts, Universal dropped the series.

Barbara appeared to be interested in having a good time and veteran columnist Harrison Carroll labeled her the new "Queen of the Night Clubs." Universal-International executives soon became disenchanted and, when she took off for a New York fling with Howard Hughes, they abruptly terminated her contract. "When Universal dropped Barbara, she couldn't have cared less," said Carol Young, also a Universal contractee in 1949. "She was so restless, and really didn't know what she wanted. I remember she would take her son to Sophie Rosenstein's (U-I's drama coach) classes. Miss Rosenstein would be furious," laughed Carol. "But it never seemed to faze Barbara. My mother was crazy about little John Lee, as we all were, and we'd have them over for dinner. He was such an adorable child." While the gossip columnists were wondering whether Barbara would lure the eligible Howard Hughes down the aisle, she had already taken up with entertainment lawyer Greg Bautzer. "Their affair went on for months," remembers Carol Young. "But it ended around the time Barbara was cast in *Trapped*."

Producer Bryan Foy assigned Barbara the lead in a cops-and-robbers drama, *Trapped* (1949), under the provision she lose a slight lisp that had plagued her since childhood. Barbara would often say that Marion Davies' and Kay Francis' movie careers weren't hurt by their speech defects. In *Trapped*, Barbara was a nightclub cigarette girl, murdered while caught up in the distribution of counterfeit money. *Film Daily* said of Barbara's disillusioned heroine: "Barbara Payton effectively renders the feminine portion of the script with looks and acting ability." The

Kansas City *Star* complimented her for being "A blond lovely, with several good scenes as Lloyd Bridges' girlfriend who loses her life while trying to help him." It was one of Bryan Foy's documentary-type crime exposes under the new Eagle-Lion banner, directed by the skilled Richard Fleischer.

After the viewing of screen tests of many contract players for the coveted role of the gun moll, Holiday Carleton, for *Kiss To-morrow Goodbye* (1950), the star, James Cagney and his brother, William, the producer, voted in favor of Barbara. She was signed to a term contract with William Cagney Productions to be shared with Warner Brothers. William Cagney was infatuated with her, but, despite rumors to the contrary, she always claimed their relationship was strictly professional.

Adapted from the Horace McCoy novel, *Kiss Tomorrow Goodbye* showcased Cagney as a hardbitten criminal with maniacal tendencies. Barbara was the woman scorned, who settles accounts with Cagney when she learns he killed her brother during a prison break. Cagney may have hurled a grapefruit in Mae Clarke's face in *The Public Enemy*, but this time the hysterical Barbara throws a coffee pot at her double-crossing lover. *The Hollywood Reporter* commented: "Barbara Payton in the difficult role of a basically good girl who turns to evil in spite of herself makes a vivid appearance. She manages the subtle transition with polished artistry." And *Variety* noted: "Barbara Payton impresses as the girl who first falls victim to Cagney's tough fascination and then kills him when he tries to run off with Helena Carter." *The New York Times* said: ". . . As the moll, a superbly curved young lady Barbara Payton performs as though she's trying to spit a tooth—one of the few Mr. Cagney leaves her." Cagney would later say, "Barbara was an actress of impressive if limited skill."

In *I Am Not Ashamed*, Barbara's infamous 1963 memoir, she recalled filming the Warner Brothers drama: "I just talked and stumbled around and wasn't formal—just had fun. The critics loved it. The word 'natural' was used in all the reviews. Sure, I was scared before I went before the cameras, but it all worked out perfectly." Barbara told the press: "Working with James Cagney was magical. He's so intense, so good—and he puts so much into every line. He's a special person."

Barbara had been scheduled to make her Broadway stage debut in S.N. Behrman's play, *Let Me Hear the Melody*, a comedy about Hollywood which never saw the light of day. There were printed items that both Metro-Goldwyn-Mayer and Twentieth Century-Fox wanted to buy up half her contract from William Cagney/WB as a result of her work in *Kiss Tomorrow Goodbye*. In a *Los Angeles Times* interview, Barbara said: "I'm not yet 24, and I haven't seen too much of life yet. I haven't suffered or starved like so many young stars have before they reached stardom. When I get to New York, I'm going to find a small place in Greenwich Village, study hard and see plays, lots of plays."

Barbara was frequently seen around Hollywood and New York with the debonair star Franchot Tone, who had recently been divorced from Jean Wallace. Tone was captivated by her and told everyone he wanted to marry the voluptuous actress; he sent her flowers and champagne every day. "I've never seen such an attentive suitor," said Barbara. His friends and even his first wife, Joan Crawford, tried to talk the suave actor out of it. Tone's obsessive passion for Barbara was apparent when he formally announced their engagement at the Stork Club in New York City.

Franchot Tone then accompanied Barbara throughout Florida to promote *Kiss Tomorrow Goodbye*. In Miami, she was given the Key to the City at the world premiere ceremonies. Her career was soaring and all the publicity was making Barbara a valuable commodity at the Jack L. Warner factory. Despite Barbara's new success, she was handed a secondary role in Stuart Heisler's *Dallas* (1950), which starred Gary Cooper, with Ruth Roman in the feminine lead. An ex-Confederate soldier, Cooper, upon finding his home and property destroyed, vows revenge on those responsible. It was a confused Western that started as a comedy and then erupted into a full action drama. Seductive Barbara was the deceiving girlfriend of Steve Cochran, who sets a murderous trap for Gary Cooper that backfires. Her role was merely ornamental in this tale of no special merit. In Hector Arce's Gary Cooper, *An Intimate Biography*, the author suggests an affair with Barbara while the Western was in production. "He'd (Cooper) also had a brief fling with Barbara Payton, a supporting player in *Dallas*, in the midst of his affair with Patricia Neal," wrote Arce. As to queries whether there was a possible romance between them, Barbara flippantly remarked, 'It was a difficult time for both of us. Let's just say Gary and I were good friends.' "

Next on Barbara's Warner Brothers agenda came *Only the Valiant* (1951), opposite Gregory Peck. Apaches go on the warpath against a cavalry troop whose commanding officer (Peck) is hated by his men. Although Barbara's part was small, as the blond-lacquered love interest, it gave her career another lift, as Peck and Gig Young battled over her affections in this bloody 1867 cavalry-Indian adventure. It was filmed on location in the New Mexico desert, near Gallup, and was one of the last remaining properties of James Cagney Productions. *The Los Angeles Times* observed: "Barbara Payton has little to do but look glamorous, quite a trick in an early day New Mexico fort." This would be the last high quality film for Barbara. Allegedly, during filming of *Only the Valiant*, Barbara had an affair with Gregory Peck. According to Barbara in *I Am Not Ashamed*: "He (Peck) barred me from the set because I upset him so much."

In 1951, the Hollywood Press Association selected a bevy of six starlets as their equivalent to the Wampas Baby Stars. Barbara was chosen to represent Warner Brothers. "I was one of the six 'Baby Stars' most likely to succeed—Piper Laurie, Mona Freeman, Mala Powers, Barbara Bates, Peggie Castle and yours truly," she wrote. "The other five are still fulfilling their promises. Me, I goofed." The same year, Barbara went before the federal grand jury in the trial of playboy Stanley Adams, who was convicted of lying about his whereabouts on February 28, 1950, the day a reputed narcotics dealer was slain. It was stressed that Barbara was not suspected of wrongdoing, but was wanted to give testimony on what she knew about the activities of Adams and his link to organized crime. She testified that Adams had been in her apartment most of the day, but her testimony did not save him from a perjury sentence.

To show their disapproval over the damaging publicity caused by the Adams trail, Warner Brothers loaned out Barbara to the King Brothers for *Drums in the Deep South* (1951). It was directed by William Cameron Menzies, the noted art director known for his stylized sets. It was a Civil War yarn of two friends (James Craig and Guy Madison) who find themselves fighting for opposite causes and a Southern belle, Barbara. Craig was the Confederate leader who takes control of a strategic mountain and Madison was the Union commander who had to retake the position in order to insure his lines would not be destroyed by Confederate artillery. Said *Variety*: "William Cameron Menzies' direction tends to drag except in some stirring sequences depicting the struggle to mount the guns on the bluff and the subsequent shelling of supply trains. Miss Payton, a busty blonde, has the only femme role in the cast. She is none too convincing either in the few romantic scenes or in her espionage activities."

While *Drums in the Deep South* was in production at the old Goldwyn Studios, *Confidential* magazine reported in a headline article, "Up in Barbara Payton's Bedroom," that she and Guy Madison carried their on-screen romance off the lot. It seems Franchot Tone obtained the services of a private detective to keep close tabs on Barbara and Madison. She was then living in a second-floor apartment at 7456 Hollywood Boulevard. Barging in on the couple, after following them from the Formosa Cafe, an angry Tone said, "I'm engaged to this girl and I'm going to marry her. Are you?" Guy Madison shocked and blushing, replied, "No, I can't. I'm already married (Gail Russell)."

Barbara began losing her brief moment of captured fame—which was unfortunate. Her timing was a fraction off. Back then, there was a certain apprehension about stars who couldn't keep a hold on their private lives. Major studios would offer no protection for their erratic behavior, unless it involved their most valuable superstars.

When boyfriend Franchot Tone left for New York on business, Barbara met rock-jawed Tom Neal at a party and soon announced she was leaving Tone to marry Neal. He projected a cockiness that was quite similar to that of the early Clark Gable—but without Gable's special charisma. Barbara, the romanticist, saw only the moonlight and roses in the swiftness with which Tom Neal rushed her off her feet. She told the press, "It was love at first sight. I saw him in a swimming pool. He looked so wonderful in his trunks that I knew he was the only man in my life."

Then, on September 13, 1951, Barbara ditched Tom Neal and was back with Franchot Tone at their favorite Sunset Strip playground, Ciro's. When they returned to her new apartment at

1803 Courtney Terrace, Tone was attacked by the furiously jealous Neal (a Golden Gloves contender) in a bloody, shocking brawl on the lawn in front of Barbara's apartment, leaving the older actor hospitalized for two weeks at California Lutheran Hospital. Franchot Tone suffered a fractured cheekbone, broken nose and a brain concussion. Barbara wound up with a black eye. She tried to break up the violent fight and was shoved aside by Neal. The encounter ended after ten minutes.

Barbara was suddenly world famous because of the ugly confrontation—not the way she had originally planned. Tone's looks were disfigured and required plastic surgery. Columnist Florabel Muir reported in her column: "What an eye opening Tone will get if he goes through with having Neal arrested and tried for assault. And Hollywood will take another beating when the hot, juicy news of this rather sordid romance goes out over the wires for all the world to read. What has always puzzled me about this romantic trio is how Tone who has a very well trained mind could play around in a league of daffy dillies and muscle developers." When Tone's injuries mended, the couple decided it was time to tie the marital knot and cement their stormy relationship. They were married far away from Hollywood, in Barbara's birthplace of Cloquet, Minnesota, on September 28, 1951. "I was shocked and terribly grieved," groaned Neal, still carrying a torch for Barbara. She said when she married Franchot Tone, it would be forever. "But forever is just a weekend, more or less," Barbara mused later. Her parents, grandparents, aunts and uncles attended the small-town wedding. The press followed them everywhere, calling the marriage a merger of brains and beauty. Hedda Hopper would report in her column, "Thank God, now we can all relax."

There was just time for a brief three-day honeymoon in New York before reporting to producer Walter Wanger for the title role in *Lady in the Iron Mask*, co-starring Louis Hayward. A week before the film was scheduled to go into production, Wanger fired her and Patricia Medina accepted the project. Barbara's later films were generally ripped by critics and ignored by most moviegoers.

Barbara and Tone separated after hardly more than seven weeks of marriage. "She couldn't forget Tom Neal," a disillu-

sioned Tone told the press. Barbara and Tom Neal then resumed their volatile relationship. Following the personal appearance tour through the South with *Drums in the Deep South*,
she dumped Neal, saying she couldn't handle his "uncontrollable temper." She and Tone briefly reconciled, until the marriage fell apart for good soon after Barbara took an overdose of
sleeping pills in March, 1952. Tone found her in time and
rushed her to a hospital. They divorced the following May.
Several years later, Tone, then in his sixties, asked her to marry
him again. "I'll be young again for you," Tone said. But Barbara, with a touch of sadness in her voice, said "No." She said
she had already messed up his life enough. Franchot Tone
would marry one more time, to actress Dolores Dorn-Heft
(1956-59).

Warner Brothers next loaned Barbara to an independent producer, Jack Broder, for *Bride of the Gorilla* (1951). The story was a
contrived version of the *King Kong* formula, wherein plantation
foreman Raymond Burr periodically transforms into an ape and
falls in love with the plantation owner Paul Cavanagh's wife,
Barbara. The foreman kills the husband but is put under a voo-
doo curse which makes him believe he is a gorilla! Tom
Conway was the doctor also lusting after Barbara. The econ-
omy horror film was written and directed by Curt Siodmak. It
provided a field day for the followers of the Payton-Tone-Neal
melee. The *Hollywood Reporter* thought: "It looked like the cast
raced through their assignment due to a restricted shooting
schedule." Producer William Cagney and Warner Brothers decided not to exercise their option and Barbara joined the ranks
of the free-lance player.

The low-budget *Bride of the Gorilla* virtually spelled "finis" to
her once promising career. Today, the campy film has developed somewhat of a cult following and was one of the films
shown at the Los Angeles City College's 1977 Barbara Payton
Film Festival. The only offers coming in for her were for personal appearances on the Eastern Minsky Burlesque circuit in
connection with *Bride of the Gorilla* openings. She was
accompanied by Tom Neal. The tour received either a semi-
brushoff from the press or tongue-in-cheek treatment. The
press still had fun pursuing Barbara and Tom Neal.

Barbara continued to make adverse news, and was reported

in the press to have been involved in the famous Palm Springs weekend battle (October 1952) at the home of Ava Gardner and Frank Sinatra, which included Lana Turner. Barbara claimed to have participated in the colorful row which gossip columns and scandal magazines had a field day recounting for years. Explaining her own version of the event, Barbara said, "I became good friends with Ava Gardner and Lana Turner. We three were in Palm Springs together. We were drinking and lying around with not many clothes on and talking about things. Ava was married to Frank Sinatra in those days. He was screaming crazy about her. Well, he didn't approve of the way we were carrying on like that, and one night he came in and caught us all together. Well, I jumped out the window and into the bushes but he caught Lana and Ava together and he was mad as hell. It got into the gossip columns and contributed to the end of their marriage."

Barbara and Tom Neal teamed up for a quickie Western, *The Great Jesse James Raid* (1953), filmed at the cemetery of burned-out stars, Lippert. It was filmed in Ansco Color and was a sizable yawn. The legendary outlaw (Willard Parker) comes out of hiding to help steal $300,000 in gold hidden in a mine. Saloon singer Barbara, appearing overweight and bloated, sang "That's the Man for Me" to real lover Neal. "Then all of a sudden you find yourself doing a Western," Barbara said in *I Am Not Ashamed*. "A Western with 'Jesse James' in the title. I did one. . . . It was no disgrace but it didn't mark a step up." In July 1952, *Variety* announced that Barbara and Neal had signed for a picture to be made in Mexico. Columnist Erskine Johnson reported that the quarrelsome lovers would star in *Prisoner of War*, an independent feature. Both projects failed to materialize.

In 1953, Barbara and Tom Neal toured in James M. Cain's *The Postman Always Rings Twice*, playing Detroit, Pittsburgh and Chicago. They were presented as "The Tempestuous Colorful Hollywood Stars." *The Detroit Times* wrote: "The dramatization is a tight, workmanlike job that captures the spirit of this novel and makes it 'play well' on stage at the Shubert Theater." *Variety* reviewing the Pittsburgh opening, said, "Payton and Neal may look the parts but their performances are indecisive and strictly summer stock. Late in the second act, she dons a white bathing suit and he puts on swimming trunks in a beach scene that's pretty embarrassing."

Barbara next succumbed to that old ploy of washed-up or fading stars—working in England. Their names, while not potent box-office, could at least help in any film's American release. She was contracted by Exclusive-Hammer for their co-production ventures with Lippert. In the first feature, *Four-Sided Triangle* (1953), she played a dual role as a scientist-creator's duplicate of his wife's best friend. *Picturegoer* magazine said, "Barbara Payton's acting range is limited, but she projects a vivacious personality."

In her second British film, *The Flanagan Boy* (1953), also called *This Woman Is Trouble* and finally released in the U.S. as *Bad Blonde*, Barbara was the evil wife of an aged promoter, Frederick Valk, who persuades a young boxing protégé, Tony Wright, to drown her husband. The advertisements read, "They call me Bad . . . spelled M-E-N!"

In the tedious U.S.-made comedy *Run for the Hills* (1953), an insurance actuary (Sonny Tufts) buys a cave to escape a possible nuclear holocaust that he feels will hit at any moment. Barbara was his sometime angry wife who moves into the cave and shares his adventures in the best B-movie fashion. The whirlwind calmed down when her movie career ended with *Murder Is My Beat* (1955) for Allied Artists. Barbara was exceptionally good as a tough-as-nails dame convicted of murder, but en route to prison sees the man she's supposed to have killed. The end result is one superior mystery. A policeman, Paul Langton, tracks her down and begins to believe in her innocence. It was directed by Edgar G. Ulmer, whose work is highly praised by film noir enthusiasts and French film critics. The suspenseful adventure is a.k.a. *Dynamite Anchorage* and *Danger is My Beat*.

The blistering on-again, off-again explosive romance between Barbara and Neal finally burned itself out. From 1955 through 1963 there were several brushes with the law. In October 1955, upon returning from living in the tiny Mexican town of Kino on the Gulf of California, Barbara was arrested on suspicion of writing bad checks at a Hollywood supermarket. "In the market where I passed the $100 check I had spent thousands of dollars over the years. And do you know why I wrote the bad check? To get liquor not food. Not that I'm a drunk. I'm

Gail Russell

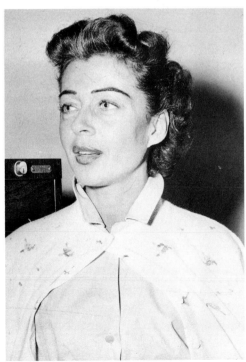

Gail Russell
leaving court
after facing
a drunk driving
charge

Sharon Tate

Sharon Tate
with Roman
Polanski

Barbara Payton

Barbara Payton
with Franchot
Tone

Inger Stevens

Inger Stevens
with Walter
Matthau in *A
Guide for the
Married Man*
(1967)

Carole Landis

Carole Landis with husband Horace Schmidlapp (1946)

Carole Landis, a suicide, on the floor of her bathroom

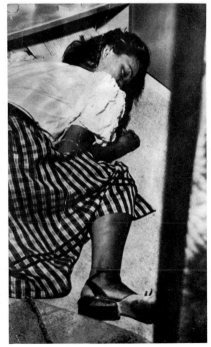

Barbara Bates

Barbara Bates
with her husband
Cecil Coan

Natalie Wood

Natalie Wood,
a little high

Suzan Ball

Suzan Ball
with new
husband
Richard Long

not. But there is something festive about having liquor around and inviting people to have a drink," wrote Barbara. She married furniture salesman George A. Provas and moved to Nogales, Arizona, for a few weeks. They divorced in August, 1958.

Back in Hollywood, a wasted-looking Barbara continued her downhill slide with more arrests for drunkenness and, finally, for prostitution. "Sooner or later you must face it," she said, explaining her nightmarish life. "You are taking money for giving a man your body for a night. Yes, but I'm no different than thousands of women every year who marry rich men for their money." Rumors that Barbara appeared in a pornographic movie remain questionable. In the book, *Movies Are Better Than Ever*, a photo of a voluptuous brunette appears next to a photo of Barbara and James Cagney in *Kiss Tomorrow Goodbye*, illustrating the course her life had undertaken. The woman in the photograph does not resemble the Barbara of that period.

In *I Am Not Ashamed*, Barbara explained how her career had plunged. She was drinking red wine during most of the taping sessions held with publisher-ghost writer Leo Guild and much of the tasteless information was told in an alcoholic haze. She said her real name was Barbara Faye and that she once appeared in a Dennis Morgan-Jack Carson comedy and also in the Frank Sinatra film *Four for Texas*. None of these facts have been verified. Barbara was living in an old shabby, rundown apartment building on the edge of Hollywood, amid unsavory characters, all her furs and jewelry gone. "The head shrinkers always told me I had the compulsive urge to see myself destroyed—that in the end it would be my final pleasure," she said. Most of her evenings were spent at a neighborhood bar, the Coach and Horses. In 1962, she was found sleeping on a bus bench at the corner of Sunset Boulevard and Stanley Avenue. Her body, clad in a bathing suit and coat, was covered with bruises. She told police she had been beaten and assaulted by a youth gang. They charged her with being drunk and with loitering. She was seen often along Sunset Boulevard, waiting for a bus or hitch-hiking. "I'm flat broke. Flat broke," she would tell drivers who stopped to give her a ride. It was a pathetic sight. But Barbara Payton never gave up.

In the last lonely years, Barbara attempted to keep a low

profile, realizing that she had become an alcoholic. She
floundered about as a shampoo girl in a West Hollywood
beauty shop, worked in sleazy Los Angeles clubs as a cocktail
waitress and, briefly, moved to the old mining town of Search-
light, Nevada. "My life has been so messed up it's hard to
know what I want to do," Barbara said. Totally dependent on
alcohol, she attended several Alcoholics Anonymous meetings,
trying to stop drinking. "Sure, drinking is self-destructive and I
do think I'm destructive at times," she said. "But then, human
reality can be very hard to take at times!" Ex-boyfriend Tom
Neal's career faded swiftly after all the notoriety and he eventually established a landscaping business in Palm Springs, where
he was accused of murdering his third wife, Gail Bennett, on
April 1, 1965. Claiming his gun went off accidentally during a
family argument, Neal was convicted of involuntary man-
slaughter and served six years. Unexpectedly, Barbara was discovered at the trial, watching from the audience at the packed
Indio Courthouse. Unlike the Barbara Payton of yore, she was
much plumper now, her skin blotched red and some of her
front teeth missing. She and Neal exchanged glances, but did
not speak. The public just wasn't interested in the notorious
pair of lovers anymore. She once confided to friends that Neal
was "the only man I ever loved." On August 7, 1972, eight
months after his release from Soledad State Prison, Tom Neal
was dead from congestive heart failure at his North Hollywood
apartment.

Barbara's personal life was complete chaos when she went to
stay with her parents in April, 1967, at their home at 1901 Titus
Street in San Diego. "I hadn't seen Barbara in years," remembers her friend from Universal, Carol Young. "She phoned and
asked if she could store some boxes in my garage. It was late,
around 11 p.m., but I said to come by. Poor Barbara, she looked
just awful, and said she was going down to San Diego to visit
her family and would be back in two weeks to pick up her
things. I felt so sorry for her and asked her in for coffee," said
Carol. "No thanks," Barbara said, "I have a friend waiting in
the car and I'm anxious to get on the road." A teary-eyed Carol
Young concluded, "I never heard from her again."

Barbara's parents had become increasingly concerned in recent months about her health and emotional problems. She
had been trying to stop drinking but by now Barbara's liver was

damaged. She seemed to be growing weaker and weaker. She refused to undergo a medical examination. Barbara's father and mother were terribly alarmed at her deteriorating condition. "For many years I journeyed into hell, now I'm ready to start over," said Barbara. Tragically, her time was running out fast and she yearned to make peace with her family. Barbara had now exhausted all sources of possible "loans" from old movie friends and acquaintances. She was in the process of divorcing her last husband, Jess Rawley.

On May 8, 1967, her father, E. Lee Redfield discovered her ravaged body on the bathroom floor, dead of heart and liver failure after a long bout with cirrhosis of the liver, aggravated by steady drinking. Her physical appearance was so drastically changed that it was two days before authorities realized who she was. The news media reported Barbara died from natural causes, replaying her tragedies, and running photos of how she once looked. The girl with the built-in destructive mechanism had come full circle.

Viewing herself in a late night telecast of *Kiss Tomorrow Goodbye*, Barbara Payton reflected in *I Am Not Ashamed*: ". . . There I am, as I was, beautiful, dashing, a big star playing opposite big stars. And there I am watching what I was. I often ask myself how it could happen. Not that I'm ashamed. I did what I had to do. But how did I fall so low? How? How?"

INGER STEVENS

The suicide of Inger Stevens still haunts many of her friends. Why would this gifted actress want to die? She had been putting up a brave front that fooled everyone. Her persona as the prototypical sunny heroine was as convincing in life as her character on her 1960s television show, "The Farmer's Daughter." But there were dark sides, also. She became self-destructive, and when she got depressed, which was quite often, slithered down into a black hole of complex misery. She once described her pain: "Once I felt that I was one person at home, and the minute I stepped out the door I had to be somebody else. I had a terrible insecurity, an extreme shyness, that I covered up with coldness. Everybody thought I was a snob. I was really just plain scared." As the years went on, Inger's fears and depressions mounted. She felt she was left with only one way out. Inger Stevens had come to the end of her journey.

Her loneliness began in early childhood when little Inger Stensland tried to understand why her mother and father didn't want to be together anymore. She was born on October 18, 1933, in Stockholm, Sweden. When she was five, her mother abandoned the family to marry another man. Inger and her brother Ola were sent to live for a time with an aunt and uncle, while her father, a teacher, continued his academic studies in America. They were kindly people, and Inger quite often referred to their generosity in later interviews.

Inger's introduction to the theatre came at six, when she was taken to see her father portray the character of Scrooge in Dickens' "A Christmas Carol." Her father, Per Stensland, a professor in the Swedish school system, was fond of directing college plays and appearing with amateur theatre groups. Her mother was also in the teaching profession, but had not shared in her husband's interest in the theatre.

She and brother Ola left Sweden when Inger was thirteen to come live with their father in the United States. Their parents had completed divorce proceedings by mail. Mr. Stensland was working on his thesis at Harvard University on a Fullbright Scholarship and was unable to meet them when the boat docked in New Orleans. Inger never forgot her fear of feeling stranded, unwanted. She wore a tag around her neck with her name on it. She hated the tag because people pointed at it. It told everyone she was a foreigner, so she quickly pushed it down inside her dress. "We came over on a freighter carrying matches," Inger later said. "We were on the ocean for nine weeks. We landed in New Orleans. The Travelers Aid took care of us first. And then a Salvation Army man took us to New York. My father had made twenty cards with Swedish phrases on one side and English on the other. But we were too proud to use them. We spoke only two words of English—yes and no, in that order." She was terrified of people discovering she didn't know English, and her shyness discouraged any further conversation.

It's hard to imagine what thoughts must have occupied her during that lonely crossing to a strange country. She was hoping to build a new and happier life with her father. What she found was a stepmother and her father preoccupied with writing his thesis on labor relations. "I fit nowhere," she once said about those early years spent in New York City where her father was now teaching at Columbia University. "Luckily I had a musical ear, so coping with the language wasn't very difficult," Inger said, "but I was . . . well . . . Swedish. I was embarrassed because I didn't look like and act like everybody else. I was a homely thing, with one tooth missing and freckles and never won a beauty contest. I remember once getting caught in the middle of an intersection when the cop who rescued me took one look and grunted, 'Oh, foreigner, eh? I can tell by the shoes.' After that I burnt the shoes and walked five blocks out of the way to avoid that cop." It was a parental decision never to speak Swedish at home, the result being that Inger eventually spoke without a trace of accent. Later, she would be required to speak with a Swedish accent on "The Farmer's Daughter" television series.

"I witnessed an awful lot of fighting in my family," she told Richard Warren Lewis in *The Saturday Evening Post*. "I got used to keeping things to myself and never really saying what was on my mind. I was always afraid of hurting somebody." When Inger was fifteen, in 1949, her family moved to Manhattan, Kansas, where Mr. Stensland had received an appointment to teach at Kansas State College. There, trouble between the teenager and her stepmother continued. Inger left home.

Inger went to Kansas City, where she worked in burlesque under the name of Kay Palmer. "There was an ad in the paper that said, 'Popcorn girl, $35 a week.' I went to the theater and the man asked me if I could dance. I thought he meant that popcorn girls had to be graceful. The next thing I knew, I was pushed out on the stage in a Statute of Liberty costume and a lot of girls were dancing around and everybody was shouting, 'Take it off!' " JoAnne Sherlock, Inger's stand-in, says, "Inger never took her clothes off and liked to joke about the teenage adventure." In three months, Inger was earning $60 a week. At Christmastime, she was given a solo number, dressed in an abbreviated Santa Claus suit and singing "Santa Claus Is Coming to Town." Her father located her and returned Inger to their Manhattan, Kansas, home. The lark was over!

Back in high school, Inger now realized she really wanted to be an actress. She became active in amateur theatricals, participating in and winning several stage competitions. She took class at Franz Schneider's ballet school. In order to finance the lessons, she taught social dancing at the college. "I enjoyed working," she said later, "And I must have been a fair teacher because one Christmas the students chipped in and bought me a set of shoe brushes." Inger took a variety of temporary jobs, working behind the counters of Penny's and Kipp's Music Store to save up enough money to get to New York City.

When Inger completed high school, her father moved to Lubbock, Texas, to become head of the adult education department at Texas Tech. Not quite eighteen, and with buoyant energy and determined ambition, she migrated to New York in 1951. Inger found a walk-up apartment over a button shop at Madison Avenue and 91st Street. To support this venture she took whatever jobs came along.

"I did odd jobs, mostly modeling in a wholesale house on Seventh Avenue in the heart of the garment district and as a movie usherette." For three months, Inger worked in the chorus at the Latin Quarter at $75 a week for thirteen shows a week. In an attempt to appear sophisticated when she went to audition, she wore white gloves. Flamboyant showman Lou Walters was appalled. "What are the gloves for?" he asked, "Are your hands cold?" Even after, Walters always called her "White Gloves."

Inger now decided to do something she had long planned on, audition for the Actors Studio, the workshop conducted by Lee Strasberg and Elia Kazan. Out of the 150 who auditioned, only 20 were accepted. Inger was among them. A small, catlike man, Strasberg was then already a living legend, known as the founder of the so-called Method school of acting, based on the theories of the Russian director, Constantin Stanislavski. According to the Method, actors were encouraged to draw on their own past experiences to project themselves emotionally in a role. The classes were held in a run-down rehearsal building, the Malin Studios, just west of Broadway in the theater district. In those dingy rooms was trained a new generation of American actors: Marlon Brando, James Dean, Rod Steiger, Carroll Baker, Eva Marie Saint, Paul Newman, Kim Stanley, Maureen Stapleton, Ben Gazzara, Geraldine Page, Julie Harris, Joanne Woodward, Jack Lord and Ellen Burstyn.

Inger subsequently won her first acting job, that of a tired housewife in a television commercial. More commercials followed. Then she met aggressive Anthony Soglio, who became her agent and manager. It was he who rechristened her Stevens and took over complete management of her career. Following their first meeting, Inger and Soglio began an immediate courtship. The early 1950s was an exciting time in television; some would later regard it as the medium's "Golden Age." Inger began appearing regularly on television dramatic shows such as "Studio One," "Kraft Music Theatre," "Robert Montgomery Presents" and "Armstrong Circle Theatre." She was perfecting her style, and was able to learn rapidly in the fast-paced world of television.

In 1954, Inger toured the summer circuits as Signe Hasso's daughter in *Glad Tidings*, beginning at the Pocono Playhouse in Pennsylvania. In a subsequent stock tour of New England,

Inger appeared with Gypsy Rose Lee in Clare Boothe Luce's *The Women,* as Peggy Day (the Joan Fontaine role in the Metro-Goldwyn-Mayer 1939 film), one of the few sympathetic parts in a play overloaded with bitchy females. Inger was a series replacement (for Kathleen Nolan) on the live ABC-Televison show, "Jamie," starring Brandon de Wilde. The eleven-year-old child actor played a likeable orphan who had been shunted from one uncaring relative to another.

On July 1, 1955, in a minister's mansion in Greenwich, Connecticut, Inger married agent Anthony Soglio. The turbulent marriage lasted just shy of six months and they were finally divorced three years later. Inger paid Soglio 5 percent of her earnings under a managerial contract that ran through 1966. It was a high price to pay and a constant frustration to her. In the same *Saturday Evening Post* article, Inger said: "That was the worst day of my life," she said. "I wanted to be anyplace but where I was. I married him for a lot of the wrong reasons. I had been dating him for about eight months, and he was the only person I knew in New York. For me, the whole marriage proved pretty much of a nightmare."

Inger broke into Broadway on February 22, 1956, at the Holiday Theater in the comedy, *Debut,* with Tom Helmore and Alberta Hunter. Critics panned the show and it closed after only four performances. Despite the hostile tone of the reviews, several critics singled Inger out for a brief word of praise. She had been noticed and was summoned to California by producer-director Albert McCleery for a "Matinee Theatre" episode and an "Alfred Hitchcock Presents" segment. Inger began drawing attention from Hollywood studios. Twentieth Century-Fox put Inger under a test option for three months. "My experience with Fox wasn't a total loss because, while awaiting the outcome of the test, I took driving lessons at the studio's expense," she once remembered.

Producers Perlberg and Seaton saw Inger's performance on "Eloise," a "Playhouse 90" production. The show had to do with the antics of a precocious little demon, Evelyn Rudie, who lives at the staid Plaza Hotel in New York. The producers had Inger test at Paramount for the feminine lead in *The Tin Star,* which was to star Henry Fonda and Anthony Perkins. Director Anthony Mann deemed Inger too young for the part, while

Paramount placed her under a term contract. Betsy Palmer won the role in the unpretentious Western.

"It was the most difficult period of my life," Inger remembered. "Running away as a teenager I survived without scars because I didn't realize the dangers. But when I came to Hollywood, I was old enough to know and I was lonely and confused. At first I had no friends, no one to really care what happened to me. I was very naïve about people and things. Everybody's main interest isn't in you, but in themselves. This is probably true everywhere, but I felt it keenly when I came to Hollywood. I had never worked in films before and it was a rather startling world to be thrown into."

Metro-Goldwyn-Mayer borrowed Inger for *Man on Fire* (1957), starring Bing Crosby. It's one of the most realistic studies of divorce ever made about a man with a custody problem concerning his son, Malcolm Brodrick, and divorced wife, Mary Fickett. Inger played the new girl in Crosby's life. "I never thought in a million years that I would get the role in *Man on Fire*. But I went in there and just sort of did it. It scared the daylights out of me. I had never done a movie before—and to work on a film with Bing Crosby!" When Inger was carried off the set with an appendicitis attack, Crosby visited the hospital with flowers every day. They soon became attracted off camera. Gossip columnists soon got word of the bedimpled beauty with the expressive gray-blue eyes and the millionaire widower. His wife of 22 years, Dixie Lee had died in 1952. Crosby was previously linked with Joan Caulfield, Mona Freeman, Kathryn Grant and Paramount dancer Betty Hannon.

"I thought Bing loved me," a sad Inger told a friend afterwards. She kept on thinking that until the very day Crosby wed Kathryn Grant in October, 1957. Inger was devastated. He had been going with the 24-year-old actress for a year, when they broke off and he started dating Inger. Apparently, she didn't know that Crosby and Grant had resumed their affair. Inger took it hard and would often say the reason they didn't marry was because she was not a Catholic. "One day he called me up and told me to go buy new drapes and curtains for the Palm Springs house," she said afterwards. "He wanted me to decorate it to my taste. He even told me that it was going to be my house so I had better fix it up the way I liked it. It may not have been a proposal but I sure took it as one. Believe it or not, I was down in the house, supervising some workmen in putting up the new drapes when I heard the news announcement over the radio that Bing had married another girl. I went into a state of shock. It took me months to recover. I actually became physically sick from all the distress." Later, the Swedish beauty would say, "After you go out with Bing, you're spoiled for young men of say 25 or 26. Being with an older man is a secure feeling for me. There was a big age difference, too. Also I was guilt-ridden because I was dating a man and I wasn't yet divorced."

Inger's stunning introduction in *Man on Fire* won respectable attention from the moviegoing public. *Variety* reported: "Inger Stevens, as a femme lawyer, is another newcomer who should be heard from in the future. She is particularly appealing as she nurses Crosby through his vicious and embittered moods." In *The Films of Bing Crosby*, Robert Bookbinder wrote: "Inger Stevens and E.G. Marshall are both excellent as Crosby's faithful friends who attempt to bring the embittered businessman back to his senses. Stevens in particular proves, in her compassionate scenes with Crosby, that she was a vastly underrated actress capable of much better roles than she was usually given." The film marked an auspicious beginning for Inger.

Although Inger possessed the curiously exciting blond quality that Alfred Hitchcock liked, she was passed over for Paramount's *Vertigo*, in favor of Kim Novak. *Life* magazine (August 12, 1957) gave a three-page color spread to Inger, May Britt and Ingrid Goude, entitled "Sumptuous Swedish Smorgasbord." *Life* thought Inger "displays a country club polish."

Cry Terror (1958), Inger's second film at Metro-Goldwyn-Mayer, remains among her best. If all but forgotten today, it contains one of her most affecting performances. She plays James Mason's frightened but resourceful wife while psychopath Rod Steiger forces Mason to aid him to master an extortion plot. The film contains some interesting Manhattan locations. In September, 1957, Inger and 11 movie technicians were felled by carbon monoxide while filming *Cry Terror* in a Hoboken railroad tunnel. Inger narrowly escaped death from the fumes spread by a gasoline generator and had to be hospitalized.

Inger's spirits were at an extremely low ebb when she became catapulted into a tumultuous affair with Anthony Quinn. "Under the personal supervision of Cecil B. DeMille," Quinn directed Inger, Charlton Heston, Yul Brynner, Charles Boyer and Claire Bloom in the lavish remake of *The Buccaneer* (1958), a swashbuckler retelling events during the War of 1812 when Andrew Jackson (Heston) is forced to rely on buccaneer Lafitte (Brynner) to help the British. It was a big-scale bomb. The reviews were lukewarm for the saga. *Photoplay* thought: "Inger Stevens makes a pretty chilly heroine, as the governor's daughter, who isn't sure it's quite proper to love an outlaw"

Quinn was married to actress Katharine DeMille, the adopted daughter of C.B. DeMille. He had warned Inger that he had no intention of divorcing his wife, due in part to their four young children. "Women can understand why Tony is so easy to fall in love," the incorrigibly romantic actress said. "He is the perfect embodiment of the virile male that all women subconsciously seek. He's Eugene O'Neill's Hairy Ape, he is the Southern aristocrat's forbidden date from the other side of the tracks. He's mysterious, he's fascinating. He's all man." The late Katy Theodore was Inger's personal dress designer and closest confidante. Inger told her, "Tony told me he couldn't live without me. It was like he was acting out a scene." Inger took a cruise to Europe in June, 1958, to try to reorganize her thoughts, and then, upon her return to the United States, went into analysis. The Quinn-DeMille union ended in 1965; Quinn then married Jolanda Addolari, an Italian wardrobe mistress, the same year.

On her third loan-out to Metro-Goldwyn-Mayer, *The World, the Flesh and the Devil* (1959), Inger, Harry Belafonte and Mel Ferrer play the only survivors of a nuclear explosion. What started as an intriguing premise gets lost halfway through, with a ridiculous conclusion. In a recent viewing of the bizarre tale, the scenes between Inger and Belafonte lend credence to the romance rumors which circulated during the New York filming. Paramount then negotiated a fourth loan-out to Metro-Goldwyn-Mayer for a courtroom drama, *Key Witness*. Inger balked at the project and was replaced by Pat Crowley. "Artistic differences" were cited as to the causes for her departure.

She subsequently underwent a long three-year contract battle with Paramount and went into debt, paying off contracts which had been negotiated by husband-agent Tony Soglio.

Inger's first break with Hollywood came in December, 1959. She was exhausted from a cross-country tour in behalf of *The World, the Flesh and the Devil* and decided to move back to New York City. She had made personal appearances in 16 cities in just 18 days. Inger moved into a spacious apartment at 24 Gramercy Park just in time for the Christmas holidays. She told JoAnne Sherlock, "I've never ever had a real home of my own. Now I can afford to have it and I don't miss Hollywood at all."

After a New Year's Eve party, Inger returned home alone to her new apartment, which was cluttered with cardboard cartons and wooden crates, all having arrived the day before from Hollywood. She proceeded, for reasons not known to anyone, to take 25 sleeping pills and swallow a half-bottle of ammonia. Three days later, her unconscious body was discovered by the building handyman. A friend, David Tebet, an NBC-Television executive, had called Inger over and over again throughout the weekend and summoned the building superintendent to break into her apartment. It was a miracle that she was still alive. Inger was rushed to Columbus Hospital. There were blood clots under her left lung, and her legs were afflicted with phlebitis and were swollen to four times their normal size, but somehow she made it through the morning. She was also blind. The sightless condition lasted for two weeks, when she finally began to regain her vision. It gradually was restored, although scar tissue always remained to cloud the corners of her eyes. The only visitors permitted to see her were younger brother Ola and David Tebet. "I was feeling lonely, very withdrawn," Inger confessed later. "I'd been in love. It ended. I tried to end myself. It solves nothing."

A Paramount executive soberly reflected on Inger's suicide attempt. "She was in love with Bing Crosby, and later Anthony Quinn. Inger tends to prefer older men. She finds them intellectually charming and I'm sure this is due to the influence of her father. She's grown up in the atmosphere of education and learning. Many of Bing's friends seemed to think it would have been a very good thing if it had worked out, if they had gotten married. Many people thought Bing and Inger were ideally suited. They seemed very much in love."

With her "Scandinavian determination," Inger bounced back to work two months later. "I lost perspective," she said, "but I benefited. . . . I can laugh at myself now!" Inger returned to Broadway in Sidney Sheldon's *Roman Candle* with Robert Sterling and Julia Meade. The comedy premiered at the Cort Theatre on February 3, 1960, and died after only five performances. She played a girl with extrasensory perception. The understudy for the two feminine leads was a newcomer from Ocala, Florida—a few years later, Elizabeth Ashley would be Broadway's brightest new star in *Barefoot in the Park*. Inger immediately returned to Hollywood after the closing of *Roman Candle*. For the next three years, she quarrelled frequently with Paramount over roles she found inferior; she guest-starred regularly on television, in such shows as "Hong Kong," "Twilight Zone," "Adventures In Paradise" and "Follow The Sun."

Returning from Europe to Los Angeles in June, 1961, Inger was the last passenger to leap from a burning jet that crashed on landing at the Lisbon, Portugal, airport. The plane exploded 20 seconds following her exit. "I still hate to talk about it," Inger said later. "The plane started burning and I thought I would be burned alive. I put on my coat, of all things, and curled up on the floor. Somehow I escaped and now I feel as if I were on borrowed time—that the worst is over and it's clear sailing." She added, "But it is reassuring to know you can continue to function under pressure and not give in to hysteria."

Inger received an Emmy nomination in 1962 for her performance in "The Price of Tomatoes" on the NBC-Television anthology series, "The Dick Powell Theater," opposite Peter Falk. He won an Emmy for his performance as a trucker racing to deliver tomatoes ahead of his rival. Slowing him down was a broke and very pregnant hitchhiker, Inger.

In 1963, Inger replaced Barbara Bel Geddes in *Mary, Mary* at the Helen Hayes Theater. It provided her with her biggest stage triumph. When she returned to California, Inger collapsed under the combined pressures of overwork, underweight and internal hemorrhaging. She had survived not only attempted suicide but also a fiery plane crash, a disastrous mar-

riage and three depressing love affairs with prominent personalities.

It was as the beguiling Swedish domestic on ABC-TV's
sitcom "The Farmer's Daughter" that Inger became television's
darling golden girl—honest, believable and successfully
capturing the ambivalence of the outspoken Minnesota farm
girl. "If we hadn't gotten Inger," said producer Peter Kortner,
"we might have abandoned the show. She was the only name
we ever talked about."

Inger was Katie Holstrum, who upsets Washington with her
frank opinions on the meaning of democracy while working as
a maid for Congressman widower William Windom and his
mother, Cathleen Nesbitt. Loretta Young won the 1947 Academy Award as the household maid who ends up elected to
Congress in the RKO Radio Pictures version. So popular had
the series become during its three seasons (1963-66) that when
one of the segments featured Inger's wedding to the Congressman, Washington, D.C.'s renowned "hostess with the
mostest," Pearl Mesta, arranged for an elaborate "real-life"
wedding reception for Inger and William Windom. The news-
media event was attended by 300 real-life ambassadors, members of Congress, high government officials, and a barrage of
photographers, newsmen and press agents.

Inger received a *TV Guide* award as the "Favorite Female Performer" of the year and the Hollywood Foreign Press Association honored her with their Golden Globe Award as "The Best
Actress on Television" She owned 25 percent of the Screen
Gems Production. "The Farmer's Daughter" was an appropri-
ate and glowing comedy series that lasted three years in the top
ten in the Nielsen Ratings. Co-star William Windom jokingly
referred to Inger as "the lady of secrets."

During the success of the television series, Inger returned to
the big screen in Columbia's *The New Interns* (1964), a hospital
soap opera. There were at least three major plots and as many
subplots. Inger played a social worker who snaps after being
criminally assaulted. It was a follow-up to the studio's *The Interns* (1962). She also returned to her native land to host her
own television special, "Inger Stevens in Sweden."

"I cannot exist for myself alone," she said. With new insight,
Inger plunged into a crusade to help mentally retarded chil-

dren. Karen Stensland Junker, the aunt with whom she had lived in Sweden, "the biggest influence in my life, there were plenty of other influences but hers was the good one," was the mother of two mentally retarded youngsters. Mrs. Junker researched the subject and wrote a definitive book on the subject, *The Child in the Glass Ball.*

The California Council of Retarded Children appointed Inger as their chairwoman and she traveled throughout the state to raise funds in its behalf. She founded the Celebrity Art Exhibit, collecting paintings by famous people to benefit these unfortunate children. She was also appointed by former California Governor Pat Brown to the Board of the Neuro-Psychiatric Institute at UCLA Medical Center. Whatever free time she had left was devoted to the Kedren Community Health Center in the Watts neighborhood, where she worked with emotionally disturbed black youngsters. If questioned about her timeless efforts, Inger would say, "It is nothing compared to what they have given me!" She also found time to take an active part in the unsuccessful 1968 presidential campaign of (the late) Hubert Humphrey.

From 1967 through 1969, Inger's hectic work schedule was stretched in eight conventional motion pictures. In 20th Century-Fox's *A Guide for the Married Man* (1967), with Walter Matthau, Inger proved to be a stylish light comedienne under the direction of Gene Kelly. *A Time for Killing* (1967), a pedestrian Western, was begun by director Roger Corman and completed by Phil Karson. It was also known as *The Long Ride Home*, a Civil War tale of vengeance and pursuit in the Utah-Arizona desert, with Glenn Ford and George Hamilton. Warner Bros.-Seven Arts' *Firecreek* (1968) was a first-rate vehicle, starring James Stewart and Henry Fonda. The tough, somber Western found bandit Fonda falling in love with Inger, the daughter of boarding house owner Jay C. Flippen. Judith Crist on NBC-TV's "Today" show said: *Firecreek* has some explosive stuff but it is, thanks to its stars and direction, a satisfyingly low-key and absorbing Western." Filmed on location in Arizona's spectacular Oak Creek Canyon, the grim Western did only mild business.

At Universal, Inger appeared with Henry Fonda and Richard Widmark in *Madigan* (1968), a cops-and-crime story, filmed in

New York City. Inger was detective Widmark's neglected wife in this thriller about Manhattan's police department and their day-to-day problems while attempting to track down a killer at the same time. The manhunt sequences were filmed with director Don Siegel's distinctive flair for pacing. Andrew Sarris reported in *The Village Voice*: "*Madigan* turns out to be the best American movie I have seen so far in 1968." Commenting on her heavy work load, Inger said in an interview, "I take great pride in my work. I want very much to fulfill my life. When I die, I don't want to have just gone down that road and just crawled into a hole and that's it. I would like to have left something behind. Not that I'm an Einstein, or anything like that. I would like to have contributed something to this generation in which I live. And maybe I would do it through my work as an actress. Because, after all, acting is your interpretation of life."

Inger went on location to Durango, Mexico, for the Hal Wallis production *Five Card Stud* (1968), with Dean Martin and Robert Mitchum. She was lost in the shuffle between sheriff Martin and a religious maniac killer, Mitchum. Film historian Leonard Maltin refers to *Five Card Stud* in *TV Movies* as "probably director Henry Hathaway's worst Western." *Hang 'Em High* (1968), was Clint Eastwood's first American-made Western after becoming an international superstar. The United Artists release successfully attempted to duplicate his *Dollar* trilogy popularity at the box-office. Inger was Eastwood's love interest, a local businesswoman, while he tracks down nine men who had tried to lynch him. It was every bit as brutal as his Italian films. "A Western of quality, courage, danger and excitement which places itself squarely in the procession of old-fashioned Westerns made with the latest techniques," said the New York *Post*.

The NBC-TV thriller "The Borgia Stick" had Don Murray and Inger as a young couple trying to break away from a modernized crime syndicate. The cast included Barry Nelson, Fritz Weaver and Valerie Allen. The two-hour drama was released throughout Europe (1968) as a Universal feature film.

The seven motion pictures increased Inger's star status and gave glimpses of the actress's range. Her professional future never looked so promising.

Inger played a widow in her last two completed films, both abysmal failures. In the compelling thriller *House of Cards*

(1969), George Peppard and Inger get involved with a fascist group, headed by arch-villain Orson Welles, in Europe. Inger looked sensational as a chic, sophisticated young mother of affluence. The action unfolds against the lush on-location splendor of Rome. In *The Los Angeles Times*, Kevin Thomas dubbed *House of Cards* "A mildly diverting so-so adventure movie that could have been lots better." National General's *A Dream of Kings* (1969) was to be Inger's farewell cinematic appearance. It is ironic that this film contains one of her most affecting performances. *Variety* wrote: ". . . Equally strong as the knotted-up widow, Inger Stevens becomes Anthony Quinn's passionate mistress and displays a voluptuous flash in her love scenes." Inger and Quinn enjoyed a good working relationship during the filming in Chicago, but it still must have been a painful experience for her. *A Dream of Kings* was her thirteenth film. "I have achieved a wonderful balance in my life now," she told Peer J. Oppenheimer in one of her last interviews.

Inger was financially secure because of her "The Farmer's Daughter" percentage deal. Her money was invested in a daycare center, a convalescent home, Malibu Beach property, a chain of pharmacies and a trust fund for herself. A great source of escape for Inger was the picturesque town of Solvang, a little tourist town north of Los Angeles. This Danish community is known for its Hans Christian Andersen atmosphere. Inger considered this Scandinavian village her personal retreat, providing her with memories of her childhood in Sweden. Inger once said, "Getting away from the work and the hours I put in, it amazes me how quickly I can forget the time I've invested in my career."

Although Inger was still suffering from recurring depression, her career was zooming. In late 1969, Inger filmed for MGM-TV "The Mask of Sheba," about an anthropological team searching for missing safari members and a priceless gold statue in Ethiopia. Also in the cast were Walter Pidgeon, Eric Braeden, William Marshall and Stephen Young. Inger appeared puffy and drawn. What was to be Inger's last TV assignment, ABC-TV's "Run, Simon, Run," co-starred Burt Reynolds, James Best and Royal Dano. The exhausting production began as "The Tradition of Simon Zuniga." In contemporary Arizona, a Papago Indian, Reynolds, is torn between his desire to avenge

his brother's death and his love for an Indian reservation counselor, Inger. During the hot Tucson location, Inger fell under
the Reynolds charm, resulting in a love affair. The actor gave
her much needed strength and support. Due to Reynolds' well-
known sense of humor, Inger finally emerged from her self-
imposed depression and misery. She began clinging to him for
comfort and security. But when the company of "Run, Simon,
Run" returned to Hollywood for interiors, the romance with
Burt Reynolds had cooled. "Let's just say our friendship is a
very special one," Inger told stand-in JoAnne Sherlock.

And then, after years of torturous self-exploration and severe
depression, Inger Stevens was dead! Her house-guest, Lola
"Butch" McNally, a studio hairdresser, found her golden-
brown negligee-clad body on Thursday morning, April 30,
1970, lying facedown on the kitchen floor of Inger's house at
8000 Woodrow Wilson Drive in the Hollywood Hills. She had
taken a high dosage of Tedral, washed down with alcohol.
McNally told the investigators that Inger opened her eyes, tried
to speak, and then slumped into unconsciousness. Rushed by
ambulance down the winding Laurel Canyon, Inger was pro-
nounced dead on arrival, shortly after 10 a.m. at the Hollywood Receiving Hospital. McNally said she had spoken to
Inger at about 11:15 p.m. the night before and the actress
seemed to be in good spirits. "There was no hint of trouble,"
the police theorized. "We believe she was trying to call for help
when she passed out."

It was only after Inger's sudden death that the public found
out that she had been married for nine years to black Isaac (Ike)
Jones, an athlete turned producer. Jones had been the director
of Nat "King" Cole's entertainment company and, following
Cole's death, produced Sammy Davis, Jr.'s absorbing drama *A
Man Called Adam* (1966) with Cicely Tyson. There are many contradictory accounts of Inger's relationship with the husband
she was never to acknowledge openly. She was afraid the public would never accept the "mixed marriage," recalling the reaction to the Sammy Davis-May Britt nuptials.

It's been reported that the last circle of acquaintances knew
Inger only a brief time, especially a well-known international
entertainer who contributed to her despondency in those last
weeks. In the opinion of many of Inger's close friends, a great

deal of conflicting misinformation was fed to the news media regarding the disheartening events. Ike Jones, as "husband of the deceased," claimed her body and made arrangements for private rites at the Angeles Funeral Home, located in the black Crenshaw district of Los Angeles. No press were allowed. Inger's body was cremated and her ashes scattered over the Pacific Ocean, four days after her demise. She left no will. A Los Angeles Superior Court Commissioner appointed Jones as administrator of the actress's estate, valued at over $171,000, with more to come through television and motion picture residuals.

Ironically, Jones was unable to produce documentary evidence of their marriage. But the couple's attorney confirmed that they had been married in Tijuana, Mexico, on November 18, 1961. But Lola McNally testified that the actress told her the couple never went through a legal ceremony. Testifying as Jones's chief witness of such conflicting claims, her brother said, "Inger wrote to me and asked me to keep her marriage a secret because it would endanger her career as an actress, and in the series ("The Farmer's Daughter") since she might lose it, and other pending contracts." The estate was eventually divided among Jones, her father who resided in New York City, and to her mother, Mrs. Lisbet Rubenstein of Stockholm, Sweden.

Although Inger and Jones officially separated in 1969, Jones said he and Inger spent the weekend together before her death and he drove her back to their home on Sunday night. On Monday, April 27, Inger and Burt Reynolds dined at La Scala Restaurant with producer Aaron Spelling to celebrate Inger's signing to star in Spelling's new whodunit series, "The Most Deadly Game," for ABC-TV, with Ralph Bellamy and George Maharis. It involved a trio of highly trained criminologists. The adventure-mystery was scheduled to begin filming in June. Producer Spelling, upon Inger's death, offered the series to Stella Stevens, who declined the offer. Yvette Mimieux took over the role as the college-trained criminologist; the show folded within three months.

When Anthony Quinn heard the news that Inger had taken her life, he said, "Inger didn't belong here. She should have stayed in Sweden and married a truck driver and had eight kids. She had idealism and purity, and maybe she came to a sort of desperation. The great competitiveness and phony sense of accomplishment we have here can be very destructive." JoAnne Sherlock, who probably knew her as well as anybody and still weeps at the memory of her death, maintains, "Inger's life had never been happier, she finally had some financial security, a new television series, and a new love, Burt Reynolds. She always had the ability to guard the dark side of her nature, even from those friends closest to her. She was very sincere and trusting." She added, "I can remember the hours she spent with mentally retarded children because she had such a compassionate and generous heart. Her childhood was not a happy one and I believe it caused her many problems later in life."

Inger Stevens once said, "A career can't put its arms around you. The thing I miss most is having someone to share things with. I always used to jump into friendships and give too much. You can't do that. You end up like Grand Central Station with people just coming and going. And there you are, left alone."

She was thirty-six years old.

CAROLE LANDIS

Carole Landis came streaking into stardom like a comet ready to burn out—and a few years later, she did. The legend is that the throaty-voiced, blue-eyed beauty was playing herself, a bright and bouncy girl, with an undertone of occasional sadness, searching for something even she wasn't sure of. She began to stagger under the strain of having to be constantly sexy on screen, "I want a fair chance to prove myself as an actress—not just a curvaceous cutie!" But no one paid her any mind. Carole joined that army of actresses who supposedly acted out their personal lives in their professional careers, their talent and unhappiness as one, propelling them headlong into quick fame and quick destruction. The intense pressures of public life caused Carole Landis to call it quits. The Hollywood cult of the failure of success.

Frances Lillian Mary Ridste was born New Year's Day, January 1, 1919, in Fairchild, Wisconsin, and was one of five children (two died at birth) of Alfred and Clara Stentek Ridste, who were of Norwegian and Polish decent. The children were all baptized in the Catholic faith. Sister Dorothy was eighteen months old and brother Lawrence was eight years older than Frances.

A few months after Frances' birth, her father, a sometime section worker, farmhand and a drifting railroad mechanic (for the Santa Fe Railroad), ended a family quarrel by walking out. The task of supporting a wife and three small children proved too much for him, and he abandoned them. Frances' mother, a strong-willed, independent woman, moved the family to California, first to San Diego and then to San Bernardino, when Frances was only three.

When Frances was seven, she took part in an amateur night contest at the Strand Theater in San Bernardino. She would later recall the event: "When the master of ceremonies made his appearance, I shouted from the back of the theater, 'I want to sing.' I ran down the aisle as fast as I could, climbed the stage and let loose with, 'That's My Weakness Now.' When I finished my last note, only two people applauded me—my mother and brother. My brother lectured me at home, though, saying that I'd disgraced the whole family. He said he was ashamed to face his friends. At fifteen, he was, too." At twelve, she won a pair of stockings as fourth prize in a bathing beauty contest. Later, in another contest, she placed second and was rewarded with an electric heater. Then Mrs. Ridste called a halt; she felt her daughter was just too young. Always star struck, Carole as a child had as her favorites Kay Francis and Mary Astor. One entire bedroom wall that she shared with sister Dorothy was devoted to the actresses. "Although I avoided dramatics at school, I shared with a million other girls the dream of making a conquest of the stage, movies or radio," Carole later said.

She attended the Jefferson School, Sturges Jr. High and San Bernardino High School. At the latter, Frances played baseball and football. She was the organizer of a girl's football team which was soon disbanded by the school authorities, who termed the game "too rough for girls." Just past her fifteenth birthday, she eloped with Irving Wheeler, 19, to Yuma, Arizona on January 14, 1934. Three weeks later, the marriage was over and she returned to school. They would later remarry on August 25, 1934. At various times, she found employment as a movie usherette, sales girl and waitress.

In 1935, Frances, with few possessions and exactly $16.82 in her purse, left Irving Wheeler and took a Greyhound bus to San Francisco. Rumors of a sometimes mysterious past as a call girl in the City by the Bay would follow Carole for years. Once asked what rumors about herself upset her the most, Carole answered, "Anyone in public life gets used to unkind rumors after a time, though all of them are very upsetting when they are published or broadcast. I've learned to stand up to them, however."

She soon changed her name to Carole (taken from Carole

Lombard) Landis, and teamed with another girl, Kay Ellis; posing as a sister act, they danced the hula at the popular Royal Hawaiian Club. It was her first official job in show business. Next she sang with Carl Ravazza's Orchestra at the exclusive Rio del Mar Country Club in Santa Cruz, south of San Francisco.

Carole decided to move on to Hollywood (1936) to try to break into the movies; she settled in an apartment at 1933 Bronson Avenue. She was soon joined by her mother and estranged husband. She can be spotted in the Santa Anita bar sequence in *A Star Is Born* (1937), David O. Selznick's classic about Hollywood's tragic ups and downs. When Metro-Goldwyn-Mayer put out a casting call for chorus girls, Carole showed up and was hired for *A Day at the Races* (1937), *The Emperor's Candlesticks* (1937) and *Broadway Melody of 1938* (1937). Beth Renner was a fellow chorine and a favorite "gypsy" of Busby Berkeley. "I danced with Carole in several musicals, but the one that stands out in my mind is *The King and the Chorus Girl* (1937). She was having marital problems with her husband (Wheeler), who was an extra and always about. In one routine, she was upset that our choreographer, Bobby Connolly, didn't put her up front during the rehearsals. When it came time to shoot the number, Carole had her way," Beth said. "The director Mervyn LeRoy liked her, and I remember Buz (Berkeley) just adored her. Carole was ambitious, independent and wanted it all," Beth Renner remembers.

At Warner Brothers, she was chosen by Busby Berkeley for the chorus of *Varsity Show* (1937), a college musical that found alumnus Dick Powell with the Lane Sisters trying to put on a "swinging" show. Berkeley designed the finale as a tribute to colleges everywhere, with a series of overhead shots in which the chorus spelled out the initials of noted places of learning. He saw to it that Carole was prominently noticeable as Sterling Holloway's dance partner. "For the two days before rehearsals started, I practiced constantly, barely taking time to eat," she later said. Warner Brothers files show that on May 13, 1937, Carole was contracted as a dancer for *Varsity Show*. She claimed to have been born in Chicago, Ill., on January 1, 1916 (?) and lied that she was single.

Busby Berkeley pulled strings to get the aspiring actress a

$50-a-week stock contract with Warner Brothers in July, 1937. For a year, Carole languished around the studio as merely another hopeful contract player. She had unbilled bits in *The Adventurous Blonde* (1937), *Over the Goal*(1937), *He Couldn't Say No* (1938), *Women Are Like That* (1938), *Blondes at Work* (1938), *Hollywood Hotel* (1937), *Girls on Probation (1938)*, *Over the Wall* (1938), *When Were You Born?* (1938) and *Men Are Such Fools* (1938). Carole first received billing (19th) in *Boy Meets Girl* (1938), as a studio commissary cashier. While working in *Gold Diggers in Paris* (1938), she became friendly with Diana Lewis (later to marry William Powell), who gifted Carole with a little gold cross, which she wore around her neck for the rest of her life. She considered it bad luck if she didn't do so. While playing Errol Flynn's secretary in *Four's a Crowd* (1938), Carole was charmed by his wit and roguish good looks. She was flattered by his flirtatious manner, despite the fact that Flynn was already married to French actress Lili Damita.

Carole, Ronald Reagan and Susan Hayward appeared on the "Warner Brothers Academy Theater," a studio-syndicated radio series designed to push Warner Brothers films with dramatizations and prolific plugs.

Two weeks after Warners dropped her, Carole made her first headlines. Or, rather, husband Irving Wheeler did, by suing Busby Berkeley for $250,000. He charged that Berkeley had wheedled Carole's affections away from him. "There has been neither affection nor consortium between myself and Mr. Wheeler since September, 1934," Carole told the court. Carole said her association with Berkeley was "strictly platonic." The suit was tossed out of court, and a year later she won a divorce from Wheeler. But Busby Berkeley did ask Carole to marry him.

Claire James was Miss California of 1938, the year Berkeley selected her for the chorus of *Gold Diggers in Paris* with Carole. Claire and Berkeley would eventually marry for a short time, three years later. "Carole was bitterly disappointed when Buz said he couldn't marry her," Claire said. "His mother, Gertrude, had heard rumors that Carole had once been a call girl and persuaded Buz to break off their engagement." It's doubtful if Gertrude Berkeley would have considered any girl good enough for her youngest son—but absolutely not Carole Landis.

Agent Louis Shurr took over Carole's career and landed her the part of Sophie Teal in the Los Angeles revival of Jerome Kern's musical *Roberta*, starring Shurr's client Bob Hope, in his original part. (Shurr's notorious bedroom closet was filled with expensive women's furs. This wasn't due to transvestism, but for his young dates' night on the town.) Producer Lawrence Schwab saw Carole in *Roberta* and offered her a part in *Once Upon a Night*, starring Ken Murray, which he had hoped to bring into New York. The satirically named musical folded after two nights in Wilmington, Delaware.

Back in Hollywood, a frustrated Carole found work with Republic Pictures in their hard-action B Westerns. In *Three Texas Steers* (1939), John Wayne as one of the "Three Mesquiteers" comes to the rescue of Carole who stands to lose her inherited circus and ranch. For Republic, she also rode the range in *Cowboys from Texas* (1939), with Robert Livingston, and did a twelve-chapter serial, *Daredevils of the Red Circle* (1939) with Charles Quigley and Bruce Bennett.

Hal Roach, Sr., was searching for someone to play a prehistoric girl in his next feature, *One Million B.C.* (1940). Producer Roach had hired D.W. Griffith to direct the film and has credited Griffith with discovering Carole for "Loana," the scantily-clad cave girl. Victor Mature, teeth gleaming and biceps bulging, had already been cast. As Roach told the story in Rosenberg and Silverstein's *The Real Tinsel*, he said, "Dave, I'd like you to cast the picture." They brought in girls (tested were Steffi Duna, Evelyn Keyes, Diana Lewis, Claire James and Beverly Roberts). "I wasn't paying any attention. He looked at them. . . . Every time these girls came in, he took them to the back lot. I didn't know what the hell he was doing out in the open spaces. Then one day, he said, 'I found your girl.' It was Carole Landis. 'Come out. I want to show you something.' We went out on the back lot where there was street scenery and, on the corner, a telephone post. He looked at the girl and said, 'Take your shoes off. Now run to that post as fast as you can. Then run back to me as fast as you can.' she did. I wasn't particularly impressed. That's a hell of way to pick our leading lady. We know she can run. He said, 'I've had fifty girls run to that post and back. She's the only one who knows how to run. You're not going to make a believable girl in a picture of that kind who runs like an average girl. She's got to run like an athlete, a deer.' And she could. Her rhythm was really beautiful. In the picture, you never noticed it. But if she ran like most girls, you would damn well have seen the difference."

Hal Roach said only that he liked the test and would consider Carole. He asked for a month's option. "Eight months of that delicate form of medieval torture," Carole later told an interviewer with bitterness. "Each month another option and me riding those nags at Republic and getting fat in all the wrong places." Whether D.W. Griffith directed any of *One Million B.C.* has never been entirely determined. Hal Roach claims that none of the footage in the completed film was directed by Griffith. Many film historians believe he was only employed as a casting consultant. Directorial credit is given jointly to Hal Roach and Hal Roach, Jr.

Carole put herself on the strictest of diets, became a willowy blonde and underwent cosmetic surgery to alter the shape of her nose. The operation refined her profile, giving her features a much softer appearance. Her new movie star image, as it would be groomed and projected by the Roach studio publicity machine, was born. The critics judged *One Million B.C.* "as primitive as the characters." The only part they really liked was the trick photography that showed shattering battles between exotic monsters. The saga of prehistoric tribesmen and their struggle for survival was a surprise hit.

Carole moved into the Sunset Tower Apartments at 8358 Sunset Boulevard, one of the Sunset Strip's most striking silhouettes. In April, 1940, Hal Roach publicist Frank Seltzer named Carole "The Ping Girl" of America—because she wants to purr (the press releases stated). The campaign proved ill-advised, as the public just didn't take to the "Ping" hype. It made no sense, but that mattered little since the equally inane "Oomph Girl," a label Ann Sheridan was branded with, received tremendous column space and parlayed her into a major star. Carole took an ad out in *Variety* to protest "this mental blitzkreig" by her press agents and to proclaim that she would "not be present at my reception (as the Ping Girl) to ping, purr or even coo."

Carole's next film for Hal Roach was *Turnabout* (1940), a screwball sex opus from Thorne Smith's novel about a husband, John Hubbard, and his wife, Carole, having their personalities reversed. She wore a man's striped pajamas and Hubbard a negligee. The comic possibilities of a female inside a male body were better used than the opposite situation, with Carole acting as a man. The concept leads to some amusing complications, particularly under the direction of Hal Roach himself, who had to work around the prevailing Production Code. As a bickering couple, Mary Astor and Adolphe Menjou were given some quick-witted dialogue and it was an unusually glossy production. The ads coyly proclaimed, "The man had a baby instead of a lady," which isn't exactly the plot.

Adolph Zukor, the powerfully influential head of Paramount Pictures, called Carole one of those rare comediennes, grouping her with Gloria Swanson and Jean Arthur. "Lovely to look at and able to play dramatic roles," he said. Zukor borrowed Carole from Hal Roach for Paramount's *Mystery Sea Raider* (1940) opposite Henry Wilcoxon. The players spent most of their time on a fog-drenched ship. The role was once announced for the studio's aggressive redhead, Susan Hayward.

In the midst of filming *Mystery Sea Raider*, on July 4, 1940, Carole made her second trip to the alter with yachtsman-broker Willis Hunt, Jr., after a whirlwind, three-week courtship. The next day she was back on the Paramount sound stages, posing with Hunt in a rowboat used in the film. Carole told writer Gladys Hall, "Every girl in the world wants to find the right man; someone who is sympathetic and understanding and helpful and strong, someone she can love madly. Actresses are not exceptions; glamour girls are certainly no exceptions. The glamour and the tinsel, the fame and the money mean very little for there is a hurt in the heart."

They separated after only two months and were divorced that November. "Everyone thought that Will and I had a beautiful romantic marriage, but we didn't. We should have just remained good friends," Carole said. "Let the blame, if any, fall where it may; we won't go into that. But I do say this. If I had been the super-smart gal I'm supposed to be, I would have made my marriages successful." She continued, "I think I have always been a sucker. By a sucker I mean someone who is very vulnerable, who wears her heart on her sleeve, who is easily hurt, who, in fact, almost asks to be hurt."

Carole wrote letters to newspapers asking that they publish no more "leg art" of her. "I want a fair chance to prove myself an actress rather than a 'curvaceous cutie,' " Carole wrote. "Leg art is valuable and appreciated during one's apprenticeship but now I want to get out of bathing suits and into something more substantial."

Back at Hal Roach, Carole teamed up with Joan Blondell in the laugh-filled *Topper Returns* (1941), a third sequel to the highly popular *Topper* series. Carole and Dennis O'Keefe helped solve the murder of Blondell, while Roland Young and Billie Burke were back as Cosmo and Henrietta Topper. The actors seemed to be enjoying themselves immensely. Joan Bennett had rejected Carole's part because she thought Joan Blondell's role too big by comparison. *Road Show* (1941) was a delightful knockabout comedy about playboy John Hubbard who falls in love with Carole, who operates (for the second time) a bankrupt carnival. Its insane asylum and circus background provided a framework for some bizarre comedy, in which Hal Roach specialized.

Darryl F. Zanuck became interested in the new sexpot and bought up half her contract from Hal Roach, but as it turned out she never returned to the Culver City lot. At 20th Century-Fox, Carole's career began to blossom. Zanuck quickly teamed her with Betty Grable in *Moon Over Miami* (1941), a Technicolor remake of *Three Blind Mice*, with Carole, Betty and Charlotte Greenwood (their aunt) as workers in a Texas drive-in who utilize an inheritance to snag rich husbands in Florida, using La Grable as bait. Carole was hidden most of the time under secretarial specs until pressed into service to help Grable handle the attention of two men at the same time, Don Ameche and Robert Cummings.

Then came the part that marked the highpoint of Carole's career, the coveted role of Vicky Lynn in *I Wake Up Screaming* (1941), an adaptation of Steve Fisher's novel. While no masterpiece, it must surely rank as one of the most underrated

thrillers of that period. Ably handled by H. Bruce Humberstone, it was like a trashy novel that you can't stop reading. A
psychological murder mystery set against the flashy background of 1940s' New York cafe society, it told of the rapid rise
and fall of ambitious Landis, built into a figure of national
prominence through the efforts of promoter Victor Mature.
(Twentieth Century-Fox also bought Mature's contract from
Hal Roach.) For the second time, Carole and Betty Grable portrayed sisters. The detective Laird Cregar, with his menacing
charisma, whose apartment is a macabre shrine to the murdered Landis, dominates the second half of the film. "Carole
was really underrated as an actress and extremely easy to work
with," director Humberstone said. "She had an energy the
camera picked up and transmitted to an audience." The screen
test scene in which Carole sings the haunting "The Things I
Love" is often missing from most television prints.

Carole was originally destined for the Rouben Mamoulian remake of Ibanez's bull-fighting story *Blood and Sand*, as the sultry
Dona Sol, the Spanish noblewoman who steals Tyrone Power
from his wife, Linda Darnell. Rumors circulated that "friends"
influenced her against accepting the role, as it was unsympa-
thetic. During a Fox press conference, Carole said she would
not dye her hair red. This seems absurd since she could have
easily worn a wig. The real reason was simply squabbles with
Mamoulian who wanted Rita Hayworth, a logical choice because of her Spanish background. Hayworth then rapidly
overtook Carole in popularity. It is interesting to speculate
what Carole might have made of the Dona Sol role had she not
been replaced by Hayworth.

When Alice Faye balked at playing in *Dance Hall* (1941),
Carole stepped in. It was a slim comedy in which blues singer
Carole is romanced by club manager Cesar Romero. She deliv-
ered a good rendition of "There's a Lull in My Life," a Mack
Gordon and Harry Revel hit. In *Cadet Girl* (1941), a tale about
West Point, she waited for George Montgomery and marriage.
It was in *Cadet Girl* that Peggy McKenna became Carole's
stand-in. She was the first person to write Carole a fan letter.
At Carole's suggestion, she came to Hollywood on vacation as
her house guest (covered by *Look* magazine) and stayed on to
become her stand-in for several years. It was Carole who intro-

duced the ex-Illinois secretary to her future husband, Elisha Cook, Jr., the memorable room clerk in *I Wake Up Screaming*.

In 1942, Claire James joined 20th Century-Fox's stock player roster and had minor roles in a number of Carole's films. "I have to give Carole credit, she succeeded in her aim to be a star. She was always full of vivacity and enthusiasm," Claire recalled. "The story around Fox was that Carole was Darryl F. Zanuck's mistress." Zanuck was so enamored with Carole, he asked Lew Schrieber, head casting director at Fox, and various producers to use her. When Zanuck's ardor cooled, as it had earlier with Simone Simon, Carole's popularity at 20th continued to slide. Darryl F. Zanuck was suddenly unavailable to her phone calls; it was a shattering blow to her ego and professional standing at 20th. In Tinseltown circles, the famed gap between Zanuck's two front teeth were known as "the passion pit."

Carole was paired again with Ceasar Romero, as a horse race bookie, in *A Gentleman at Heart* (1942) as the socialite who introduces him to the world of culture. Romero, a close personal friend, was also her favorite leading man. Then came a baseball yarn, *It Happened in Flatbush* (1942), with Lloyd Nolan as the manager of the Brooklyn Dodgers and Carole as the chic heir to a ball club. Carole's romantic interludes also kept her in the columns. Gossip columnists reported her dates with Charlie Chaplin, Gene Markey, Victor Mature, Cesar Romero and George Montgomery.

The glittering Tin Pan Alley musical *My Gal Sal* (1942) was to be Carole's last important role for 20th Century-Fox. She received sympathetic reviews for her warm performance as an understanding performer, Mae, who befriends composer Victor Mature on his way to success. Columbia loaned Rita Hayworth to play the musical stage star opposite Mature. (It was Carole's third and final film with "the beautiful hunk of man.") Gene Ringgold reported in *The Films of Rita Hayworth* that Alice Faye, then Irene Dunne and Mae West were approached to play the role of Sally Ellis in *My Gal Sal*. And then Ringgold went on to say: "At this conjuncture, he (Darryl F. Zanuck) decided to groom Carole Landis for the role, deciding to showcase her first as Dona Sol in *Blood and Sand*. When she balked at doing that film, Zanuck retaliated by giving her a secondary role in *My Gal Sal,* as she had already been announced to appear in it anyway." Said the *Hollywood Reporter*: "Carole Landis is wasted on a part much too brief for her career at this point—but plays it like a trouper."

Carole was in a clique of neglected wives who follow their musician husbands around the country in *Orchestra Wives* (1942), a musical drama involving assorted members of the Glenn Miller Orchestra. Ann Rutherford was the smalltown girl who got more than she bargained for when she hitched up with band member George Montgomery. Carole and Mary Beth Hughes kept things moving with their snappy dialogue and icy charms. *Manila Calling* (1942) involved the Japanese invasion of the Philippines, with entertainer Carole and guerrilla fighter Lloyd Nolan doomed to die by enemy bombs.

Producer Charles R. Rogers borrowed Carole for *The Powers Girl* (1942), based on the book by John R. Powers. She was Anne Shirley's stylish sister who becomes the top Powers Girl of 1943. The sisters clash over George Murphy, of all people. Although Carole was exquisitely gowned by Adrian, she had begun an endless assortment of color and hair-styles so that whatever image had been established at Hal Roach and her first year at 20th Century-Fox was destroyed. All Carole's 1942 output did well at the box-office, during this entertainment-starved war period. But these were not star-making parts, and they did little to help her overall career.

In October, 1942, with Martha Raye, Kay Francis and Mitzi Mayfair, Carole flew to Bermuda, Northern Ireland and England to entertain U.S. troops abroad, as part of the Hollywood Victory Committee tour. The unexpected climax of the tour of England occurred on January 5, 1943 in London, when Carole married ex-Eagle Squadron Captain Thomas Wallace. Carole said, "Everything stopped inside me when I met Tom, everything went boom, boom, crash! And my knees felt weak." The elaborate marriage received a great deal of publicity space. Carole's childhood idol, Kay Francis, tried to talk her out of the marriage. "You can't be sure. You haven't known him long enough," Francis said. But Carole had made up her mind, "Why wait if you're sure about something and you know it's right? Why wait and take the risk of things going sour on you?" Wallace was an active participant in the Battle of Britain. Because her earlier marriages had only been civil ceremonies, the Catholic Church permitted Carole a church wedding. Dancer Mitzi Mayfair was the maid of honor. Three days later, the group continued their tour path to North Africa and encountered two powerful bombings by the Germans while performing in Algiers. The actresses averaged five hours' sleep each night while playing to thousands of GIs.

The group returned to the United States in March, 1943, and 20th Century-Fox awarded Carole with the thankless second lead in *Wintertime* (1943), Sonja Henie's final Fox skating whirl. As the cunning torch singer with Woody Herman's Orchestra, Carole sang "I Like It Here" and "Wintertime." In *Secret Command* (1944) for Columbia, Carole and Pat O'Brien played FBI agents seeking to put a halt to sabotage in California shipyards. (Carole's mother, Mrs. Clara Ridste, was helping in the war effort by operating a rivet machine at North American Aircraft.) On radio, Carole co-starred with Robert Young on Screen Guild theater's CBS rendition of *Design for Scandal*, recreating the role Rosalind Russell had performed in the MGM film (1941). Carole told the story of her first USO adventures in a book, *Four Jills in a Jeep*, which was published serially in *The Saturday Evening Post* and later by Random House. She also spent many evenings entertaining servicemen at the Hollywood Canteen.

A fictionalized recreation of the USO tour based on her book was filmed by 20th Century-Fox with Carole, Martha Raye, Kay Francis and Mitzi Mayfair appearing as themselves. *Four Jills in a Jeep* (1944) was not a popular picture; servicemen in particular seemed to dislike Hollywood's obvious attempt to capitalize on the well-publicized USO tour. Carole's good friend George Jessel played the master of ceremonies for the radio broadcast sequence, where Fox stars Betty Grable, Carmen Miranda and Alice Faye sang tunes associated with them. It was the Fox debut of recording star Dick Haymes. The New York *Herald Tribune* analyzed: "There are two definite reasons why this picture should have been left in its tin container. Primarily, its silly actual experiences, its bad acting and production and its retakes of dead and buried Fox musical numbers make it one of the dullest bits of entertainment ever. Secondarily, its self-praise, its recurrent theme of 'Look what we girls did for our country' is almost sickening. Undoubtedly the studio couldn't resist making capital on its girls' USO tour, but it has done it in the worst possible taste. Even if the picture itself were gay it would still labor under all embarrassing lack of shame."

On tour again in 1944, Carole contracted amoebic dysentery in North Africa, and malaria in the South Pacific. She almost succumbed to pneumonia in New Guinea. An enlisted man hacked his way through 18 miles of jungle to give her a bouquet of flowers while she lay on her sickbed. In October, Carole and Thomas Wallace separated.

The following summer, Carole obtained a divorce in Reno, Nevada. "He didn't like my friends and I didn't like his criticism," she said. "It was a marriage which, I believe, we would have discovered was not meant to be had we disciplined ourselves and waited." Wallace's only comment was, "I've had enough of being the guy Carole Landis married."

For RKO's *Having Wonderful Crime* (1945), Carole and Pat O'Brien engage in a lighthearted suspenseful farce about the disappearance of a magician. The *Motion Picture Herald* said, "Although the three stars (Carole, O'Brien and George Murphy) work hard to give the screen version of Craig Rice's play animation and humor, and succeed in several sequences, the film as a whole suffers from a confused story line." It was handsomely photographed on the grounds of the Del Monte Lodge in Carmel, California.

On January 10, 1945, Carole made her Broadway debut in *A Lady Says Yes*, a musical comedy that managed to run for ten weeks. The J.J. Shubert production had previews in Boston and Philadelphia prior to its New York opening at the Broadhust Theater. The plot was a Commedia del'Arte situation with touches of plastic surgery and reincarnation. The show was originally titled *Lady in Question*. The press blamed *A Lady Says Yes*'s dismal failure on poor material. One critic explained: "No amount of face lifting can save it." Observed Ward Morehouse in the New York *Sun*: "Carole Landis of the films and darling of GIs makes her Broadway debut in *A Lady Says Yes* and comes through surprisingly well. She wears stunning costumes and is a joy, whether the book places her in the waiting room of a hospital, on a street in old Venice, or in a garden party in Washington." *Time* magazine noted: "*A Lady Says Yes* is a $200,000 musicomedy blunder redeemed only by the shapely figures of

Carole Landis and Christine Ayres. The critics said No." Included in the cast were Jacqueline Susann and Jack Albertson. During the out-of-town tryouts, Carole became friendly with Susann (before her literary fame). They soon began an intimate relationship. In *Lovely Me: A Biography of Jacqueline Susann*, by Barbara Seaman, the author describes Susann's lesbian affair with Carole: "Carole fell in love with Jackie and was not reticent about showing it. She sent flowers, followed by a tiny pair of perfect pearl drop earrings, even tried to present a mink coat from her personal wardrobe. And Jackie, no doubt flattered, reciprocated, later describing to her girl friends how sensual it has been when she and Carole had stroked and kissed each other's breasts." Their brief encounter is echoed in two Susann blockbusters, *Valley of the Dolls* and *Once Is Not Enough*.

Choreographer Joe Paz was one of the dancers in *A Lady Says Yes*, his first Broadway show. "I was just a young kid and very impressionable," said Paz. "I remember Carole's famous smile, her kindness and generosity to the other cast members. Despite the closeness of her friendship with Jacqueline Susann, it never occurred to me they might be lovers." The novelist modeled the vulnerable Jennifer character in *Valley of the Dolls* on composites of Carole and Joyce Matthews. A former New York show-girl and Paramount actress, Matthews is the ex-wife of Milton Berle and impresario Billy Rose.

For the world premiere of Rogers and Hammerstein's *State Fair*, in August, 1945, Fox sent Carole, Dick Haymes, George Jessel, James Dunn, Peggy Ann Garner and Faye Marlowe to Iowa for the opening day ceremonies at the Des Moines and Paramount Theaters. In December, 1945, Carole made her last stab at marital success by marrying millionaire producer W. Horace Schmidlapp. They were introduced by Jacqueline Susann. "Carole is everything I want in a woman," said Schmidlapp. Carole kept very active during the latter part of the war in the bond sales campaign and after its conclusion in work for the American Cancer Society, through the sale of benefit tickets. In these charitable efforts she gained a distinction her Hollywood roles seldom gave her. Once, speaking at a rally on Wall Street during a downpour of rain, she shouted to the crowd, "You can't stop a war for the weather! The boys over there don't."

Carole's position in the studio hierarchy was definitely diminishing. She returned to 20th Century-Fox for two minor-league murder mysteries, *Behind Green Lights* (1946) and *It Shouldn't Happen to a Dog* (1946). In the first, socialite Carole is suspected of murdering a blackmailing private detective. The latter title speaks for itself. Carole was a police-woman with troublesome doberman pinscher, who helps her nail a racketeering mob. The tepid direction of both films didn't help. Carole was now free of her 20th Century-Fox contractual obligations.

In United Artists' fascinating *A Scandal in Paris* (1946), Carole was sophisticatedly directed by Douglas Sirk in a brief but memorable role as the wife of deposed police chief Gene Lockhart, who eventually murders her. It was based on *The Memoirs of Francois Eugene Vidocq*, with George Sanders as a crook who became head of the French police. As the ill-fated singer in a nineteenth-century cafe, Carole sang "The Flame Song." An almost surrealistic film, it is considered one of director Douglas Sirk's most delicate works. Carole was fifth billed in the oddball *Out of the Blue* (1947), an undistinguished but engaging comedy for Eagle-Lion. Ann Dvorak creates a supposedly comedic marital situation between a husband, George Brent, and his shrewish wife, Carole, when she (Dvorak) is discovered in an unconscious condition in their Greenwich Village apartment. Virginia Mayo and Turhan Bey also starred.

On a weekend trip to Palm Springs, Carole was introduced to British actor Rex Harrison at the Racquet Club by Charles Farrell. Harrison was married to actress Lilli Palmer. Carole and fourth husband Schmidlapp had been going their separate ways for over a year, although they continued to reside together. Harrison was quite taken with Carole's all-American spirit and sense of freedom. She was a feminist long before the launching of the women's liberation movement. They soon fell in love.

With work at a minimum in Hollywood, Carole left for England for two films. In *The Brass Monkey* (1948), she investigates a murder involving a brass monkey charm and winds up accused of the crime. It was an exceptionally well-made, traditional style mystery. The other, *The Silk Noose* (1948), in which she played a newspaperwoman who brings a black market op-

eration to justice, was finally release in the United States by
Monogram Pictures in 1950. The original British title was *The
Noose*. Both films played regularly on early television, but have
since virtually disappeared. While filming in London, Carole
continued to see Rex Harrison, who was working in 20th
Century-Fox's *Escape* with Peggy Cummins. Carole and
Harrison managed to spend most weekends away from the
bustling city in Plymouth.

Harrison completed *Escape* and returned to Hollywood to
begin filming *Unfaithfully Yours* with Linda Darnell. On his return to New York, he was asked by the press about his reported romance with Carole, "Of course, I am fond of Miss
Landis. We are great friends and that is all. She is also a good
friend of my wife." In March, 1948, Carole returned to California and immediately began divorce proceedings against Horace
Schmidlapp, although she was totally exhausted from the long
months of filming in England. In April, Carole wrote her friend
Lilyan Miller of Detroit, Michigan, "I had a wonderful time in
England making *The Brass Monkey* and *Noose* (*The Silk Noose*),
and am going back late this summer to make another picture
there in September."

Of the last few months of Carole's life, Rex Harrison would
reveal in his memoir, *Rex*: "Our feeling for each other showed
no sign of abating. From time to time Carole seemed to with-
draw from what was going on around her, as though
temporarily she had gone elsewhere, except in the physical;
but in a few minutes she would be herself again, and I attached
little significance to these times."

On July 3, 1948, Harrison (Lilli Palmer was in New York) had
an early dinner at Carole's new home at 1465 Capri Drive in
Pacific Palisades. He had been offered the part of Henry VIII in
Maxwell Anderson's play *Anne of the Thousand Days*. "She
seemed a little down, but I was so high myself on the idea of
getting back into the theatre that I'm afraid I didn't notice the
extent of her downness," Harrison would remember later.
"She also told me she had general financial problems." Rex
Harrison left the house around 9 p.m. to visit with actor Roland
Culver and his wife. Later that night, Carole called Marguerite
Haymes, the mother of Dick Haymes, in New York but was
unable to reach her. Mrs. Haymes was a friend of many years

and had once taught Carole singing. She found a message that Carole called from California. But Mrs. Haymes hadn't returned the call, because it was past midnight and she thought Carole would probably be asleep.

When Rex Harrison called the house late the next afternoon, July 4th, the maid Fannie May Bolden said there was no response to her knock on the bedroom door. He rushed over and found her dead on the bathroom floor. There was an empty bottle of Seconal by Carole's side. An autopsy would also reveal a considerable amount of alcohol in the blood. She was still dressed in a full skirt, peasant blouse and sandals. both arms were bent under her as if she had been trying to raise herself. Mrs. Bolden later told police, "We both went into the bedroom and found a suicide note. Harrison started to cry and said, 'Oh darling, why did you do it, why did you do it?' " In his autobiography, Harrison attributed Carole's Hollywood downfall to her being a rebel caught in establishment values of the 1940s. Harrison wrote, "I hadn't realized that she had been many times before at the end of her tether, that there was so little stability in her life, and that, as I learned later, she had already attempted to take her life on previous occasions. She was an enormously sweet person, and a good person, and I was simply knocked over by feeling what a damnable shame it was that such a marvelous girl should be brought to this—not really by our relationship, which was all for the good, but by her background and circumstances catching up on her."

The suicide note was addressed to her mother: *Dearest Mommie: I'm sorry, really sorry to put you through this. But there is no way to avoid it. I love you darling. You have been the most wonderful Mom ever. Everything goes to you. Look in the files, and there is a will which decrees everything. Good-bye, my angel. Pray for me. Your Baby.* As to reports that she had left a second note to Harrison, it was explained at the coroner's inquiry that the second note only contained instructions to the maid to take the kitten to the vet, because it had a sore paw. Harrison would testify in court: "I don't know of anything that could clear up the suicide mystery. She appeared to be in good spirits, although I don't believe she was entirely happy with her career." Later, Harrison would say: "I felt no guilt complex—no, none at all, but I did spend months afterwards going to psychiatrists, discussing the

suicide with them, seeking the reasons for it. The plain fact is
that Carole Landis had a death wish!"

Rex Harrison retreated to the home of friends Roland and
Nan Culver on the evening of the discovery of Carole's body.
He recounted in *Rex*, "There I was given a small suitcase that
had been found just outside a gate in the lane by their house.
Carole must have left it there while I was with the Culvers the
night she took her life, for it contained the letters I had written
to her in London. She had taken them out of the house, evi-
dently, to prevent my being embarrassed by them. It was typical of Carole's sweet nature to act so thoughtfully when she
was in such an appalling state of mind. If the press had discovered those letters, what whooping and jubilant screams would
have gone up from the Hearst and other newspapers, determined to increase their circulation at the expense of her tragedy." In Cincinnati, Horace Schmidlapp told the press, "This is
a terrible shock." He soon flew back to California. Carole's lawyer, Jerry Giesler, said, "I take little stock in the idea that
financial distress contributed to Miss Landis's death. Money
from the sale of her house would have paid all her bills and left
a considerable sum besides.

Many of Carole's friends and columnist Louella Parsons believed the suicide was over Rex Harrison's efforts to break off
the affair. In *Hedda and Louella*, George Eells reported: "Rex
Harrison outraged both Hedda and Louella when he and wife
Lilli Palmer attacked Hollywood after the columnists felt
Harrison had been protected against a scandal following the
suicide of Carole Landis. Hedda lambasted him on that point
and thereafter sarcastically referred to him as 'Sexy Rexy.' "
Carole's funeral was held at Forest Lawn Cemetery. She was
clad in an evening gown with a purple orchid held in one hand.
A purple and white orchid was pinned on each shoulder. An
over flow crowd of 600 attended, including Rex Harrison who
came with Lilli Palmer, Mr. and Mrs. Roland Culver and agent
Jack Bolton. The pallbearers were Dick Haymes, Cesar Romero,
Pat O'Brien, Lou Wasserman, Ben Nye and Willard Parker.

When the $150,000 estate was finally settled, debts slightly
exceeded the assets. In order to cut liabilities, her personal possessions were auctioned off. "My baby Carole had her troubles," her mother said. "She had married a rich man, but she

was in deep financial trouble. She had sold her car, her home. Little things. But things just piled up for her. Carole told me of her financial worries, despite her marriage. Why, only a short time ago, in bitterness, she said to me, 'Mother, marry a rich man and then support yourself!' "

Carole was scheduled to start filming *The Hypnotist* in late July for Eagle-Lion, opposite Turhan Bey. The film eventually reached theatres as *The Amazing Mr. X* (1948) with Lynn Bari in the role Carole had been slated for. Just three days before Carole Landis ended her young life, she recorded a message to her many fans. The recording conclude with: ". . . Time's up. But invite me again soon and I'll have some games for you. Good-by, Carole."

BARBARA BATES

Barbara Bates' breathtakingly beautiful face gained her entrance to motion pictures during the middle 1940s. Although she steadily progressed in the next decade, her roles, with the possible exception of *All About Eve*, never matured beyond that of dull ingenues. She always underestimated her own talent. "I have no illusions about being a star," she once said. "Every time I did something really important, they ended up cutting it." Barbara's role opposite Danny Kaye in *The Inspector General*, only led to another terrible disappointment. All her key scenes with Kaye (whom she adored) were edited out. There were rumors of an affair between the two. Barbara possessed a curious chemistry of sensual appeal mixed with vulnerability and naturalness. On the surface, she created an indelible impression. But in reality, she had a tremendous amount of emotional suffering, a paralyzing self-doubt and an obsessed older husband.

Barbara was born on August 6, 1925, in Denver, Colorado, the daughter of Eva I. and Arthur W. Bates. Her father was a postal clerk, and she had two younger sisters, Joanne and Claudine. Of Scotch-Irish descent, Barbara was preoccupied with ballet until she was 13, studying with Claire Deane and performing regularly in annual group recitals. With her sisters, Barbara loved to spend summers with their grandparents in Manitowoc, Wisconsin. She attended Emmaus Latheran Grade School and North Denver High School, where, besides dramatics, Barbara was active in winter sports (a talent acquired on snowy weekends in the Rocky Mountains) and bowling.

It was while modeling "back-to-school" clothes for the Denver May Company that Barbara was persuaded by friends to enter a local beauty contest. She felt awkward parading before a jury with no special talent to demonstrate. To Barbara's astonishment, she won the contest. One of the prizes was two round-trip train tickets to Hollywood. Accompanied by her mother she arrived in Los Angeles in early 1944. Two days before they were set to return to Denver, Barbara met the man who would alter the course of her life—Cecil Coan, an outgoing, influential publicist for United Artists. Coan would have a growing obsession with Barbara's future destiny.

They met at Pickfair at one of Mary Pickford's Sunday charity affairs in which the actress would invite aspiring young starlets to mingle with servicemen around the pool and gardens. Something particularly appealing about her prompted Coan to help her. She reminded him of Susan Hayward. "By the way," he said, "You're a remarkably pretty girl. I suppose you know that?" "I've heard," she answered seriously. Further conversation disclosed that she had ambitions to become an actress. Star-making was the kind of game that appealed to Coan's publicity instincts. "Well," he said, not too seriously, "if you decide to stay in Hollywood, perhaps I can be of some help." Mrs. Bates returned to Denver alone.

Coan arranged an interview with producer Walter Wanger at Universal Pictures, who was searching for "The Most Beautiful Girl in the World" to star in his "cinema curiosity," *Salome, Where She Danced* (1945). Wanger was intrigued with Barbara's sweetness of disposition but found her too inexperienced; nevertheless, Universal signed her to a contract in September, 1944, and then cast Yvonne De Carlo in the title role of Salome.

Barbara made her screen debut as one of Yvonne De Carlo's handmaidens in *Salome, Where She Danced* and gathered much publicity as the most promising of "The Seven Salome Girls," as they were known. The others were Kerry Vaughn, Karen Randle, Poni (Jane) Adams, Jean Trent, Kathleen O'Malley and Daun Kennedy. Kathleen O'Malley, the daughter of silent screen star Pat O'Malley, recalls, "We signed our Universal contracts the same day. In the year we spent there, Barbara worked very hard, but I never really thought she was that interested in a career. She had a Madonna-like quality and a happy-go-lucky nature. I guess Jean Trent (also from Denver) and myself were her two closest friends back then. I remember

Barbara's immense emotional dependence on Cecil Coan. He absolutely charmed her off her feet." O'Malley was impressed at how fiercely ambitious Coan was for Barbara.

Barbara's relationship with Coan became serious, despite the fact he was much older, married and the father of three young sons. Talk was spreading about their romance. The Coans separated and were soon divorced. Coan probed the problem of Barbara's youthfulness and had qualms about a permanent commitment to a girl young enough to be his daughter. In his dilemma over the age difference, Coan sought the advice of his old friend, Charlie Chaplin, who married 18-year-old Oona O'Neill, daughter of playwright Eugene O'Neill, two years before (1943). The comedian asked, "Are you in love with Barbara?" Coan replied, "Yes, unfortunately." "Then marry," Chaplin said. They were secretly married on March 27, 1945, a few days after Coan's divorce was final. Barbara was 19, Coan gave his age as 40 (he was 45). Actress Kathleen O'Malley remembers driving with Barbara and Julie London to location to shoot some publicity pictures. "Julie happened to notice that Barbara was wearing a diamond wedding ring," O'Malley said. "When Julie asked if she was married, poor Barbara became terribly embarrassed and said no she wasn't, then looked away."

Barbara's professional and personal life soon became dominated by her new husband. In the next year, Barbara toiled at Universal without any appreciable success, in such films as *This Love of Ours* (1945), as a guest at a birthday party; *Blonde Ransom* (1945), as a cigarette girl; *Here Come the Coeds (1945); Lady on a Train* (1945) as a hatcheck girl, *Easy to Look At* (1945), as a model and *Shady Lady* (1945), as a party guest. In *A Night in Paradise* (1946), Barbara and the other six "Salome Girls" did duty as Merle Oberon's palace maidens.

As a result of the *Salome, Where She Danced* promotion, Barbara found herself committed irrevocably to cheesecake art. A top pin-up girl during the closing months of World War II, especially after her *Life* magazine cover story (May 28, 1945), Barbara admitted later, "I suppose it was good at the time. Helping to spread your name around. I was never the pin-up girl type." When their second year option came due, Universal informed the "Salome Girls" they could remain at the studio, but at the same salary. "We had a secret meeting and all of us, except one (Jane Adams), decided to move on," remembers Kathleen O'Malley. "I often think of Barbara and the fun we had at Universal. The business is all so different now."

In United Artists' *A Scandal in Paris* (1946), Barbara can be seen wading in a pond, with *Salome* pal Daun Kennedy, behind one of the film's stars, Signe Hasso. The drama was also released as *Thieves' Holiday*. A screentest at Paramount followed; but it was Hal Roach, Jr., who offered her a contract. Barbara's first feature role was as Walter Abel's daughter in Hal Roach/ UA's *The Fabulous Joe* (1947). She enacted the romantic interest, opposite Johnny Miles, in this featurized segment from *The Hal Roach Comedy Carnival*. It was the last in Hal Roach's modestly-budgeted "Streamliner" comedies, produced by Bebe Daniels in Cinecolor.

In the first years of their marriage, Barbara's fondest desire was to have a child. Cecil Coan had grown children from his previous marriage. They enjoyed a Pygmalion-Galatea relationship which was more than that of mentor and pupil. It was a deep and genuine love. The Hollywood-wise Coan became engrossed with the idea of her becoming a star, while the withdrawn Barbara was infected by his ambitions for her. The personalities seemed to balance each other perfectly. But others didn't see it that way. Many found Coan to be meddlesome and arrogant when it came to what was right for Barbara and her work. Trying to find a new "image," Coan advised Barbara to become a blonde and perhaps change her name. Agent Henry Willson tried to convince Barbara to take the name Bets Dawson. She hated the sound of the name and told Willson so, "It sounds like a B-Western heroine." Then Willson replied, "And so does the name Jennifer Jones."

In between studio contracts, Barbara went back to modeling for photographers Paul Hesse and Tom Kelley. It was the short *Camera Angles* in which four top still photographers each chose their favorite model to photograph that brought her to the attention of Warner Brothers talent executive Solly Baiano. Barbara had been the personal choice of cameraman Paul Hesse. A review in *Motion Picture Exhibitor* noted: "The rarely seen man behind the camera is viewed at work photographing various Hollywood actors and actresses (for magazines and newspapers). Much of this has a humorous slant, and the cameramen include Paul Hesse, Bob Wallace, Earl Thiesen, Hymie Fink, and Sprague Talbot, while the subjects are Hedy Lamarr, Sonja Henie, Jack Carson, Alexis Smith, Barbara Bates, Andy Russell and Della Norrel." It wasn't released until 1949.

On May 26, 1947, Barbara was signed to a term contract with Warner Brothers. The studio gave her the standard ingenue buildup, minimizing the fact that she was married. Of Barbara's two year association at "The Factory," as Warner's players sometimes sarcastically called it, she would say, "Well, it was quite an experience!" A WB biography lists her favorite actors as Ronald Reagan and Laurence Olivier! Barbara was enrolled in coach Sophie Rosenstein's classes to help her lose her Rocky Mountain accent. "I wish I were a sponge so I could just mop up all the things there are to learn about acting," she said. Her contract began inauspiciously with *That Hagen Girl* (1947); *Always Together* (1947); *April Showers* (1948), as a secretary; *Romance on the High Seas* (1948), as an airline stewardess; and *Johnny Belinda* (1948), as Jeff Richards' date at a dance.

More importantly, Barbara was assigned the title role in Warners' *June Bride* (1948). A New York magazine editor, Bette Davis, and Robert Montgomery go to Crestville, Indiana, to cover a typically American wedding for the June issue. The trouble is that the bride, Barbara, and groom-to-be, Ray Montgomery, elope instead. It was the image Barbara would quickly become type cast in—sweet, charming and demure. Her "big break" provided few opportunities, but she did her best with a few brief scenes in the slow-moving comedy. Most of the attention went to the affectionate relationship between Bette Davis and the younger sister, played by Betty Lynn, on loanout from 20th Century-Fox. The nifty Lynn magaged some amusing moments and stole nearly every scene she was in. The film was based on the play *Feature for June* and marked the film debut of a 16-year-old Debbie Reynolds. Barbara was at this point in her career doing slightly better than other Warner Brothers starlets such as Lila Leeds, Kyle MacDonnell, and Joan Vohs.

In the last of Errol Flynn's swashbuckling films, *The Adventures of Don Juan* (1949), Barbara sparkled as the innkeeper's decorative daughter. Off-camera, she attempted to resist Flynn's ardent advances. In *One Last Fling* (1949), Barbara was a record store employee; and in *The House Across the Street* (1949), one of Warner Brothers' action programmers, Barbara had some good moments as gangster James Mitchell's sexy mistress. The three films were filmed prior to *June Bride* but released later.

When Danny Kaye accepted a lucrative contract from Warner Brothers, to star in *The Inspector General* (1949), he obtained the right to choose his director and leading lady. With a publicity fanfare Barbara was handed the role of Kaye's servant girlfriend, Leza. Henry Koster was signed to direct the color-splashed production. Set in an 1800s French mythical kingdom, the story has Kaye masquerading as an Inspector General friend of Napoleon's, then exposing a crooked political system by his blunderings. It was freely adapted from a Nicolai Gogol comedy, and was an unusual background for Kaye with its heavily foreign atmosphere and Graustarkian goings-on.

Danny Kaye's wife, Sylvia Fine Kaye, served as associate producer and wrote eight songs for the comedy. The gymnastic Kaye calmed down long enough to croon "Lonely Heart" to a starry-eyed Barbara. In Michael Freedland's *The Secret Life Of Danny Kaye*, William T. Orr, then head of production at WB, described the climate on the set of *The Inspector General*: "Danny and Sylvia gave us a lot of problems—particularly with Sylvia, who did most of the talking at our meetings." Orr continued, "Sylvia was the one who appeared to take the decisions—and if not to take them, then to convey them to studio executives or to other people who could make life difficult for them."

The couple felt that working together would benefit their strained relationship. Unfortunately, the reverse happened. Their numerous squabbles on the set almost ruined their marriage. Danny Kaye was very compassionate toward Barbara in her first prominent role, while his wife's coolness and bitchy remarks were a disturbing factor. As Barbara grew closer to Kaye, Mrs. Kaye became more difficult and quarrelsome in her demands with Warner Brothers and producer Jerry Wald. Barbara was flattered by his attentions and found Kaye to be gentle, considerate and extremely disciplined, nowhere near the idolized extrovert he projected on the screen. Some friends of Barbara suspected they became romantically involved, though the true depth of the liaison remains a mystery.

Due to Sylvia Kaye's final cut approval, Barbara's role was trimmed considerably. The German-born director Henry Koster felt protective toward Barbara, and sympathetic to her personal problems during the filming. "She was a warm human being, vulnerable and very sensitive," remembers Koster. "My wife (actress Peggy Moran) and I frequently invited Barbara and her husband to dinner at our Pacific Palisades home."

The Inspector General proved to be merely forced, witless and silly. *Fortnight* reported: "For romantic interest Barbara Bates shines as a pert little scullery maid with whom Kaye would spend all of his time if he could." And the *Hollywood Reporter* evaluated: "As the romantic femme lead, Barbara Bates is required to look only beautiful. She does." Barbara said years later, "I have mixed feelings about *The Inspector General*. Except for Danny Kaye's affection and warmth, it was an absolutely terrible experience."

Emotionally affected over her shabby treatment at Warner Brothers, Barbara was asked to take part in a publicity trek with the cast of *The Younger Brothers*, cancelling out a proposed trip to New York to promote *General*. Barbara was hurt and humiliated, refused the tour, and thereupon was sent a telegram by Jack L. Warner, stating her services with the Burbank lot were immediately terminated in May, 1949.

As Mickey Rooney's faithful sweetheart in United Artists' *Quicksand* (1950), Barbara sticks by Rooney, an auto mechanic, as his troubles snowball after borrowing twenty dollars from the garage where he's employed. According to *Daily Variety*: ". . . and Barbara Bates, who loves Rooney, is particularly excellent, especially in a difficult dramatic scene." And the *Hollywood Reporter* was flattering: "Pretty Barbara Bates comes out of the background for several impressive scenes with Rooney toward the end of the picture. The young actress's looks are matched by a lovely speaking voice and moving dramatic ability."

Columbia Pictures expressed interest in testing Barbara for *Born Yesterday* and studio czar Harry Cohn agreed to a meeting to discuss a possible contract. Cohn took a hard look at her beguiling quality and apparently like what he saw. "You have a great future before you, provided you let the right man take charge," Cohn said. "I will personally guide you at Columbia but only under the condition you divorce Cecil Coan." Barbara couldn't believe what she had just heard. His piercing blue eyes made Barbara even more uncomfortable. "Your marriage is interfering with your career," Cohn continued. "I had the same problems with Rita Hayworth (wed to much older Ed Judson), until she wised up." Barbara became nervous and frightened, got up and walked out of his office. She was certain she'd never hear from "that lecherous man" again. But two nights later, Harry Cohn phoned Barbara in the middle of the night, "sounding a little drunk." He was inviting her to spend the weekend on his yacht and "don't bring that midget husband of yours," Cohn said. "I told him I wasn't interested in any cruise, especially without my husband," Barbara replied and hung up. *Edith Gwynn's Hollywood* column reported: "Harry Cohn wishes he'd grabbed faster at Barbara Bates, signed at Fox after leaving Warners. We ribbed him how this beauty would be perfect for *Born Yesterday* and why did he let her get away, etc. He said, 'I missed signing her by minutes—dammit!' "

Agents Charles Feldman secured a 20th Century-Fox contract for Barbara and announced her first at Fox would be *Night Without Sleep*. Instead, she was switched to *Cheaper by the Dozen* (1950), as the second oldest daughter (Ernestine) of efficiency expect Clifton Webb and his psychologist wife Myrna Loy.

It was director Joseph L. Mankiewicz's fancy to close his "inside" look at the Broadway theatre, *All About Eve* (1950), with an unfamiliar face monopolizing the screen. Thus, Mankiewicz chose Barbara, in a piece of inspired casting, as the wide-eyed Phoebe, bent on repeating nemesis Anne Baxter's scheme to win over tempestuous older trouper Bette Davis. Barbara had the climactic fade out all to herself, posing in front of a three-way mirror, holding the Sarah Siddons Award, which Baxter had just won. This single sequence would give Barbara her greatest recognition. The film was praised by the critics and has withstood the test of time. Drama critic George Sanders asks, "And tell me Phoebe, do you want to be an actress?" She eagerly replies, "More than anything else in the world." Reviews for *All About Eve* had praise for the entire cast and Barbara charmed the critics in her brief role. Noted the *Hollywood Reporter*: "Barbara Bates comes on the screen in the last few moments to more or less sum up the whole action and point of the story. She's quietly beautiful and refreshingly simple in her acting. It's odd that a bit should count for so much, and in the hands of Miss Bates all the required points are fulfilled."

Life magazine singled out Barbara twice again. Photographer Philippe Halsman recorded in his own special way what the movies thought Americans in 1949 liked in the way of women. A classic pose, titled "Barbara on the Beach," had Barbara appearing to be rising out of the sand at Malibu Beach in her favorite two piece white bathing suit. Others in the portfolio were Janet Leigh, Alexis Smith, Ann Blyth and Linda Darnell. In 1950, *Life* spotlighted Barbara, along with Marilyn Monroe and Debbie Reynolds, as movieland's most promising young players, being tutored for bigger things. Barbara was still being heralded as a "new face"—after more than six years in Hollywood!

Barbara's husband was instrumental in securing a test for her with Charlie Chaplin for *Limelight*, a tale of an aging vaudevillian who saves a young ballerina from a suicide attempt; together they inspire each other to go on. The role paralleled Barbara's own life, a beautiful girl, lacking in self-confidence, falls in love with a father figure and becomes completely devoted to him. Charlie Chaplin sent Barbara to his friend, actress-coach Constance Collier, to work on a British accent for her screentest. The star-making part opposite Chaplin was narrowed down to Barbara, Joan Winslow, Cloris Leachman and Claire Bloom. Columnist Sheilah Graham announced that Barbara had won the role of the ballerina, with a banner headline, *Barbara Bates Wins Top Role In Chaplin's Limelight*. According to Cecil Coan, Fox vetoed the loanout, fearing Chaplin's political leanings were too far left and would result in a hostile press—which is exactly what happened after a stormy U.S. premiere, with a boycott by the American Legion. "It was the one part Barbara really wanted to do," Coan said. "Her test, which Charlie directed himself, was magnificent and Chaplin said, 'You've got the part.' It absolutely broke her heart when Fox stubbornly refused to okay the loanout." Charlie Chaplin then decided to cast Claire Bloom.

Twentieth Century-Fox cast Barbara in director Henry King's *I'd Climb the Highest Mountain* (1951), with Roy Calhoun, filmed in Dawsonville, Georgia, near Atlanta. They were the young lovers of a subsidiary love affair involving a Methodist minister, William Ludigan, and his wife, Susan Hayward, and their adjustment to a new life in the picturesque red-clay Georgia hills. It was based on Corra Harris' best-seller *A Circuit Rider's Wife*. There was little social contact between Barbara and other crew members during the location filming, except in the last few weeks when Coan visited her. They became good friends with Rory Calhoun and his then wife, Lita Baron. The foursome dined regularly at a restaurant near their motel. As the film neared completion, director John Sturges in Hollywood saw Barbara's *Limelight* test and wanted her to play Spencer Tracy's daughter in Metro-Goldwyn-Mayer's *The People Against O'Hara*, but, due to delays on *Mountain*, the role went to Diana Lynn. Barbara was deeply disappointed a second time.

Modern Screen magazine chose *I'd Climb the Highest Mountain* as "Picture of the Month": There's something very nice and warm about this picture. The hill people, the kind of parties they hold, the way they talk and look, the scene where the mourners at a small funeral walk along slowly singing an old hymn—these seemed wonderfully authentic and flavorful to me," wrote Christopher Kane.

In *The Secret of Convict Lake* (1951) an innocent Barbara is one of eight pioneer women who encounter escaped convicts while their men are away. Under Michael Gordon's direction, the cast, which also included Glenn Ford, Gene Tierney, Ethel Barrymore and Richard Hylton, turned in genuinely effective performances. *The Los Angeles Times* praised her performance: "Barbara Bates is excellent as a young girl whose emotional curiosity has near-fatal results when she centers her interest on Richard Hylton, a youthful sex maniac." The sizzling rape assault scene between Barbara and Hylton was chopped down just before the film's release due to censorship problems. Barbara always felt a warm sisterly interest for the impassioned Hylton from the moment they met, while rumors abounded that he was gay or bisexual. Hylton was a fine, sensitive actor whose looks and talent were suffocated in the Hollywood closet. *The Secret of Convict Lake* marks an interesting teaming of two remarkably vulnerable actors. Barbara attempted to help Hylton when his personal life began a downhill slide a few years later. "Richard was on the quiet side," she used to say. "I guess it's what attracted us to each other. There were problems in his private life that got in the way of his career. He was far more serious about his work than I was." Richard Hylton was to die tragically, alone and forgotten, at 41, in 1962.

Barbara was next cast with Claudette Cobert, Macdonald Carey and Marilyn Monroe in *Let's Make It Legal* (1951), a well-stuffed turkey masquerading as a light, airy souffle. Colbert and Carey were a battling couple who decide on a divorce, but change their minds in the end. As their dutiful daughter, Barbara, married to Robert Wagner, helps them to get back together again. "Claudette was wonderful to all of us newcomers," Robert Wagner told author Laurence J. Quirk in *Claudette Colbert, An Illustrated Biography*: "I know she was wonderful to Marilyn. And Barbara Bates and I, to coin a phrase, 'heroine-worshipped' her. She was always pleasant, had good camaraderie with everyone. I am sure she realized she was in a picture that was no world beater, but being an inventive, resourceful, never-say-die person, she probably felt she could save it. I was only twenty or twenty-one at the time, and I was as nervous as Marilyn and Barbara were. The girls would get sweat on their brows and around their mouths when they got keyed up ('It's the hot lights,' they'd always say') but I just got a regular guy's nervous stomach."

Director Joseph M. Newman fashioned the uneven *The Outcasts of Poker Flat* (1952), from the Bret Harte classic. It found Barbara, wed to Craig Hill and an expectant mother, caught up with a group of social rejects who are trapped together in a mountain cabin during a snowstorm. The intriguing premise was not sufficiently developed, nor were the cardboard characters. Anne Baxter, Dale Robertson and Miriam Hopkins were top-billed.

Barbara was disenchanted with her dowdy role in *Belles on Their Toes* (1952), repeating as Jeanne Crain's sister in this *Cheaper by the Dozen* sequel, about the further adventures of the Gilbreth family. The film was minus Clifton Webb, who died in the original. Although Barbara is prominent throughout the follow-up comedy, the film was designed as a showcase for Darryl F. Zanuck's new favorite, Debra Paget. When the film was completed, 20th Century-Fox failed to exercise its option on Barbara's contract. The late Jeffrey Hunter, who played Jeanne Crain's beau in *Belles on Their Toes*, once commented, "Barbara seemed very disturbed. Quite frankly, I felt uncomfortable in her presence and felt she was a very troubled young woman." The daughter of Stan Laurel, Lois Laurel Hawes, was Barbara's closest friend. "Cecil felt he had to exert complete control over her," said Lois. "He told her what roles to take or turn down, what friends she should be with—he ran her life, but I never knew Barbara to rebel."

Barbara promptly signed for a Columbia musical, *All Ashore* (1953), about three sailors on leave and their frivolous adventures. It was Columbia's lesser effort answer to Metro-Goldwyn-Mayer's tremendous hit, *On the Town*. The mild audience pleaser was scripted by Blake Edwards and had Mickey Rooney in love (again) with rich Barbara. She next traveled over to Paramount as scatterbrain Jerry Lewis's love interest in *The Caddy* (1953). Golf addicts Lewis and Dean Martin enter a tournament, with disastrous results, and end up in show business. Although it was one of Martin and Lewis's weakest comedies, their brand of outrageous mugging appealed tremendously to audiences of the 1950s.

As a lustrous blonde, Barbara next moved over to Metro-Goldwyn-Mayer for the handsomely produced *Rhapsody* (1954), an Elizabeth Taylor deluxe vehicle. Barbara, beautifully photographed, was a jet set debutante who tries to snatch musician Vittorio Gassman away from spoiled rich girl Taylor. On the syndicated television series, "It's a Great Life," which debuted on September 7, 1954, Barbara provided the romantic interest for William Bishop. It was a saga of three ex-GIs (Michael O'Shea, James Dunn and Bishop) plagued by financial matters and their harebrained attempts to terminate monetary burdens, while living at Frances Bavier's rooming house. Barbara played the daughter of Bavier. The situation comedy lasted until June 1956.

In the final phase of Barbara's career, she accepted an offer to join J. Arthur Rank's stable of contract players in England in the hope of recovering her fleeting movie magic. Since she was only thirty-one (Rank biographies said twenty-four) in 1956, it appeared that perhaps Coan's big dream of making his wife a major star might happen after all. They sold their Beverly Hills home and their 52-foot yawl, the "Bayadere," and Coan, a British subject, transferred to United Artists' London office as publicity director. "Hollywood is wonderful but I didn't want to stay there all my life," Barbara told the British press. "And so many of the big parts in Hollywood movies these days are going to British actresses like Jean Simmons and Audrey Hepburn. Of course, they are all wonderfully talented but it's their British qualities that set them apart from the American girls back home. I figured that an American actress in British films might have a similar rarity value. I've always wanted to travel and see new places, so here I am."

Triple Deception (1956), provided Barbara with one of the few interesting characters she ever portrayed on screen. Seaman Michael Craig posed as a member of a gold smuggling gang involved with international spy Barbara. The suspense mystery was well-executed, filmed on location in Paris and directed by distinguished Guy Green. The J. Arthur Rank Organization next assigned Barbara to co-star with Rod Steiger and David Knight in *Across the Bridge*, then "due to illness," filming was halted after three weeks and the press reported she was replaced by Marla Landi.

Columbia Pictures borrowed Barbara to play Charles Coburn's attractive niece in *Town on Trial* (1957), about a police investigation into a mysterious killing filled with many unexpected twists and turns. It was based on the *Nylon Murders* series by F. Durbridge. The mystery was a tepid exercise in suspense that started off slow and never gained momentum. So much time was spent setting up the situation that the story was practically over when the suspense began. *The Los Angeles Times* said: "Barbara Bates handles some difficult scenes with ease and dignity."

J. Arthur Rank then attempted to cast Barbara opposite Britain's top box-office attraction Dirk Bogarde in the ill-fated *Campbell's Kingdom*. Shortly after the announcement, Barbara collapsed, reportedly from exhaustion, then dropped totally out of sight for several days. One press report speculated that she suffered a nervous breakdown; and another hinted that due to frequent depressions and mood changes, she had attempted suicide. Barbara Murray was hastily substituted in Barbara's role.

Gradually, Barbara began to pick up the threads of her life again, but the events in England had taken their toll on her, both physically and mentally. She and Coan decided to relocate to the United States when the Rank contract was cancelled. At Columbia Studios, Barbara was saddled up with pal Rory Calhoun in *Apache Territory* (1958), an underrated Western. A close personal friend of Barbara and her husband, producer-star Calhoun had requested her for the sagebrush tale. They had been friends since playing lovers in *I'd Climb the Highest Mountain*. "Barbara had the most tender nature of anyone I've ever seen," Rory Calhoun recalled. "Maybe there were problems I didn't notice, but she wasn't the kind to burden others with them. Barbara reminded me in many ways of Gail Russell." Filmed as *Papago Wells*, the film was an adaptation of a Louis L'Amour novel. The *Hollywood Citizen News* allowed: "The filmization of L'Amour's novel is a good suspense Western from fade-in to fade-out." *Variety* noted: "Thesping, topped by Calhoun's good performance, is creditable, with a fine job turned in by Barbara Bates."

Sadly, Hollywood had washed its hands of her—it was evident Barbara's career had lost its impetus. She worked sporadically on television including a "Millionaire" episode, a couple of commercials, one for a floor wax product, and another with comedian Buster Keaton. Barbara made a second excursion to England, where the British movie industry offered only a cold shoulder, except for the segment of "The Saint," entitled "The Loaded Tourist," with Roger Moore. This was to be her last acting assignment. Money was another problem for Barbara and Coan; they had lost a great deal of cash in poor land investments in Spain. In 1960, the couple moved back to Hollywood, rented a Beverly Hills apartment (445 North Doheny Dr.) near Saint Victor's Catholic Church, which they attended regularly after converting to Catholicism.

When it was discovered that Coan was suffering from cancer, Barbara never left his side. When he was moved to the Motion Picture Country Hospital for further treatment, Barbara moved into the living quarters of Saint Victor's, working as a church volunteer. Unable to deal with Coan's terminal illness, a distraught Barbara slashed her wrists and was discovered lying unconscious in her room by a parish priest, and rushed to nearby Cedars-Sinai Hospital. After Barbara recovered, Cecil Coan phoned Lois Laurel to ask if Barbara could stay in her guest house temporarily. Lois remembers, "Barbara didn't like to drive the freeways and our house was just a short distance from the Motion Picture Country Hospital. I knew nothing about her recent suicide attempt and was shocked when I saw the terrible scars on her wrists. I guess it was a cry for help. We were happy to have Barbara and she was so loving to our children."

Barbara was at Coan's bedside as his life slipped away on January 25, 1967, when he gave up the struggle with the painful disease. "She absolutely fell apart when Cecil died," Lois said. "She used to spend every day at his bedside." A week after Coan died, a despondent Barbara decided that the only possible cure would be a change of atmosphere. She had a hard adjustment ahead. Barbara severed all ties with Hollywood and with the help of a friend, Ron Tonkins, packed up all her belongings and returned to Denver, Colorado. "I could always rely on Cecil when I was down. He always knew what to say and what to do. There is nothing left for me in Hollywood," Barbara told Lois. She began to carve out a new life as a nurse's aide at a Denver hospital where her mother was employed as a registered nurse, while attending a secretarial school in the evenings.

In December, 1968, Barbara married a former childhood sweetheart, sportscaster William Reed, and her emotional state of mind seemed to be lifted. No one saw the impending doom. Lois Laurel Hawes received several letters from Barbara, "All very positive, except for some minor problems with a stepdaughter. I didn't notice any warning signs in her letters." Her mother, Mrs. Eva Bates, was quoted as saying, "Barbara was finally at peace with herself." But despite her newly found happiness, the intent to commit suicide was still lodged in the back of her mind. The new happiness proved to be only an uneasy reprieve.

On March 18, 1969, Mrs. Bates returned to her suburban Denver home after a day at the hospital to a frightening nightmare. Unlocking the garage door, she had an eerie feeling. Barbara's Volkswagen was parked in her mother's garage. It was a grisly sight—she was dead in the front seat of her automobile in the sealed garage. Following completion of toxicological tests, the cause of death was listed as carbon monoxide poisoning. Reportedly, Barbara was pregnant.

Why Barbara chose to return to her mother's home for this final tragic act remains a mystery to her grief-stricken mother. Her new husband William Reed and family were shocked. "Barbara was making such great progress and seemed so tranquil in her new marriage with Bill Reed," Mrs. Bates said. "But the manner in which she took her life proved to all of us that she was absolutely determined to succeed in ending her life." Then her mother broke down, "She will always be in my heart."

Barbara Bates' road to self-destruction had started long ago, perhaps the day she decided not to return to Colorado but instead pursue a movie career. The Hollywood goal proved unfulfilling and the ethereal beauty simply stopped searching and gave up her painstaking quest for happiness.

NATALIE WOOD

"What a waste. What a waste," sighed a bereaved Robert Wagner some time after his movie star wife Natalie Wood suddenly drowned in 1981. "It was a terrible, tragic accident, the memory of which I will have to live with all the rest of my life." Natalie Wood's course was set early. It has been said that she was "enchanted" by cameras at the tender age of seven months, when she posed for her first official portrait. The feeling was mutual. In just a few years, she would become "Hollywood's child." Some of her fellow movie striplings were able to assimilate massive doses of fame and still flourish, although early adulation is almost certain to have effects on most recipients. If nothing else, it places them in a goldfish bowl so that all the world can see their mistakes. Finally, there is the trauma of gauging the transition from movie moppet to sophisticated actress. Natalie would say later, "I was a child actress, never a child star. If I missed the fun of growing up, I didn't know about it." She was one of the exceptions, achieving major stardom as an adult. Starting with *Rebel Without a Cause*, she became an ideal for other teenage girls, most likely because youth icon James Dean included her in his outcry for understanding. With her flashing dark eyes and sensitive ability, Natalie was able to have it all—for a time: a happy marriage to Robert Wagner, motherhood, a timeless kind of beauty and self-respect as an actress. Just before her death, she was preparing her next career move—the legitimate stage. But Natalie Wood's path crossed the unexpected and the brutal unfairness of her chilling loss stunned Hollywood and saddened the world.

Natasha Gurdin was born on July 30, 1938, in San Francisco, California, the daughter of Russian-born immigrants Nicholas and Maria Kuleff Gurdin. Her parents fled Vladivostok and Harbin, respectively, and met and married in San Francisco around 1937. Nicholas Gurdin's real name was Zacharenko, which he decided to Americanize soon after arrival in the United States. He was a carpenter/wood-carver and his wife an ex-ballerina. The family lived in the Richmond District, a predominantly Russian area of the City by the Bay. There was an older half-sister, Olga (Teddy), born in China in 1929 from Mrs. Gurdin's first marriage, and later, another sister, Lana (Svetlana), born on March 1, 1946. The Gurdins made sure that little Natasha was instructed in Russian, German and English, as well as piano and ballet. In 1942, the family moved to Santa Rosa, California. A bright child, Natasha skipped the first and fourth grades. Very early, too, Natasha exhibited a strong tendency to daydream and play-act.

The sleepy town of Santa Rosa became Hollywood's "all-American town"—the architecture being solid Midwest. The paragon of normalcy was discovered for films by director Alfred Hitchcock while scouting locations for Universal's *Shadow of a Doubt*. When 20th Century-Fox sent the company of *Happy Land* to film exteriors there in June, 1943, Mrs. Gurdin registered herself and four-year-old Natasha with Charles Dunwoody, manager of Santa Rosa's Chamber of Commerce. Dunwoody had turned his offices into a central casting bureau for the duration of the filming there. He catalogued vital statistics on every man, woman and child within a fifty-mile radius who wanted to work as extras. The Gurdins owned a trailer that 20th Century-Fox had rented to use as an outdoor dressing room. One of the stars, Ann Rutherford, was enchanted with little Natasha and would often show her off to other members of the cast.

Happy Land (1943) was the story of a simple, hardworking Iowa family caught in the tide of war. Speaking to Natalie between takes, director Irving Pichel became increasingly impressed with the child's poise and personality. Recalled Natalie, "My mother led me over to the director, Mr. Pichel, and said, 'Why don't you sing your little song for him?' I sang 'In my arms, ain't I ever gonna get a guy in my arms?' " Pichel chose her for a bit in the opening scene as a tyke who drops her ice cream cone and cries. Mrs. Gurdin didn't know it, but her little darling had been discovered. As the story goes, her parents were unconvinced that their child should have a film career and thought *Happy Land* would be the end of it.

Irving Pichel remembered the bright-eyed youngster, however, and in 1945 when he as casting the strong role of the little European refugee in his *Tomorrow Is Forever* (1946) he brought Natasha and her mother to Hollywood. She was successfully tested for the film which would be made by the newly formed (and short-lived) International Pictures producing company founded by William Goetz and Leo Spitz. The latter pair christened her Natalie Wood because of their friendship with director Sam Wood. Years later, when asked if her mother had pushed her into a career, she replied, "My mother is the farthest thing from a stage mother, she's just not interested. My father didn't want me to act. It was against his wishes that Mother brought me to Los Angeles when Mr. Pichel sent for me." The Gurdins bought a two-bedroom bungalow at 9060 Harland Street in West Hollywood, just cross the Beverly Hills line, and Natalie was enrolled at West Hollywood Grammar School.

In the plot of *Tomorrow Is Forever*, Claudette Colbert's husband (Orson Welles) returns home after having been thought killed in the war twenty years before. The emotionally and physically altered Welles is accompanied by his adopted German daughter (Natalie, with bleached blonde pigtails and a German accent). Said Louella O. Parsons in the Los Angeles *Examiner*: "Little Natalie Wood, as a tiny refugee, gives a remarkable performance for a child. She eats your heart out." The Hollywood *Citizen News* reported: "There's some expert work, too, by Natalie Wood, a tot who can cry and laugh with the aplomb of an adult." *The Independent Journal* went on to laud Pichel's direction as "warm and understanding. He is responsible for a sparkling performance from six-year-old Natalie Wood, who steals scenes from Colbert, Welles and George Brent, all of whom are at their best." For this, her first major acting part, Natalie won the Box Office Magazine Blue Ribbon Award. She and her mother attended the New York premiere of the film.

Betty Henry, who lived next door to the Gurdins on Harland

Street, retains a clear memory of young Natalie as a great animal lover with two dogs, six canaries and three turtles, "all at the same time!"

"Natalie was a well-mannered, spirited child, utterly unspoiled and natural. She loved to draw and was forever brushing her doll's hair. She played beautiful piano and studied classical dancing. When Natalie signed a contract with 20th Century-Fox, my children accompanied her and Mrs. Gurdin to court. Shortly before Natalie died, I was gardening in the front yard, and hadn't seen Natalie in years. She drove by with her two young daughters to show them the house she grew up in. She also visited some of the other neighbors who still lived in the area and wanted to know what happened to some of her playmates. Her parents were lovely people," remembered Betty Henry.

Within two years, as Natalie's popularity grew, the family purchased a larger home at 15036 Valley Vista Boulevard in Sherman Oaks. Gurdin, an accomplished carpenter, worked at various times for Warner Brothers studio and Desilu, designing miniature props.

Director Pichel next cast protegée Natalie in Paramount's *The Bride Wore Boots* (1946), a weak comedy about a wife (Barbara Stanwyck) who loves horses and her husband (Robert Cummings) who doesn't. Natalie is Stanwyck's niece. Universal Pictures announced they were signing her to a seven-year contract, but the deal fell through. The studio was already grooming Beverly Simmons as a rival to MGM's supermoppet, Margaret O'Brien.

Next came perhaps Natalie's best-loved role as a child actress, the cynical little girl who finds it difficult to believe in Santa Claus in 20th Century-Fox's *Miracle on 34th Street* (1947), which opened at New York's Roxy Theatre on June 5, 1947. As directed by George Seaton, it was a delightful combination of fantasy, whimsy and heart-warming humor. Divorced Maureen O'Hara is the advertising manager for Macy's who wants Edmund Gwenn to be one of their holiday Santa Clauses. As it turns out, Gwenn actually believes he *is* Santa, and in court proceedings attorney John Payne proves that the elderly gentleman is right. The film earned several Academy Award nominations (Valentine Davies won the best original story, and Gwenn for best supporting actor), and Natalie picked up her second *Box Office* Blue Ribbon Award as well as "A Most Talented Juvenile Star of 1946" honor from *Parents Magazine*. The film has become a television staple at Christmas time.

Maureen O'Hara would later recall how young Natalie made little gifts in school for the cast and crew, and brought them to the set. On December 22, 1947, Natalie, Maureen O'Hara, John Payne and Edmund Gwenn recreated their roles on "The Lux Radio Theatre." Natalie soon became 20th Century-Fox's answer to MGM's boxoffice champ, Margaret O'Brien. Other child actresses who twinkled brightly at the time, then dropped from sight, were Connie Marshall (Fox), Gigi Perreau (Goldwyn), Sharyn Moffett (RKO) and Luana Patten (Disney).

In 20th Century-Fox's *The Ghost and Mrs. Muir* (1947), a romantic comedy about a widow (Gene Tierney) and the ghost of a sea captain (Rex Harrison), Natalie played Tierney's daughter who "grew up" to be Vanessa Brown. For her role as June Haver's kid sister in Fox's *Scudda-Hoo! Scudda-Hay!* (1948), Natalie won the Critics Award from *Film Daily* for giving one of the five best performances by a juvenile actress. Natalie's Fox schoolteacher, Gladys Hoene, remembers her as an average student, but a competent actress even then.

Natalie next reported to Republic Pictures for *Driftwood* (1947), about a backwoods spotted fever epidemic in which Walter Brennan and Dean Jagger adopted Natalie when her grandfather dies. In Peter Bogdanovich's book about him, *The Last Pioneer*, the director Allan Dwan stated, "Writer Mary Loos discovered some information about a virus carried by squirrels that hits people in a certain section of the country and that intrigued her. So we got involved in that and brought in a young doctor who's developing a serum, and a little girl—an orphan with a dog. But what intrigued me after we got going was the ability of the child we found—little Natalie Wood. She had a real talent for acting, an ability to characterize and interpret, and that was a pleasure. Her folks were Russian and her mother was ambitious for her daughter to be a ballet dancer. Any Russian would rather have their daughter be a ballet dancer than anything else. Anyway, it was a nice picture to make." The working title was *Heaven for Jenny*.

Director George Seaton asked for Natalie again for 20th Century-Fox's *Chicken Every Sunday* (1948), turn-of-the-century Americana about get-rich-quick schemer Dan Dailey and his long-suffering wife (Celeste Holm). Natalie is their daughter. She went on loanout to Texas oilman/producer Glenn McCarthy for *The Green Promise* (1949). In this one, Walter Brennan and his four children struggle to keep their farm going, while Robert Paige encourages pig-tailed Natalie to join the 4-H Club movement and raise a pair of lambs.

Natalie always said she was terrified of deep water, her phobia perhaps commencing with *The Green Promise*. In one scene she was supposed to cross a bridge that would collapse just as she reached the other side. "However, somebody pulled a lever too quickly and the bridge collapsed while I was halfway over," she said later. "I was thrown into the water and it was unbelievably scary." Due to the childhood mishap, a small bone on her left wrist jutted out slightly, which is why for the rest of her public life Natalie's left wrist was usually concealed by large bracelets, gloves or long-sleeved clothing.

Marguerite Chapman, the feminine star of *The Green Promise*, recalls, "Natalie's mother was always on the set, keeping track of everything, taking very good care of her. This is what the parents did then. Natalie was a well-behaved, well-bred, very, very professional little girl—so much so that she scared the hell out of me! To tell the truth, I was getting a little jealous. As the baby on the set, she was getting all the attention from everybody."

Once asked if she thought she was pushed into a career, Natalie swore, "I had no such problem. Something in me obviously wanted to act. When I was told to do something, I cooperated and enjoyed it. But the idea of free will didn't occur to me. Not until my middle teens did I get a clue that I had some say in the matter." Other sources claim Mrs. Gurdin was very ambitious for her daughter.

Back at Fox, Maureen O'Hara became her mother again for *Father Was a Fullback* (1949). The comedy focused on college football coach Fred MacMurray's domestic problems and efforts to win the big game, while daughters Natalie and Betty Lynn have their share of growing pains. Now an eleven-year-old, Natalie received yet another trophy—as Child Star of 1949 by the Children's Day National Council of New York. With her busy work and schedule, Natalie still found time to study at the Mikhail Panaieff Ballet Center, where her classmates included Stephania "Taffy" Federkiewicz (Stefanie Powers) and Jill Oppenheim (Jill St. John). As she approached the difficult stage of adolescence, she began working more and more. For his Book *Twinkle, Twinkle, Little Star*, ex-child actor Dick Moore interviewed Natalie shortly before her death. In it, she confessed, "As a very young child, acting for me was just like playing house or playing with dolls, but when I entered adolescence, I became self-conscious. I guess I didn't look awkward, because I continued to work and didn't go through the 'awkward age' professionally, but I certainly did emotionally. There was no adult I could confide in, and I was very withdrawn, very shy."

Columbia's moving *No Sad Songs for Me* (1950) had a dying Margaret Sullavan preparing her husband (Wendell Corey) and daughter (Natalie) to go on without her. It marked Sullavan's last film appearance—she died in 1960, probably by suicide. In Samuel Goldwyn's *Our Very Own* (1950), Natalie was the bratty kid sister of Ann Blyth, who accidentaly learns that she was adopted by Jane Wyatt and Donald Cook. Then she went to RKO for *Never a Dull Moment* (1950), in which songwriter Irene Dunne marries rancher Fred MacMurray and has to adjust to rural life and two step-daughters (Natalie and Gigi Perreau). Producer Harriet Parsons vainly tried to imitate the recent Universal success, *The Egg and I*. The last film on her 20th Century-Fox contract was *The Jackpot* (1950), which spoofed the radio giveaway craze. Natalie and Tommy Rettig are the children of department store executive James Stewart and his wife (Barbara Hale).

Next, Paramount's *Dear Brat* (1951), a tepid follow-up to the family series previously including *Dear Ruth* and *Dear Wife*. Mona Freeman had the title role, while Natalie enacted the daughter of rehabilitated criminal Lyle Bettger. Natalie is particularly appealing in RKO's *The Blue Veil* (1951), as entertainer Joan Blondell's lonely child. The sensitive, beautifully made tear-jerker centers around nursemaid Jane Wyman and her charges and was a remake of a 1942 French film starring Gaby Morlay. Wyman earned a best actress Oscar nomination, Blondell a supporting nomination. In Paramount's *Just for You*

(1952), musical comedy producer Bing Crosby is torn between romance with Jane Wyman and raising his children (Robert Arthur and Natalie). As a student at Ethel Barrymore's exclusive girls' school, Natalie has some memorable screen moments with the legendary Barrymore. After appearing in two Jane Wyman vehicles, Natalie became infatuated with Wyman's acting skills. She told columnist Hedda Hopper, "My ambition is to be just like Miss Wyman when I grow up." Monogram obtained her services for the role of Rose Princess Vera Miles' little sister in *The Rose Bowl Story* (1952). For the Cinecolor feature set against Pasadena's annual Tournament of Roses parade, Natalie's parents are Jim Backus and Ann Doran, who, three years later, would play the parents of Natalie's co-star, James Dean, in *Rebel Without a Cause*. Commented *The Los Angeles Times*: "Natalie Wood is the cutest cutie seen in a long time—has beauty and appeal plus an impish humor all her own."

The Star (1953) deals with fading movie queen Bette Davis' attempts to make a comeback, featuring Natalie as her neglected twelve-year-old. She was third-billed, after Davis and leading man Sterling Hayden, in this Bert Friedlob independent production released through Fox. Wrote Charles Higham in his book *Bette: The Life of Bette Davis*: "During the shooting of *The Star*, Bette formed a new friendship that would last the rest of her life. There was a scene in which a child, Natalie Wood, was to fall in water from a pier. Stuart Heisler (the director) wanted to throw Natalie in; the little girl was terrified and cried hysterically. Bette heard Natalie's cries, came out of her trailer, picked Natalie up and said to Heisler, 'If you make Natalie do this, I'll walk off the picture. Who do you think she is? Johnny Weissmuller? You mustn't do this kind of thing to a little child.' Heisler backed down and Bette took over the direction of the scene." Although they finally used a double, the scene was cut out of the picture. Later, Natalie would say, "I learned more about acting from Bette Davis than the Actors Studio could teach me in a lifetime."

Natalie went on to play a seductive fifteen-year-old in Warner Bros.' *The Silver Chalice* (1954). A four-and-a-half-million-dollar flop, it tells the story of a Greek sculptor (newcomer Paul Newman) who designs the "Silver Chalice" of the Last Supper. The film was adapted from Thomas B. Costain's pious best-seller. Natalie's last "awkward age" role came with Universal's *One Desire* (1955), starring Anne Baxter and Rock Hudson. In this Ross Hunter-produced soap opera, Baxter is a gal from the wrong side of the tracks who tries to cross over while becoming a foster mother to an orphan (Natalie).

Natalie's only television series, "Pride of the Family," aired from October, 1953, through September, 1954, on ABC-TV. She and Bobby Hyatt were the teenage children of Paul Hartman and Fay Wray. Hartman played a character not unlike Dagwood Bumstead, always getting into misunderstandings both at home and as the head of a local newspaper's advertising department. It was put into reruns on CBS-TV during the summer of 1955. Natalie's early TV career also included: *Ford Theatre's* "Too Old For Dolls," with Laraine Day, Franchot Tone and Robert Kendall; *The Schaefer Century Theatre's* "Playmates"; *Hollywood Opening Night's* "Quite A Viking," with Ann Harding and James Dunn; *Studio 57's* "The Plot Against Miss Pomeroy"; "Heidi" with Jo Van Fleet, in which Natalie portrayed the crippled girl; and guest starred on two short-lived Warner Brothers TV series, *Conflict*, a dramatic anthology series, and *King's Row* with Jack Kelly, Nan Leslie and Dennis Hopper.

In December, 1954, Natalie was in an automobile accident along Mulholland Drive, the press reporting that she narrowly escaped serious injury. Her car left the road, knocked down forty feet of guardrail and turned over. Natalie walked away with only minor bruises. That same month, Natalie was cast with Eddie Albert and a pre-stardom James Dean on TV's General Electric Theatre. The show, titled "I'm a Fool," was an adaptation of the Sherwood Anderson short story about a young man's lost love. The producers originally wanted to use John Smith, first noticed in *The High and the Mighty*, but they finally chose James Dean.

"Rehearsals were held in a dilapidated theatre in downtown Los Angeles and everyone arrived on time except Jimmy," Natalie told *Photoplay* magazine. "Like everybody else in Hollywood, I'd heard the stories and was frankly afraid of him. The longer we waited the more frightened I became, and as I went through the script I found that he was going to make love to me. After a half-hour with everyone watching the door for

Dean's arrival, he came in—through a large window of the building. All I could think of was, 'He sure knows how to make an entrance!' He was dressed in a dirty sport shirt and had a large safety pin across the front of his pants—jeans, of course. He jumped down on the floor, looked around, picked up a script from the table and sat in a corner. The director said, 'C'mon, Jimmy, sit next to Natalie. You're going to have to make love to this girl.' Jimmy didn't even look up. He just grunted."

After the first rehearsal, Dean asked Natalie to lunch. "We found a cafe," Natalie remembered, "and, like most actors, gabbed about the script we were working on and the show. Then in the middle of his sandwich he said, 'I know you. You're a child actress.' I said that was true, but it's a lot better than acting like a child. He didn't get it for a moment. Then he started to laugh. Then I started to laugh and that's how our wonderful friendship began." The program provided Natalie's first "grownup" role.

When Warner Brothers began its search for the ingenue lead in *Rebel Without a Cause*, columnist Hedda Hopper reported that Margaret O'Brien, Debbie Reynolds, Lori Nelson and Jayne Mansfield were under consideration to play "Judy." The film's star, James Dean, preferred a friend from the Actors Studio, Christine White. Director Nicholas Ray told David Dalton in the Dean biography, *The Mutant King*: "I wasn't going to cast Natalie Wood in the picture because she's a child actress, and the only child actress who ever made it as far as I'm concerned was Helen Hayes." Ray went on to explain that actor Dennis Hopper, Natalie and a friend named Faye had been in a car accident. Hopper called Ray, said there had been some trouble and that he thought Natalie had a concussion. When Ray arrived at the police station, the doctor was just leaving and said Natalie was all right. "I went in and Natalie was lying down, and she grabbed me and pulled me close to her and whispered in my ear, 'You see that son of a bitch? and she pointed to the precinct doctor. 'Well, he called me a juvenile delinquent. *Now* do I get the part?' " She did, and it changed her life.

Rebel Without a Cause (1955) is the sensitively acted classic about alienated youth to which young people everywhere related. It probably marked the beginning of the world's subsequent "youth rebellion," precursing the "beat generation" and "hippies," making a legend of James Dean. *The New York Times* described *Rebel* as "Brutal and excessively graphic. . . . It's a picture to make the hair stand on end." Although Natalie received generally good notices, *The Harvard Lampoon* castigated her "saccharine, whining caricature of American girlhood." The film was shot on location in and around the Los Angeles area, using Santa Monica High School, the "Norma Desmond" house from *Sunset Boulevard* and the Griffith Observatory. Tourists still try to locate the Desmond villa, but it was torn down years ago.

James Dean was nominated for the best actor Academy Award for the same year's *East of Eden*, but Natalie and Sal Mineo were nominated in the supporting category for *Rebel Without a Cause*. Today, though the performances remain powerful, *Rebel* appears somewhat hysterical and silly from a contemporary viewpoint.

On June 14, 1955, Natalie was graduated from Van Nuys High School, where one of her fellow students was Robert Redford, although they didn't know each other then (the San Fernando Valley school alumni also included—from various years—Marilyn Monroe, Jane Russell, Gail Russell and Stacy Keach). Natalie celebrated the occasion by having a swimming pool installed in the family home and buying herself a pink Ford Thunderbird. In early September, Natalie was placed under contract to Warner Brothers at four hundred dollars a week.

The night *Rebel Without a Cause* was sneak-previewed in Huntington Park, Natalie attended with Nicholas Ray, James Dean, Sal Mineo and two other actors in the film, Nick Adams and Jack Simmons. They later retreated to the then popular Googie's restaurant on the Sunset Strip to celebrate. Afterward, Warners sent Natalie on a promotional tour to New York, where she was joined by Nick Adams, one of Dean's closest friends. Natalie, Nick, Sal Mineo, Richard Davalos and his wife Ellen, having just seen Davalos in *A View From the Bridge*, were having dinner on a Friday evening (September 30th, 1955), the night James Dean ran into another car in his Porsche sports car and was killed instantly in California.

Warners took full control of Natalie's career and began the process of turning her into a star. But first there was a small but crucial role in *The Searchers* (1956), as the young white child captured by Comanche Indians and rescued after five years' pursuit by her uncle (John Wayne). The distinguished John Ford directed the well-received Western saga that was filmed largely in Monument Valley, Arizona. In a novel bit of casting, Natalie's real-life kid sister, nine-year-old Lana Wood, portrayed Natalie in the early scenes.

The Burning Hills (1956) found Natalie and new teen heartthrob Tab Hunter as a pair of young lovers battling a ruthless cattle baron's son (Skip Homeier). Natalie plays a spirited "half-Mexican, half-Yankee girl." In Warners' *A Cry in the Night* (1956), Natalie is kidnaped on a lovers' lane by Raymond Burr and later rescued by her father (Edmond O'Brien). During the filming, gossip columnists noted that Natalie was dating the much older Raymond Burr, when not in the company of Nicholas Ray or actor newcomer Scott Marlowe.

With movie audiences growing younger and more vocal, Warner Brothers realized they had a hot new team in the youthful persons of Natalie Wood and Tab Hunter. They were tossed into the modest but pleasant *The Girl He Left Behind* (1956), which was reminiscent of the service comedies of the previous decade (and particularly *See Here, Private Hargrove*). Hunter essays a spoiled peacetime Army draftee whose prime concern is getting out and back to his girl (Natalie). Even more routine is *Bombers B-52* (1957), starring Natalie with Efrem Zimbalist, Jr., and Karl Malden as her father who opposes her relationship with the older Zimbalist. Marsha Hunt is her understanding mother and there is some good aerial footage of jet plane maneuvers, but not much else. The comedy was filmed on the Fort Ord, California, Army base.

Nevertheless, Natalie's career was now in high gear. She joined Elizabeth Taylor as that rarest of screen creatures: the child star who makes the transition to adult star while remaining continuously in the public eye. On suspension during most of 1957, Natalie and her agents eventually settled with Warner Brothers for a salary raise from five hundred dollars a week to seven hundred and fifty dollars a week. Her final bachelor girl flings included a turbulent romance with hotel heir

Nicky Hilton and a highly publicized invitation to Elvis
Presley's Southern estate, Graceland. Two days into the visit
with Presley, Natalie called her sister Lana. Referring to
Presley's domineering mother, she revealed, "Gladys has
wrecked everything. I don't have a chance. Get me out of this,
and fast." Returning to California due to a "family emergency," Natalie confessed to Lana, "God, it was awful. He can
sing, but he can't do much else."

Natalie had first spotted the handsome, 19-year-old Robert
Wagner in 1949 while the child actress and her mother were in
the 20th Century-Fox executive building. She told Mrs. Gurdin,
"I'm going to marry that man." They began dating on Natalie's
18th birthday in 1956. And in a private ceremony on December
28, 1957, they were married at the Scottsdale Methodist Church
in Arizona. Natalie's friend and sometime stand-in Barbara
Gould was maid of honor and Robert Wagner, Sr., acted as best
man. The Wagners would become "Hollywood's dream couple," the most photographed, talked-about young marrieds
since Tony Curtis and Janet Leigh. Later, she would say of their
honeymoon, "The best part was the last week. We spent it on
R.J.'s boat, off the coast of Catalina, in a dense fog for four
days. . . . We're happiest on the boat, and we intend spending
as much time there as possible." (Years afterward, this state-
ment takes on eerie connotations.) Natalie was about to have
her first major vehicle as a star.

Warners tested several other actresses before assigning
Natalie to the film version of Herman Wouk's glossy bestseller,
Marjorie Morningstar (1958), the story of a Jewish girl (Natalie)
who dreams of going on the stage but winds up a contented
housewife. Gene Kelly, as the Catskills resort director with
whom she falls in love, is miscast, and the lack of chemistry between the two stars hurt the film, which was still a popular success.

This was followed by *Kings Go Forth* (1958), co-starring Frank
Sinatra and Tony Curtis, on loan to United Artists. It was a
three-cornered romance set in wartime on the Cote d'Azur,
with Natalie the offspring of a mixed marriage. Said the Los
Angeles *Mirror-News*: "The cast's reactions often don't ring
true. One doesn't even believe that Sinatra is really stunned,
for instance, when he learns that the girl (Wood) is half Negro.

Still, Sinatra is the best of the three." Natalie and Sinatra became good friends. "Frank can think of the most wonderful things to do to people who have done him wrong," she once remarked cryptically. "I don't think he does them often but he always tells me about them and I save them up in my head."

Back at Warner Brothers, Natalie starred in a charming comedy, *Cash McCall* (1959), opposite James Garner, who had been a featured player in *The Girl He Left Behind* three years before. Garner plays the unscrupulous tycoon who acquires a new set of values while romancing Natalie, the daughter of failing businessman Dean Jagger. Natalie's quarrels with Warner Brothers over salary and parts continued; she refused to be loaned out to Universal for *This Earth Is Mine,* starring Rock Hudson, because she felt the role was a supporting one, and was suspended for eighteen months. She said, "You get tough in this business, until you get big enough to hire people to get tough for you. Then you can sit back and be a lady."

Natalie and Robert Wagner co-starred in a theater film for the only time in Metro-Goldwyn-Mayer's pretentious *All the Fine Young Cannibals* (1960). As a headstrong, mixed-up girl, Natalie is loved by Wagner but marries George Hamilton. Also thrown in are such topics as drinking, babies, broken-down singers and religion. The New York *Herald-Tribune* called it "An oversimplified, over-excited picture which nobody could be expected to rescue from absurdity."

In Warner Brothers' *Splendor in the Grass* (1961), Natalie gives what many consider her finest portrayal as an emotionally broken girl who loses the love of her live (Warren Beatty). From the pen of William Inge and under Elia Kazan's direction, the 1920s Kansas story unfolds as poignant, romantic, human and timeless. Natalie would say of her experience on *Splendor,* "Elia Kazan is exciting to work with, he's an education for any actor. He cuts right through to the core of a characterization. And with Kazan, there are never any waits between scenes. It's the most exciting creative experience I've ever had." Her performance bears this out, and she is particularly touching as she wilts under the knowledge that Warren Beatty has left her for someone else in frustration over their unconsummated love. She was rewarded with her first Oscar nomination in the best actress category. In *The New York Times*, Bosley Crowther wrote, "The authority and eloquence of the theme emerge in the honest, sensitive acting of Beatty and Wood. And Miss Wood has a beauty and radiance that carry through a role of violent passions and depressions with unsullied purity and strength." And *Variety*: "Natalie Wood and Warren Beatty are the lovers. Although the range and amplitude of their expression is not always as wide and variable as it might be, both deliver convincing, appealing performances."

Playwright Mart Crowley told writer Gavin Lambert: "Back in 1960, I was working for Elia Kazan as a production assistant on *Splendor in the Grass*. Warren and Natalie didn't get along well on the film at all. No one predicted that eighteen months later they would be dating. Gadge (Kazan) was a real devil. Natalie was terrified of water and she didn't want to do the swimming sequence, so Gadge promised her it would be done by a double. I don't know whether he ever intended to have anyone else do it, but at the last minute he told Natalie she'd have to do it herself. She got terribly upset and refused, but Gadge really soothed her, convincing her to do it. He had the grips build a plywood platform sunk under the water, so that Natalie could touch ground if she wanted. And so she went ahead and did the scene. She was a very brave person. Right after *Splendor*, Warners wanted to put her in *Rome Adventure* with Troy Donahue. Natalie felt so strongly about not doing the movie that she decided this was a great time to have her tonsils out—which she did."

The same year as *Splendor in the Grass* was released, 1961, United Artists brought forth *West Side Story*, making it Natalie Wood's greatest professional year. She starred with Richard Beymer in the Leonard Bernstein-Stephen Sondheim musical re-telling of *Romeo and Juliet* in a contemporary Spanish Harlem setting, and with Shakespeare's families transformed into rival street gangs. The result, as it had been on Broadway, was a smashing success, with the Robert Wise-Jerome Robbins co-directed production garnering ten Academy Awards, including best picture plus supporting actress and actor Oscars for Rita Moreno and George Chakiris. As the Puerto Rican heroine, Maria, Natalie's singing was dubbed by Marni Nixon. "Unless she chooses bad scripts, Natalie will be a big star for years to come," correctly predicted director Robert Wise. "About her personal life—I don't know."

During the three years following their marriage, Natalie and Robert Wagner continued to be extolled as Hollywood's happiest couple. Sometimes they seemed to have invented togetherness—they refused to be parted even when working. When Wagner worked, Natalie sat on the set and he returned the compliment, giving up a film at one point so he could go on location with her. Suddenly, however, it was a case of their relationship being "too hot not to cool down." The Wagners' marriage broke up abruptly on June 20, 1961; they finally divorced on April 28, 1963. An affair between Natalie and Warren Beatty was said to be the reason. Although columnists reported that their marriage was imminent, Beatty proved (and proved again) not to be the marrying kind. Natalie had less publicized flings over the next few years with Arthur Loew, Jr., Robert Evans, Stuart Whitman, David Niven, Jr., Guy McElwaine, Steve McQueen, Tom Courtenay and Frank Sinatra. There was also a brief engagement to South American jet-setter Ladislav Blatnik. She went into analysis and once said her psychiatric bills totalled "at least the equal of the annual defense budget of most Central American nations."

Then came another transferred Broadway musical hit, *Gypsy* (1962), the campy saga about the early life of stripper Gypsy Rose Lee (Natalie) and her ambition-consumed mother (Rosalind Russell in the role created by Ethel Merman on the stage). The familiar story begins during the 1920s vaudeville heyday with Russell pushing talented daughter "Baby June" (Ann Jillian). As years pass, and Jillian elopes, Russell concentrates on making her more demure daughter (Natalie) into a burlesque star. As a whole, the movie just missed, perhaps because Natalie, petite and slim, is the unlikeliest stripper ever, and because harmful cuts were made just before release. The Jule Styne-Stephen Sondheim score, though, is always a joy. And Rosalind Russell troupes with astonishing gusto, especially in view of the fact that she had recently had a mastectomy (although this was not revealed until after her death in 1976 of cancer complicated by severe rheumatoid arthritis).

Still, director Mervyn LeRoy would remember in his autobiography *Take One:* "Natalie Wood was my first and only choice for the mature Gypsy, and she was excellent. At the time, she was going with Warren Beatty and he was on the set almost every day. Natalie's striptease was done in the days before Hollywood went on its 'freedom' binge, so the strip was very decorous—Natalie never took her bra off. Nevertheless, it was exciting and it raised the blood pressure of the male cinemagoer a few points." Once again, Marni Nixon did most of Natalie's singing. When *Gypsy* was completed, Natalie flew to France to attend the Cannes Film Festival.

Natalie passed on doing *Term of Trial* in England with Laurence Olivier and Simone Signoret, instead reporting to Paramount for *Love With the Proper Stranger* (1963), co-starring Steve McQueen—the closest she had yet come to projecting the ordinary American girl. Robert Mulligan directed, and the film provided a touching, optimistic slant on what was a fresh and provocative topic of controversy in the early 1960s: unwanted pregnancy and abortion. McQueen enacts the shitftless trumpet player who impregnates Natalie, a salesgirl at Macy's Department Store. It was popular with the public, and generaly well reviewed, although *Time* felt the production "recalls the tenement symphonies of the 1930s—working-class misery in a minor key." Natalie won her second best actress Academy Award nomination. Tom Bosley, who played a boyfriend of Natalie's in *Love With the Proper Stranger*, fondly remembered how, as he prepared to fly home to New York after completion of his role, he discovered that his plane reservations had been cancelled by Natalie, who had other plans for Bosley and his wife. Natalie gave them a lavish, surprise going-away party at Chasen's Restaurant.

Natalie had now reached the zenith of her profession and was surrounded by an ever-growing entourage, including Mart Crowley, now her secretary; hairstylist Sugar Blymyer; make-up artist Eddie Butterworth; and stand-in Roselle Gordon. Warners' *Sex and the Single Girl* (1964) had little to do with Helen Gurley Brown's spicy best-seller of that title. Instead, it was turned into an innocent farce about the sexual daydreams of scandal magazine editor Tony Curtis. Natalie was a research psychologist, and Fran Jeffries, wife of the director Richard Quine, had a role in the slick comedy, and she recalls: "Richard and I were living in the old Ingrid Bergman estate, and Natalie came by several times during the weeks of preparation. She was usually in the company of Mart Crowley or Howard Jeffrey (her new secretary). Natalie was enthusiastic over the script and had final cast approval. She spoke with an appealing directness and was concerned about every detail of *Sex and the Single Girl*. As I remember, Richard wanted Natalie for his next film, *Oh, Dad, Poor Dad*, but she just wasn't interested." As it turned out, refusing the latter part was fortuitous, because neither Rosalind Russell nor Barbara Harris was able to save that dismal black comedy.

The Great Race (1965), advertised by Warner Brothers as "the greatest comedy ever made," wasn't. Director Blake Edwards' slapstick romp chronicles the first New York-to-Paris car race in the early 1900s. A few funny moments manage to creep in, but basically it is an over-produced dud. Natalie adds the female allure to the contest between hero Tony Curtis and villain Jack Lemmon.

Inside Daisy Clover (1966), produced at Warners from a Gavin Lambert novel, is an uneven story of 1930s Hollywood. Moviemakers periodically have taken a look at their own, and the results generally deal with characters who seem to have crawled out from under a rock. *Inside Daisy Clover* is very much in that tradition—a rags-to-riches story in which Natalie is a teenager with a great singing voice (shades of Judy Garland/ Deanna Durbin) who is taken in by executive vampires. Conniving relatives and a gay leading man (Robert Redford) complete the circle around Natalie, whose indomitable spirit prevails in the end. Natalie has some effective sequences, notably her nervous breakdown in a dubbing booth during a recording session. While filming a sailboat scene with Redford, Natalie was horrified when a severe swell rose, separating them from the rest of the company. In James Spada's *The Films of Robert Redford*, director Robert Mulligan said: "There was no way we could get them off the boat, and the lines to keep them in place were breaking right and left. One of the crew members broke his leg as a cable snapped and we had to rush him to the hospital. All the time we were worrying about Bob and Natalie, and it was obvious that she was terrified and he was having a great time. He was laughing like hell and turning the whole thing into a wonderful adventure. When he found out about the broken leg, of course, he didn't think it was so funny, but I think his sense of fun kept Natalie from having a heart attack."

Inside Daisy Clover opened to negative reviews and was not a success. "By the Hollywood standards of 1936, the time of the story, the picture would have been pretty bad, and by today's standards it is still pretty bad, its weaknesses all the more embarrassing for being inadvertent," commented *The New Yorker*. "Natalie Wood isn't very plausible either as a 15-year-old or as a singer." The musical numbers were choreographed by future director Herbert Ross. The late distinguished actress Ruth Gordon, who plays Natalie's mother in *Daisy Clover*, once reminisced, "I learned a lot about being a star from her. She never threw her weight around, but one day when we were on location in Pasadena, I said, 'Oh, I forgot my lucky bracelet with my St. Christopher's medal.' Natalie said, 'Send a limo for it.' It was in my dressing room back at Warners and I said, 'Oh, no.' she said, 'That's what limos are for.' "

Tennessee Williams' *This Property Is Condemned* (1966), the sad fable of an idealistic Southern girl (Natalie) crushed by sordid reality, was enhanced by beautiful camerawork by veteran cinematographer James Wong Howe. Under the direction of Sydney Pollack (in his second feature), Natalie and Robert Redford gave creditable performances in this expansion of a one-act Williams play said to have contained an early development of the character Blanche DuBois from *A Streetcar Named Desire*. Paramount's *This Property Is Condemned*, while never totally satisfying, somehow manages to leave a pleasant aftertaste.

Metro-Goldwyn-Mayer's *Penelope* (1966) was received with ho-hum reviews, its forced gaiety being all too evident. Natalie plays a zany girl who befuddles even her psychiatrist when she holds up her husband's bank for sixty thousand dollars. Peter Falk, doing his "Columbo" detective turn, gives the silly comedy's best performance.

One of the most startling revelations from Lana Wood's *Natalie: A Memoir* is that Natalie, soon after the poor reception for *Penelope*, attempted suicide by swallowing a bottle of sleeping pills. Mart Crowley found her unconscious and rushed her to Cedars of Lebanon Hospital. Reportedly, the near fatal attempt followed a "loud visit" with her ex-lover, Warren Beatty.

Natalie was off the screen for the next three years, admitting she was going through a personal catharsis, rearranging her life. "I have been working steadily since I was five," she said. "I had to have two years of just—just living. Catching up. And I was thrilled to discover that I didn't have the need to work. There was a time when if I wasn't working, I felt at a loss." She continued, "Sometimes, when I pass 20th Century-Fox, I think 'That's where I went to grammar school.'" Or, if I was at Warner Brothers, 'That's where I went to high school.'"

While traveling through Europe with Lana, Natalie met and fell in love with British film agent Richard Gregson, the brother of actor Michael Craig. He was president of London International Artists. On May 30, 1969, they married in a Russian Orthodox ceremony at the Holy Virgin Mary Church in Los Angeles. The best man was Robert Redford. A daughter, Natasha, was born on September 29, 1970. Natalie's close friend, Ruth Gordon, was the child's godmother. The marriage proved to be a stormy one and they divorced in April, 1972. Gregson, now a producer, returned to England.

Natalie returned to the screen in Columbia's *Bob & Carol & Ted & Alice* (1969), a wife-swapping comedy—this time, wisely, for a percentage of the profits as opposed to her customary seven hundred and fifty thousand dollars. The film earned her over four million dollars. (She had been offered a percentage of *West Side Story* and didn't take it.) Representling Paul Mazursky's directorial debut, *Bob & Carol & Ted & Alice* is a shrewd blend of satire, sharp gags and sentiment. In this antic lampoon of California lifestyles, which was considered daring, even revolutionary in 1969, Natalie and Robert Culp try to "modernize" the thinking of close pals Elliott Gould and Dyan Cannon.

Meanwhile, Robert Wagner had married Marion Marshall, ex-wife of director Stanley Donen. But the union, like Natalie's second marriage to Richard Gregson, was destined to fail. The Wagners separated in 1970, and divorced the following year. "Bob's single again," girlfriend Asa Maynor told Natalie. In a 1973 interview, Natalie explained: "When R.J. heard I was getting a divorce, he phoned me. We had a lot of telephone contact. Then I just got on a plane and flew to Palm Springs. We were going together a very long time before people knew about it. First in Palm Springs and then Lake Tahoe. Mickey Ziffren (the wife of her lawyer, Paul) gave me a birthday party last year. And halfway through the evening the writer Leonard Gershe leaned over and said, 'Oh, I get it! You're together again!' "

Natalie and Robert Wagner remarried on July 16, 1972, on board a chartered, fifty-five-foot cabin cruiser, moored in Paradise Cove, off the coast of Southern California. They purchased a home in Brentwood and later bought singer Patti Page's sprawling, two-story New England-style house on Canon Drive in Beverly Hills. "Lots of people walk away from a relationship rather than try to make it work," Natalie said. "And that's not really very healthy. I'll always love R.J."

In Warner Brothers' *The Candidate* (1972), Natalie plays herself, a star at a fundraising event for United States Senate candidate Robert Redford. In a funny cameo, Natalie is introduced to Redford, who asks an aide, "Who *is* she?" Then Natalie and Wagner co-starred in the 1973 sentimental love story for ABC-Television, "The Affair," made for Spelling-Goldberg productions. As a crippled songwriter who had polio as a child, she experiences her first love affair with Wagner, a sensitive lawyer. Bruce Davison, who plays her brother, was a big fan of James Dean and asked Natalie what she thought of her former costar. "I really didn't know him at all. He was a very odd boy," she said. At the same time, Tab Hunter, who had co-starred with Natalie in films and on TV, and who once had done magazine layouts with her and was photographed escorting her to premieres, was asked about Natalie. "I hardly knew her," was his similarly curious reply. Noticeably pregnant in "The Affair," Natalie also sang the TV film's theme song. On March 9, 1974, the Robert Wagners became parents of a daughter, Courtney Brooke; Courtney was the name of Natalie's character in "The Affair."

"Natalie was actually very intelligent in terms of money," remembers her attorney, Paul Ziffren. "She was not only very bright, but she could understand the most complicated financial matters. She could also remember ten-year-old conversations verbatim. But the most extraordinary thing about Natalie is that she was the only one of the child stars to grow into an emotionally adult woman. She looked so very young that it was hard for her to find correspondingly mature roles. Although she had developed real emotional maturity, she was still looking for a vehicle to express it."

Natalie began to work less frequently during the 1970s, although she appeared in more varied roles toward the end of the decade. Twentieth Century-Fox' *Peeper* (1976) was an occasionally engaging take-off of private eye yarns, with Michael Caine as a British detective working in 1947 Los Angeles. Natalie is the long-lost daughter of Caine's client, and the film appeared to be a send-up, in particular, of the 1947 Bogart-Bacall classic, *The Big Sleep*.

In the autumn of 1976, Natalie attended the 20th Annual San Francisco Film Festival held at the Palace of Fine Arts Theater. As one of the honorees in a retrospective glance at past films, Natalie submitted to a question-and-answer period. She was thrilled, she said, to be back in her hometown and spoke about her latest performance as Maggie in a television production of *Cat on a Hot Tin Roof*, co-starring Robert Wagner and Laurence Olivier. Excerpts were then shown. Wagner played the sexually tormented Brick, Olivier Big Daddy in Tennessee Williams' powerful study of a Southern family actually filmed in Manchester, England. "It was a weird experience looking at all those clips from my films," she said. "It was all so odd. I looked so much like my daughter Natasha when I was about eleven. Some of the movies I remember very well and others I don't." Natalie was accompanied to the festival by Wagner and ex-secretaries Mart Crowley and Howard Jeffrey. Crowley had become a successful playwright with *Boys in the Band* and Jeffrey a producer. While in the Bay Area, Natalie visited with eldest sister Olga and her family.

To the consternation of loyal Wood-watchers, a nervous twitchiness, especially around the mouth, had become apparent circa *Cat on a Hot Tin Roof*. Fans began to worry about her well being.

Natalie was off the screen for the next three years to devote more time to her children Natasha and Courtney and her step-daughter, Katharine Wagner. When Natalie did decide to return to filmmaking, she did so with her usual intensity of purpose. She enrolled for strenuous exercise classes with physical fitness instructor Tybee Brascia. An accomplished dancer, Brascia had worked with Fred Astaire in MGM's *Silk Stockings*. Shortly before her death from cancer, Brascia reminisced about her "serious talks" with Natalie between workouts. "Natalie became a movie star at an age when most children are playing with dolls, and it's no secret that she suffered horribly from starting her career too soon," Tybee Brascia said. "And she had tremendous problems through adulthood."

In American-International's *Meteor* (1979), Natalie portrays a Soviet scientist and interpreter for Russian astrophysicist Brian Keith. They come to the United States to join forces with NASA in an effort to deflect a meteor zipping toward Earth. Sean Connery, a disgruntled former NASA person, is Natalie's love interest. If nothing else, *Meteor* gave Natalie the opportunity to speak Russian on the screen for the first time.

In 1979, Natalie went to Hawaii for the NBC-Television miniseries *From Here to Eternity*, based on James Jones' novel about military life on the eve of Pearl Harbor. Appearing with William Devane and Steve Railsback, Natalie won a Golden Globe Award for her role as Karen Holmes, played by Deborah Kerr in the much-honored 1953 film. Natalie chose not to continue in the subsequent TV series, and Barbara Hershey tookover the part.

The same year, Natalie starred in the ABC-Television movie *The Cracker Factory* as an alcoholic housewife who found herself in a psychiatric ward after a drunken attack on her husband (Peter Haskell). Ex-actor Burt Brinckerhoff directed. Natalie also had a cameo role in Robert Wagner's "Hart to Hart" pilot film, which aired in May, 1979. She did a bathtub scene and had one line acknowledging Wagner's startled look. Continuing a busy year, Natalie starred for producer Irwin Allen in the CBS-Television drama, "The Memory of Eva Ryker," in which multimillionaire Ralph Bellamy begins the salvaging of a torpedoed luxury liner on which his wife (Natalie) and others perished years before. In the complicated plot, Natalie plays a dual role, the title's Eva Ryker in flashbacks and then her heiress daughter. It was filmed aboard the *Queen Mary* in Long Beach, California.

Natalie satisfied a lifelong desire to visit Russia in 1979. With her husband and novelist Thomas Thompson, she spent two weeks in Leningrad where she filmed a documentary with Peter Ustinov for NBC-TV on the treasures of the Hermitage Museum. It was supposed to have been shown as part of the Olympic year, but the Soviet invasion of Afghanistan caused it to be shelved until April, 1981.

Director Gilbert Cates, who had directed "The Affair," teamed Natalie, George Segal, Valerie Harper and Dom DeLuise in Universal's *The Last Married Couple in America* (1980). A limp sex comedy about a happily married couple (Natalie and Segal) so upset by divorcing friends that they question their own relationship, it did nothing for Natalie.

Natalie and Robert Wagner had ridden in the Hollywood Christmas Parade with their children for a few years, and served as grand marshals for 1979's 48th annual parade. Natalie first participated in 1947, when the event was known as the Santa Claus Lane Parade. An enthusiastic art lover, Natalie owned works by such artists as Courbet, Dali, Matisse and Giocometti, as well as a collection of over five hundreds pieces of pre-Columbian sculpture. In 1965, having devoted considerable time to the theatre arts workshop at UCLA, she established an annual scholarship award there to provide recognition and financial support for theatre students. On November 5, 1980, her father Nicholas Gurdin, died following a long illness.

Natalie was announced to star with Rock Hudson and Kim Novak in Agatha Christie's *The Mirror Crack'd*, playing a faded movie queen. However, when the producers insisted she test for the role she dropped out and Elizabeth Taylor stepped in. Discussing Taylor's then weight problems and need for public adulation, Natalie once remarked to Lana Wood, "God, I hope I have enough sense not to be that pathetic."

On September 28, 1981, Natalie began work on what was to be her last film, MGM's *Brainstorm* (1983), in which she plays the wife of research scientist Christopher Walken. Following rumors that during the location filming in Raleigh, North Carolina, Natalie and Walken were having an affair, Wagner made two trips to the set before the company returned to the Culver City studio in California in late October. Just five days away from completion of her role in *Brainstorm*, Natalie's life came to a tragic, sudden end.

She loved the *Splendour*, a sixty-foot luxury yacht that she and Wagner bought soon after their second marriage, and they often made weekend crossings from Marina Del Rey to Catalina Island routinely in late spring and summer. During a Thanksgiving weekend cruise to Catalina on November 29, 1981, just past midnight, Natalie, dressed in her nightgown and a red parka jacket, appears to have gone up on deck of the *Splendour* to secure or board the rubber dinghy.

In his book *Coroner*, Dr. Thomas Noguchi, the ex-chief medical examiner of Los Angeles, said that Natalie probably fell overboard and drowned as she was trying to re-tie the dinghy so it wouldn't bang against the stern and disturb her sleep. "The wind was strong and would have pushed the dinghy away from the yacht," Noguchi wrote. "And it is quite possible that, instead of trying to step into the dinghy, she might have been reaching for it and lost her balance." When she fell into the cold dark water, her cries for help were not heard by Wagner, reportedly down below in an argument with Christopher Walken, their only guest that weekend. Allegedly, some small quantities of drugs (Quaaludes) had been used aboard earlier that evening.

Although there were wind and heavy rain that Thanksgiving weekend, Wagner was not immediately concerned that Natalie was missing, along with the dinghy known as *Prince Valiant* (the title of the film Wagner considered his worst). Natalie had often taken the motorized dinghy out alone. But later, Wagner became worried. At 1:30 a.m., Wagner called Doug's Harbor Reed and Saloon, where they had dined and quarreled that night, consuming much champagne and wine.

"There was real tension in the air that weekend," *Splendour* skipper Dennis Davern would state later. "Natalie was being very flirtatious with Christopher Walken and R.J. was getting annoyed." Patrons dining near them that last evening overheard Wagner say, "Let's do this in the privacy of our boat, not here in front of strangers." The argument raged on once they returned to the *Splendour*, when, claimed Davern, Wagner screamed at Walken, "What are you trying to do? Seduce my wife?" A distraught and angry Natalie, not knowing where to turn, ran to the master bedroom, exclaiming, recalls Davern, "R.J., I won't stand for this!" According to all testimony, that was the last time anyone saw Natalie Wood alive.

The search for Natalie intensified. It ended at 7:45 a.m. when a search helicopter finally spotted Natalie's body floating in Isthmus Cover, a mile and a half from the *Splendour*. The dinghy was two hundred yards from the body. The harbor patrol reported that "Natalie's hands were scratched, as if she had tried to climb up some rocks to save her life and then had slid back down." When Wagner was notified, he embraced Davern and sobbed, "She's gone, she's gone. Why did this have to happen?" Natalie's weak left wrist, caused by a childhood filming accident and known only to her closest friends and family, could have been one of the reasons why she was unable to hang on to anything and save herself, though this has never before been mentioned in any reporting of the tragedy.

Natalie's seventy-four-year-old mother, Maria Gurdin, was actually the first to receive the heartbreaking news. She answered the phone in the home she was sharing with daughter Lana and granddaughter Evan. It was a childhood friend of Lana's calling. "Did you hear?" asked Sheri Herman. "Natalie's body has been washed up on the beach." "Mother fell where she was standing," Lana said later, "passed out cold, her blood pressure over two hundred and twenty." Lana confirmed the many reports that her sister had had a terrible fear of water. Robert Wagner, "absolutely devastated" with grief, was unable to identify the body. Dennis Davern did the grim task.

Robert Wagner gathered with family and close friends at the Westwood Memorial Park for their sad farewell to Natalie on December 3, 1981.

Eulogies were delivered by friends Hope Lange, Tommy Thompson and Roddy McDowall. Lange said, "She was part imp . . . full of mischief, capable of going from a depressed state to extremely high spirits. Natalie, you put us to a very severe test today. It's difficult to feel joy and laughter when you're not here to share it." And McDowall said, "It is a joy to think that one individual can accomplish so much beauty in so few decades. She found a way to put life in her heart and to put heart into her life." Because they were not in season, it was necessary to obtain white gardenias, Natalie's favorite flower, from florists in eight states so that her casket could be covered with four hundred and fifty of them.

Natalie was preparing to make her stage debut that next February in *Anastasia*, with Wendy Hiller and Perry King, at Los Angeles' Ahmanson Theater. Her friend Tommy Thompson then planned to write a screen version of the drama for her. The star chosen for dedication on the Hollywood Boulevard "Walk of Fame" in celebration of Hollywood's 100th birthday honored Natalie Wood. Robert Wagner dedicated Natalie's star (the 1,842nd) on February 1, 1987.

Not long after Natalie's death, Lana Wood, who had had her differences with her sister, remarked, "Nothing bad ever happened to Natalie. I always thought she was born under a lucky star." There were no stars shining the night Natalie Wood died.

SUZAN BALL

One of the saddest stories in Hollywood concerns the courageous beauty Suzan Ball. Even at a very early age, she could turn heads. An ethereal creature with an abundance of talent and supreme courage, she fell victim to a crippling disease that cut short what was becoming an illustrious career. In the best tradition of Movieland fairy tales, the studio publicity mills called her "The New Cinderella Girl of 1952." "I've always felt I was a driven girl," Suzan once said. "Driven mostly by myself." Suzan's career was in high gear. The story of glitzy Hollywood has had its share of Cinderellas, but time was running out for this young actress. Unbeknownst to anyone, Suzan Ball had only three more years to live. Suzan's fade into premature obscurity took away her moment of prominence and the glass slipper turned into just another Movieland statistic. The dreams, the happiness, the fairy tale were soon all wiped out.

On February 3, 1933, a baby girl was born to Howard Dale and Molly Ball of Buffalo, New York. They were of French, English and Irish descent. The parents called their first child Susan; four years later brother Howard Jr. was born. Suzan's studio biography listed her mother's occupation as an aerodynamics engineer.

Susan, a second cousin of Lucille Ball, was born in Jamestown, New York, a farming and manufacturing community some sixty miles south of Buffalo. Susan's ancestry dated back to the *Mayflower*. She was a direct descendant of both John Alden and the first governor of Massachusetts. In 1938, when Susan was five, Mr. Ball moved the family briefly to Miami, Florida. They later moved back to Buffalo, and lived at 43 Warren Avenue, while she attended Washington and Kenmore Junior High Schools.

As Suzan described in a *Modern Screen Magazine* interview, "I had already reached my present height of 5'7" and I was so self-conscious I was getting round-shouldered. Mother enrolled me in a modeling school, not for a career, but to teach me to walk and carry myself gracefully. After a while, I became proud of my height instead of feeling handicapped." The family next migrated to California in 1947, settling in North Hollywood, around the corner from Universal Studios. Susan enrolled at North Hollywood High School as a music major. She became president of the school's choral group and vice-president of the girl's club. Susan appeared in several school operettas, while harboring ambitions to be a professional singer. "My happiest memories are of growing up in North Hollywood while attending North Hollywood High," she once said.

When Susan was just fifteen, she saw actor Richard Arlen's "Hollywood Opportunity" show on a local television station. Viewers were invited to telephone in for an audition. It wasn't long before she got a chance to sing on the show. Susan didn't win first prize, but band leader Mel Baker was watching and offered her a job as the band's vocalist. For the next three years, Susan sang with Mel Baker's Orchestra in and around the Los Angeles area, at various college dances, local aircraft plant functions and occasional appearances at the popular Florentine Gardens nightspot.

In 1951, Susan's mother, suffering from asthma, was forced to move to Santa Maria for her health. Meanwhile, her father purchased the Valley Airline Travel Agency in the then sleepy California community of Santa Maria. As Suzan would later recount the move, "I begged my parents to allow me to stay in Hollywood and graduate with my class in June. Actually, my big idea was to get on with a movie career, something I dreamed of all my life."

With the small sum Susan earned with the Mel Baker Orchestra and a $15-a-week allowance from her family, she went to live at the House of the Seven Garbos, the home of movie pioneer Jesse Lasky high in the hills on La Brea Avenue. At one time, the boarding house (first located in the old Wallace Reid mansion at Sweetzer and DeLongpre) sheltered such aspiring actors as Ruth Roman, Linda Christian, Leonard Nimoy, Hugh O'Brian, William Phipps and writer Doris Lilly. The large comfortable home, which was always home for future screen performers, was then owned by actress Karen X. Gaylord and her husband, actor-writer Don McGuire. It was operated by Mrs. Marie Cote, who served as a surrogate mother to the young hopefuls, and contained a large garden, tennis court and an Olympic-size swimming pool.

To celebrate her new independence, Susan signed with agent Ynez Seabury, a onetime Cecil B. DeMille contract player. Seabury secured her a job at Monogram as one of several harem girls in *Aladdin and His Lamp* (1952). Susan decided to change the spelling of her name to the more unusual Suzan Ball. There were several rather cloudy and contradictory stories about how Suzan came to the attention of Universal-International Studios. The most popular was that her mother had invited several servicemen to Sunday dinner from nearby Camp Cooke Army Base while Suzan was spending the weekend at her parents Santa Maria home. The GIs took a few snapshots and the photos found their way to Universal. In another publicized story, Suzan won first prize at a Santa Maria charity bazaar for baking a chocolate layer cake and a Universal-International scout spied her photograph in a local newspaper.

Despite many claims to the contrary, it was actress Mary Castle who arranged an interview with the head of Universal-International's talent department, Robert Raines. Mary had switched to Universal from Columbia Pictures where she was heralded as the Rita Hayworth look-alike. "I had once lived at the Seven Garbos," she recalled, "and went over quite often to visit with my friend, Marie Cote, the house mater. That's where I first met Suzan, who had only been there a short time. I believe she had done a minor picture in Tahiti [unable to confirm]. She was so beautiful, with a sense of innocence about her. I thought this girl is going to be a big star. I took her out to Universal, to meet with Bob Raines, the studio's top talent executive. He was totally overwhelmed with her. Suzan was one of those bright, shining people."

Robert Raines had Suzan read for Sophie Rosenstein, who was in charge of young talent and screen tests. Rosenstein, the wife of actor Gig Young, had Suzan placed under the studio's test-option arrangement for a period of four months. Sophie Rosenstein was Frances Farmer's first drama instructor at the

University of Washington and was respected as a gifted acting coach.

Suzan's screen test, in which she performed scenes from *Crossfire* and *The Postman Always Rings Twice*, impressed executive Robert Raines, and she signed a standard term contract on October 24, 1951.

Her Universal-International career was launched with a bit in *The World in His Arms* (1952), in which Gregory Peck and Ann Blyth co-starred. In November, Suzan appeared as the "Lux Girl" on the "Lux Radio Theatre's" broadcast of *Winchester 73*. She joined the press junket of Universal stars going to Portland, Oregon, for the world premiere of *Bend of the River*. During this juncture, Suzan was taking evening courses at the Art Center Institute.

Suzan received "introducing" billing in *Untamed Frontier* (1952), as the blackmailing mistress of Scott Brady. She was in the solid company of Joseph Cotten and Shelley Winters. *The Hollywood Reporter*, for one, praised her performance: "The production is an eye pleaser, beautifully photographed in very attractive Technicolor and serving to introduce newcomer Suzan Ball, a looker as well as a competent actress. Miss Ball is most persuasive as a female menace." But *Daily Variety* wasn't so sure: "Picture serves to introduce Suzan Ball, but the dance hall girl role is hardly an auspicious debut." The story line was reminiscent of *Duel in the Sun*, revolving around the efforts of an old cattle baron to keep his empire intact. It was long and rambling. When asked to explain her sudden rise to stardom, Suzan said, "It's because I played a bad girl in *Untamed Frontier*! I could have gone on for years and I never would have been noticed. I had the role of a mistress with a fiery temper. When a gal like that enters the room, she takes command of the scene."

Meanwhile, Suzan and Scott Brady had a fleeting romance. They met when Brady helped prepare her screen test. Columnists were convinced that they planned to marry. Shelley Winters, already noted for being temperamental on the set, was especially kind to the newcomer. "She tried to help me all she could on the picture (*Untamed Frontier*)," Suzan would reveal later. "We even went double-dating to nighclubs, and Shelley would try to get the photographers to take my picture too. I think she's wonderful and a great pal."

Suzan was an instant hit in *Untamed Frontier* and was next rushed into *Yankee Buccaneer* (1952), as a Spanish countess, achieving star billing with Jeff Chandler and Scott Brady. The swashbuckling epic film dealt with the trio being involved in Brazil's struggle for independence from Portugal. "I loved working with Jeff Chandler," Suzan told Hedda Hopper, and Chandler felt similarly and expressed a desire to work with her again. "Suzan Ball, with little to do but look beautiful, does that most successfully, aided by Bill Thomas's period costumes which are truly gorgeous, if somewhat incongruous aboard a fighting vessel," said *Variety*.

Universal-International sent Suzan to Texas and her hometown of Buffalo, New York, for the grand opening of her first starring role, *Untamed Frontier*. Kenmore Junior High remembered their famous alumna with a special assembly. During the personal appearance tour, she was stricken with acute appendicitis while en route to the Buffalo Statler, following an interview on the Bob Wells' 970 radio show. Suzan was rushed to the Millard Fillmore Hospital for an emergency appendectomy.

Upon Suzan's return to Hollywood and encouraged by her new popularity, she changed agents and signed with the William Morris Agency. She was slated for the top feminine lead in *Horizons West*, opposite Robert Ryan and Rock Hudson, but was cancelled out and the role went to Julie Adams. Instead, director Budd Boetticher, who had wanted her originally for *Horizons West*, cast Suzan in *City Beneath the Sea* (1953), which was essentially a vehicle for its male stars, Robert Ryan and Anthony Quinn. The overladen drama bordered on science fiction with Ryan and Quinn as divers seeking stolen treasures and finding a submerged city. Suzan did get a chance to sing "Handle With Care," as Venita, a waterfront cafe singer. The story was taken from the Harry F. Reisberg novel, *Port Royal, The Ghost City Beneath the Sea*. "About as banal and uninspired as they come," is the way *The New York Times* described it.

Suzan fell deeply in love with Anthony Quinn during the filming of *City Beneath the Sea*. He was a man of considerable charm and fascination. From their first meeting, she chased him relentlessly. The romance would endure about a year. The couple made no secret of their affection for one another, while

U-I feared this storm of adverse publicity might harm Suzan's budding career, since Quinn was still very much married to Katherine DeMille and notorious for his extramarital wanderings. "Tony was very passionate and very possessive," she told a close friend. "We would argue about almost anything." Suzan bore a striking resemblance to the exotic Katherine DeMille of the 1930s. Many actresses found Quinn magnetic; many admitted they were "momentarily" in love with him, including Ingrid Bergman, Shelley Winters, Ruth Warrick and Inger Stevens.

The editors of *Modern Screen* magazine named Suzan among fifteen promising winners of the first annual Golden Key Awards. Some of the other winners were Anne Bancroft, Penny Edwards and Virginia Gibson. And columnist Hedda Hopper picked Suzan as one of the most important "New Stars of 1953."

In 1953, Mara Corday was a young Universal-International contract player. Like Suzan, Mara had the same brunette coloring and exotic look. She would play a principal part in Suzan Ball's short life. "I was Suzie's understudy in *The Big Knife*, one of the plays Universal put on for producers and casting directors," Mara Corday said. "At first, I didn't think she liked me. Barbara Rush and Russell Johnson were also in the cast. Two days before the show was to be presented, for some unknown reason, Suzan was unable to perform. Our coach, Estelle Harmon, said I was to play the part. After watching Suzie rehearse for so many weeks, I told her, I am such a mimic, I was probably going to imitate her completely. That broke the ice and after that we became very close friends."

Mara disclosed that Suzan appeared to be accident prone. On Suzan's next assignment, *East of Sumatra* (1953), the first signs of her doomed illness began to manifest itself. "It was during *East of Sumatra*, that Suzie had the first injury to her right leg," pointed out Mara. "She was rehearsing this sensuous dance number and had dancer Julie Newmeyer (Julie Newmar) set to photo-double her in the more strenuous steps. Anthony Quinn was on the set and I think Suzie wanted to show off a bit and prove to him that she could do this number herself, without the help of Julie. But it was a little more intricate than she thought, because when you do a knee drop, you don't go forward—you have to give to the side and then fall or you can crack your bones," remembered Mara. "She didn't know that and put all her weight on her right knee and hit the knee on the cement floor." Suzan told columnist Louella Parsons in a *Los Angeles Examiner* interview, "I'm not really a dancer and I had worked very hard on this dance sequence. I was finally doing my dance before the cameras when I slipped and banged my right knee hard on the cement floor. It hurt like the blazes. Annoyed at my clumsiness, I picked myself up and started again. After the studio doctor treated my leg, I went right back to work. The knee was sore for a few days but I forgot about it."

The second of Suzan's Budd Boetticher-directed films, *East of Sumatra* was a brawling adventure saga. As Anthony Quinn's alluring voluptuous fiancée who goes on the make for mining engineer Jeff Chandler, she gave a splendid performance. In this film, Suzan displayed a strangely sympathetic side to her acting. Universal-International sent Suzan back East for a series of personal appearances. While she was driving up to the Berkshire Mountains with studio publicist Gail Gilford, their car was sideswiped by another vehicle. Nobody was hurt and their auto was damaged only slightly. However, when they received the jolt, the upper part of Suzan's knee struck the window crank handle of the car. She didn't think much of it at the time.

When Suzan returned to Hollywood, she decided to break off the affair with Anthony Quinn and to rent an apartment in Toluca Lake with her menagerie of pets, which included a Siamese cat named Chata, a toy poodle called Cezanne, and a spider monkey. Rebounding from her broken romance with Quinn, she met Richard Long. He was tall, had dark hair and handsome features.

The initial meeting between Suzan and Richard Long occurred in the U-I studio commissary. He had seen her in *Untamed Frontier*, while stationed overseas and was anxious to meet her. Long's dashing, debonair personality and delightful sense of humor instantly captivated the actress. They clicked right from the start and gradually Richard began to assume the place Anthony Quinn had initially occupied. The two became inseparable. They began attending baseball games, acting classes and parties. It wasn't too long afterward that Richard moved into her three-room apartment near the Universal Studios at 1025 Moorpark Avenue.

Suzan was next seen in *War Arrow* (1953), another Technicolor vehicle for Maureen O'Hara and Jeff Chandler. The new romantic duo had previously starred in *Flame of Araby*. Suzan was the tempestuous daughter of a Seminole chief with eyes for Major Chandler. During the filming, she was told by her doctor that she had developed tumors on her leg. By the time the adequate Western was completed, she was walking on crutches much of the time, because of the throbbing pain. Throughout the ensuing months, Suzan was determined that the condition wasn't that serious; she continued her studies with studio coaches, posed for publicity photos and gave intimate dinner parties at the apartment on Moorpark Avenue. "I didn't understand what was happening to me," she would say later.

Mara Corday would often come by with "Mickie the mailroom girl," a studio messenger whom Suzan befriended and had now attached herself to Mara. Ann McCrea, who had been one of the "Seven Garbos" and had become Suzan's stand-in, was often there. Frequently, Richard Long would be away on location. "Suzie would hop around on one leg and serve dinner, never spilling anything. Which, if you've ever tried to do it, is almost impossible," Mara said. She would remember yet another unpublicized car accident that Suzan was involved in, while driving on the Hollywood Freeway with Long. The new black Cadillac convertible was a gift from Universal Vice President Matty Fox.

Suzan switched doctors and began a new course of treatments. By now, she couldn't walk without the crutches. Doctors told her the malignancy appeared to be arrested. Long was scheduled to leave for Banff, Canada, to film *Saskatchewan* with Alan Ladd and Shelley Winters. Two days later, despite the ever present crutches, an anxious Suzan flew off to Banff. They had a marvelous week together. "I've rarely seen two people who loved each other that much," said Shelley Winters.

Shortly afterward, a weary Suzan boarded a flight to Mexico for further treatment at a health farm. Long completed the Alan Ladd Western and embarked on a nationwide personal appearance tour for U-I. Suzan had been told by at least two doctors

that her leg eventually would have to be amputated. But she
was pinning her hopes on some new treatments, and Long
supported her. Boldly, they went ahead and made arrangements to marry.

While preparing lunch in her apartment kitchen, Suzan
slipped on some water that her poodle, Cezanne, had spilled
on the floor from his drinking dish. The leg was now broken.
She was immediately hospitalized and remained in traction for
two weeks. Surgeons removed the tumor area and replaced it
with a bone graft from her hip. At first the operation was diagnosed a success and declared cancer-free. She was convinced
she'd licked the dread disease. But further tests revealed that a
malignancy was still present and amputation of the leg would
be necessary. Secretly, Suzan underwent agonizing months of
chemotherapy. In early December, 1953, Suzan and Long had
become engaged. Their December 12th wedding plans in Las
Vegas were postponed when Suzan was told of the pending
operation.

Some sources around Hollywood hinted that Suzan was a
victim of cancer. The late Mike Connolly, a columnist for *The
Hollywood Reporter*, telephoned Long to inquire if the rumor
were true. Long rebuffed the story and begged him not to say
anything, because it would break Suzan's heart if it appeared in
print. Mike Connolly was known to be very treacherous when
he wanted to be. Connolly printed the story and Suzan read
the item. The next day, Richard encountered Connolly shoved
him up against a wall, took him by the throat and slugged him,
knocking Connolly out cold.

After her share of tears, Suzan entered Orchard Grove Sanitarium to prepare for the surgery. Universal assigned a private
nurse, Kay Biddle, to personally attend her. The Cinderella
Girl's life of only two short years before had turned into a hideous nightmare. On January 11, 1954, on the night before the
operation, Richard Long, Hugh O'Brian and her father sat at
her bedside at Temple Hospital. Suzan whispered to Long that
she wouldn't expect him to marry her after the surgery. Long
just brushed aside her protests. "I love her, not her legs," Long
told friends. "And I couldn't get over her lack of self pity. She
always found fun and laughter in whatever turned up."
Suzan's unfortunate illness was the subject of numerous news-

papers and fan magazine articles commenting on her bravery. "I felt awful when I heard the news that I would have to have an amputation," Suzan said following the operation. "They told me that a year ago and it appeared I was getting well. But I pulled out of it. When something like this happens, you find the courage somehow. After the surgery, I was sure my days as an actress were over. I was determined to find other things to do."

On April 11, 1954, on Palm Sunday, Suzan walked down the aisle of the El Montecito Presbyterian Church in Santa Barbara. She was radiantly beautiful in a wedding gown, designed by the studio's Bill Thomas, to become Mrs. Richard Long. She wore her new artificial limb. "I'm going to use my new leg," she told her father. "I always said I would walk down the aisle at my own wedding and that's just what I'm going to do." U-I's top echelon turned out, including such Hollywood immigrants as Rock Hudson, Lori Nelson, Jeff Chandler, Barbara Rush, Tony Curtis and Janet Leigh, David Janssen, Julie Adams, Mary Castle, Hugh O'Brian, Mala Powers and more than 100 other guests. They all crowded into the tiny Spanish-style chapel for the ceremony and then proceeded to the Biltmore Hotel's Loggia Room for the reception. Suzan's nurse, Kay Biddle, was the matron of honor and Robert Long, the bridegroom's brother and his brother-in-law Marshall Thompson, were the ushers.

The newlyweds appeared together for the only time in CBS-TV's live "Lux Video Theatre" presentation of the tele-feature, "I'll Never Love Again." Suzan was an accident victim, confined to a wheelchair, who with Long's encouragement, walks at the end. Her work as the tragic heroine was "beautifully sustained," said *The Los Angeles Times*.

George Sherman who had directed Suzan in *War Arrow*, asked for her again to star opposite Victor Mature in *Chief Crazy Horse* (1955), to be filmed on authentic locations in the rugged Black Hills of South Dakota. When U-I executives attempted to replace her with Susan Cabot, director Sherman insisted on casting Suzan. "She doesn't act with her legs, she acts with her face, with her mind, with her spirit."

"Dick and I picked up the leg, tossed it in back of the car, and set off for the airport. I figured I'd have to get my gait training

on and off the set. The important thing was to be working,"
said Suzan. Even though the role was difficult, with tempera-
tures well over one hundred degrees, her energy level was
boundless. Suzan maintained a cheerful attitude on the set,
kidding with all the technicians and leading man Victor Mature. Suzan's high spirits promoted Long to say, "She has a
new thing in her face now and it comes through to everybody
who knows her. It's a different quality of depth and compassion. She's the same carefree, independent, even reckless kid
but she's concerned about others now." A double was used for
scenes that required walking and in close-ups, Suzan managed
to move her shoulders to suggest she was in motion normally.
To conceal her noticeable limp, cameraman Harold Lipstein,
skillfully covered her movements. During the production,
Suzan began to lose weight rapidly and was fifteen pounds
lighter by the time *Chief Crazy Horse* was completed. She managed to deliver a moving portrayal as Black Shawl, the wife of
the legendary Indian Crazy Horse. Suzan had thrown herself
wholeheartedly into the part and had her share of very touching scenes. It was almost as if she had a premonition this was to
be her last motion picture.

Observed *The Hollywood Reporter*: "Of side interest, and also
with sympathetic angle, is the fact *Chief Crazy Horse* gives
Suzan Ball her first camera outing since her leg amputation.
The doubling-in scenes requiring movement are very good,
and elsewhere she acquits herself well in handling the role of
the bride of Victor Mature, seen in the title role as the Indian
who lives out a tribal prophecy."

The offers for public appearances continued to pour in. The
public wanted to see the brave beautiful actress and her handsome husband. It gave Suzan an incredible ability to want to
bounce back and survive temporarily. They embarked on a
nightclub tour, playing Phoenix and Palm Springs. "I couldn't
believe how beautiful and composed Suzan looked on stage.
You'd never know how much discomfort she was in," said
Mara Corday.

There were several major television guest shots on variety
shows, including the Ed Sullivan and Horace Heidt Shows.
"I'm not really possessed with driving ambition," Suzan told
writer Doug McClelland in New York. "My marriage is all im-

portant to me. When Dick and I have had, say, three children I
may retire to wherever we're living in California and rest on
what I hope will be laurels. Right now I enjoy performing, and
our night club act has augmented my interest in it. Working is
good therapy for me. Perhaps, too, my small accomplishments
will serve as an incentive to other handicapped persons, as well
as the not-so-handicapped, to face life unafraid."

Suzan had no illusions about what first brought most audiences to their nightclub act. "Many, I know, came to get a look
at the movie star who lost a leg," Suzan told Doug McClelland,
"But, in all modesty, I think they went away entertained. The
critics have been kind and now I feel that if we fill a club it's on
our act's merits." From the start, Suzan was a hit with the press
and fans. Hollywood photographer Frank Edwards was a teenage fan of Suzan's during that last visit to New York. "She
never once hesitated to stop to give her fans an autograph
wherever she and Dick Long went," Edwards remembers.
"That's the kind of girl she was."

Suzan and Long's nuptial bliss wasn't to last. When they
were rehearsing a "Climax" television drama, she was rushed
to the City of Hope Hospital in a state of collapse. She was seriously ill. It was then that doctors made the grim discovery that
the cancer cells had now spread to her lungs. Richard Long and
nurse Kay Biddle watched over her around the clock. The doctors told Long that Suzan had only a few more weeks to live.
Her condition was kept a secret from the press and the doctors
gave special orders that she was not to know the truth.

Suzan's mother was visiting the hospital one day and asked
Suzan if she could have certain household possessions for
various members of the immediate family. The incident an-
gered Long so he immediately ushered her out of the room and
asked that she never return again! Suzan suddenly burst into
tears, realizing for the first time that she must be dying.

As Suzan's condition worsened and the pain grew more ex-
cruciating, her personality would undergo dramatic changes.
The pain had transformed the sweet girl into another person,
often to her own bewilderment. Reportedly, because of the
pressure put upon Richard Long, which, in conjunction with
the strain he must have been undergoing in trying to keep up
the pretense that she was going to pull through the deadly ill-

ness, he slid into an affair with Suzan's nurse Kay Biddle. The relationship became something of a bond among the three but ended with Suzan's death.

Mara Corday remembers what a traumatic time it was for everyone who loved Suzan. "I could never get over Suzie's total lack of self pity. She was a warm and affectionate girl—that was until the heavy doses of morphine to alleviate the extreme pain turned her into a female Jekyll and Hyde. She was in so much pain. The most important thing was keeping Suzan comfortable. So whenever she asked for a pain shot, she got it. Those last weeks of her life were horrible," recalls an emotional Mara.

Universal-International stood by Suzan, personally assuming all medical expenses, although legally they weren't liable. Fans from all over the world sent flowers and wrote their good wishes for recovery. On the night of August 5, 1955, Suzan lay in her hospital bed in a semi-conscious state. With Long at her side, she opened her eyes and in a glazed stare looked at him and in a weakened voice murmured "Tony." She had come to the end, quietly slipping away.

Richard Long suffered a tremendous emotional blow because of Suzan's final word in reference to Anthony Quinn. This unfortunate incident was to haunt him for many years. But, being a romantic soul, the happy times of their short life together prevailed. "I will always love her," he tearfully declared. "My love remains eternal."

Suzan Ball was finally free of the years of pain. She was only 22. Her death set off a tidal wave of emotion. The grief of her Universal co-workers and friends was genuine and obvious as they bid their last farewell atop a hill at the Forest Lawn Cemetery. Active pallbearers and ushers at the ceremony included John Agar, Hugh O'Brian and writer Danny Arnold.

Two years later in 1957, Richard Long broke out of his shell by marrying Mara Corday. They had three children. In the will of Suzan Ball, the amount of $10,000 was bequested to her younger brother, Howard, stipulating that the money be used for a college education. But Howard had disappeared and an intensive search to locate him proved futile. Nearly twenty years later, at the funeral services of Richard Long, his wife Mara and her business manager were approached by Suzan's father, Dale Ball. He had some important information regarding his son, Howard. He had been found and now wanted to collect his $10,000 inheritance Suzan left him. An astounded Mara, in total disbelief of the insensitive timing of what she had just heard, could do nothing but turn and walk away.

Perhaps the words Suzan Ball said a few weeks before she died best sum up the gallant grit of the tragic young actress: "I felt no pity for myself, nor have I any feeling of regret. Sometimes I pondered, 'Why has this thing happened to me?' But it was never in terms of a complaint, I sought a real answer. It is not an easy one to find, and perhaps I will never know."

Jean Seberg

Jean Seberg at
the start of her
career, as *Saint
Joan* (1957)

Jean Seberg
at a Paris opening
(1979)

Susan Peters

Susan Peters with Richard Quine and adopted son

Marie McDonald

Marie McDonald
showing signs of
beating she had
received from
husband Harry
Karl

Gia Scala

Gia Scala and Don Burnett at their wedding reception (1959)

Jayne Mansfield

Jayne Mansfield
and husband
Mickey Hargitay

Marilyn Monroe

Norma Jeane
Baker and James
Dougherty

Thelma Todd

Thelma Todd,
slumped over the
wheel of her
roadster

Pina Pellicer

Dominique Dunne
with Vito Scotti

Maggie McNamara

Peggie Castle

Bella Darvi

Pier Angeli

Dorothy Stratten

JEAN SEBERG

It all started like a fairytale. A lot of aspiring young actresses had as many stars in their eyes as free-spirited Jean Seberg did when she was plucked, reportedly from 18,000 aspirants, to play the title role in Otto Preminger's screen version of *Saint Joan*. The script followed the tested Hollywood plot—unknown girl from the heart of the corn belt ushered into stardom! Jean was canonized as Iowa's answer to both Grace Kelly and Ingrid Bergman. The formula only works on the screen where truth can be altered by fantasy. The overnight successes were part of the myth that Hollywood kept alive when people still flocked to the movies. In real life, stardom is not achieved without high risks to the ascending star. For Jean, the costs beneath the phony tinsel were multiplied. Her career always seemed like a seesaw, charted by critical acclaim and critical disdain. Somehow, the tragedy of Jean Seberg seems the more poignant because the story line began in Marshalltown, Iowa, and ended what must have become a tortured life in the most romantic city in the world, Paris.

The archetypal All-American girl from Marshalltown was born Jean Dorothy Seberg on November 13, 1938, a Friday the 13th, to Edward and Dorothy Benson Seberg, Jr. She was of Swedish extraction and had an older sister, Mary Ann, and two brothers, Kurt and David. Her father was a pharmacist; her mother, a primary schoolteacher.

Back in the fourth grade at Rogers Elementary School, Jean won a prize for writing a playlet entitled, "Be Kind to Animals." She told Gordon Gow in a 1975 *Films and Filming* magazine interview: "I became aware of acting 'per se' at the age of 12, when I saw Stanley Kramer's film *The Men*, which was Marlon Brando's first film. I was completely overwhelmed by the power of Brando in that. Next day I went to the public library in Marshalltown, and told them I wanted to be an actress; and there were a couple of books they could recommend, both by Stanislavsky, *An Actor Prepares* and *My Life in Art*. Well, I took them home, and couldn't make head nor tail of them. But from there on in school, I began getting involved in all the plays I could, and all the declamatory contests. There had been an earlier period, when I was seven or eight, when I went to Betty Grable movies and took tap-dancing lessons. But I was fascinated by her in a totally different way. Acting as the conveying of emotions—that was Brando, and I guess it still is, and will always be Brando for me."

In late December, 1955, Jean was named chairman of the Iowa March of Dimes campaign. In her senior year at Marshalltown High, Jean was elected lieutenant governor of Iowa Girls State and taught Sunday School. Jean's mother had wanted her to be a writer and her father had wanted her to be a doctor. In 1956, she agreed to spend one term at the University of Iowa, mostly to satisfy her parents. But Jean dreamed only of one thing—acting. She sometimes looked after neighbors Dolores and Forrest Supinger's three little daughters, Andrea, Mary Beth and Emily. One of the daughters, Mary Beth, became the actress Mary Beth Hurt. Also a graduate of Marshalltown High School, Hurt has refused to discuss her former baby sitter in all interviews.

In the same *Films and Filming* interview, Jean remembered her discovery for Shaw's Joan of Arc: "At the end of my high school studies, when I was seventeen, I received a scholarship. Every year our school gave one for about 500 dollars to the person they considered their most promising actor or actress. As a result I played summer stock in Massachusetts and New Jersey (the Priscilla Beach Theatre in Plymouth, Massachusetts, and the Cape May Playhouse in New Jersey). I owe a great deal to a woman in my home town. Her name is Carol Dodd Hollingsworth. She was herself a frustrated actress, and also a wonderful dramatic teacher. It was she and our local millionaire, a man named J. William Fisher, who wrote a letter to Otto Preminger saying that they thought he ought to see me if he was really looking for a new St. Joan. A letter came back, asking me to prepare a certain speech and come to Chicago to read for Mr. Preminger. Previously, I had won prizes doing Anouilh's version of Joan, *The Lark*. But, of course, that is nothing like Bernard Shaw. At the time I was due to audition for Preminger, I was enrolled to study dramatic art at the State University of Iowa, my eventual goal being stardom on Broadway, hopefully. So it was a toss-up in the family as to what I should do. My father is a druggist (Seberg's Pharmacy), my mother a schoolteacher; they're quite separate from the whole world of acting. But they said that if I wanted to try for St. Joan, they'd drive me to Chicago. So I took my suitcases into the University and met my roommate and then left immediately for Chicago—where there were several hundred girls waiting to see Preminger. He went all over the world for that auditioning. And after I read for him, he talked very seriously to my parents and said he wanted to do a screen test of me in New York, as well as testing two other girls. They agreed, although they were reluctant that I should give up my education."

Jean's first drama teacher, Mrs. Hollingworth, now lives in Gilman, about ten miles from Marshalltown, and she is more than 80 years old. "Jean was a lovely, talented girl," Hollingsworth says now of her former pupil. "I wasn't the only one who recognized her talent. You see, Jean wanted this career from childhood. But it's all turned out so sad."

"I remember at Marshalltown High School, Jean starred in *Our Town* as the smalltown girl who senses the joy of life only after her death. She also did *The Happy Journey to Trenton and Camden*," says a friend from high school. "And in *Sabrina Fair*, she played this middle-class girl who heads off to Paris. Now that I think about it, that's all pretty spooky." Jean joined the Des Moines chapter of the National Association for the Advancement of Colored People. "Jean," her father said, "Folks will say you're a communist." She angrily replied, "Papa, I don't care what people say." Toward the end of her life, Jean would recall, "Marshalltown had no real problem with blacks. They lived apart—the poorest, the most underprivileged down by the railroad tracks. They had their own churches, their own social life. The whites ignored them. Only when the racial tensions began to mount did I become involved."

Director Otto Preminger's memories of the Seberg discovery are only slightly different: "United Artists had rented a ballroom at the Sherman Hotel in Chicago for about three hundred contenders from the Midwest. One of them was the daughter of a druggist from Marshalltown, Iowa. Her name was Jean Seberg. She was seventeen years old and had no professional experience whatever. She read for me and I was impressed. I asked her to come with her parents to my hotel and we made a contract. A number of other young women seemed very talented, but she appeared to have the strength and simplicity that I wanted." He was taken with Jean's special aura of youthful innocence and spontaneous acting ability. Preminger decided on Jean for his production of the Maid of Orleans. It was announced to the nation on the Ed Sullivan show that Jean had won the starring role in *St. Joan.*

Graham Greene wrote the screenplay from Bernard Shaw's "Saint Joan," the very successful 1923 play. Preminger's *St. Joan* (1957) was filmed during a gruelling winter in London. It also starred Sir John Gielgud, Richard Windmark, Richard Todd and Anton Walbrook.

Drama critic David Richards who wrote *Played Out, The Jean Seberg Story,* told an interviewer: "If the film was a success, it would be a double success for him (Preminger) because he not only would have directed the film, but he would have made the star. And he promptly set out to do that—to shape Jean Seberg in exactly the image he wanted. He did so ruthlessly and brutally, frequently belittling her efforts, making fun of her and submitting her to his huge tantrums." The movie was panned brutally with most of the blame put on the inexperienced actress. It was a disastrous film debut and a severe disappointment to everyone.

Variety acknowledged: "Jean Seberg is helped most by her appealing looks. She has a fresh, unspoiled quality and she photographs well. But the fact remains that her Joan has no dimensions and her delivery of the lines after a while becomes monotonous. Shaw's Joan is more than just an innocent country maiden. Her faith can move mountains and the flame within her kindles the faith in other men. There is no flame in Miss Seberg, just stubbornness and the almost casually-voiced belief in God and her 'voices.' When she speaks of her yen for soldiering and battle, it is hard to believe she means it. And throughout the film she never matures."

Preminger subsequently cast Jean in the movie adaptation of Francoise Sagan's first novel, *Bonjour Tristesse* (1958), with an equally lusterless outcome, in which she was the daughter of a wealthy Parisian playboy, David Niven, and resents his romance with an attractive widow, Deborah Kerr. It was filmed lushly on the French Riviera. *The New York Times* suggested sending her back to "That Iowa High School whence she came," and the New York *Herald Tribune* found Jean "About as far from a French nymph as milk is from pernod." The high-gloss Technicolor photography of the Cote d'Azur scenery helped the handsomely mounted production.

Referring to her relationship with Preminger, Jean said years later, "He's the world's most charming dinner guest and most sadistic director. Preminger was attacked for his presumption for trying to make an actress out of a country bumpkin like myself, and I was told to get back to the farm. It was amazing, the cruelty of some of the reviews." On September 5, 1958, Jean, 19, and Francois Moreuil, 24, were married at the Trinity Lutheran Church in Marshalltown, where she once taught Sunday School. She met the wealthy Moreuil while waterskiing in St. Tropez during the *Bonjour Tristesse* location. He was an attorney, Harvard-educated, suave and a distant relative of the late director William Wyler. The nuptial was doomed from the start.

Jean's childhood friends at the wedding noted she had acquired a tough sort of lingo to go with her put-on blasé manner. But she still had a lot of the smalltown girl in her, so it wasn't one of her better lines when Jean told the local photographers: "OK, boys, I think we should call it quits on pictures now."

Otto Preminger sold Jean's contract to Columbia Pictures. Preminger finally gave up on her, "Jean," he said, "I have sold you." Columbia immediately put her into the comedy, *The Mouse That Roared* (1959) with Peter Sellers, which did well in Europe and on the American art house circuit. She played the daughter of a United States scientist who's kidnapped by Sellers' private army. "Otto got rid of me liked a used Kleenex," Jean noted bitterly.

Jean and Francois sublet an apartment in New York for six months. She studied speech with Alice Hermes and applied for membership in the Actors Studio, which never bothered to answer her. Jean also took mime lessons from Jean Louis Barrault and Etienne Decroux. She sought the companionship for a while of Martin Goldblatt, a Columbia Pictures publicist. They would often have dinner and spend many late hours in Goldblatt's cozy Greenwich Village apartment discussing her career uncertainties. He also enjoyed the same close relationship with another Columbia star, Kim Novak. The publicity agent recognized Jean's sincere vulnerability and fear of revealing her true feelings. Several years later, the disturbed Goldblatt would take his own life.

Husband Francois Moreuil introduced Jean to a dissident group of avant-garde moviemakers, including young director Jean-Luc Godard. He requested Jean for *Breathless* (1959), opposite "the most exciting young actor in Europe today," Jean-Paul Belmondo. As the languid American hawking the *Herald-Tribune* on the Champs-Elysees, she harbors a petty hood who shoots a policeman and then betrays him to the police. The first "new wave" film, made in chronological sequence, was mainly an improvisation between Godard, Jean and Belmondo. They strove for spontaneity and in so doing so provided the 1960s with a new archetypal hero and brought all three to world attention. The innovative director, Godard, offered Columbia Pictures $12,000 to borrow Jean, or alternatively—Columbia could have half of the world profits of *Breathless*. Columbia immediately replied that they would take the $12,000, which proved to be a big mistake on the studio's behalf. Jean's new boyish coiffure was copied all over Europe. With the immense international popularity of the film, Jean represented the beginnings of feminism throughout France.

In David Richards' *Played Out*, the author commented on Jean's reaction to her sudden fame with the public: "I still don't know why I should have meant anything to the French," Jean noted later. "This strange awkward creature with rather bad teenage skin and extremely short-hair—what could she possibly have symbolized? . . . But it was a triumph in the funny old Hollywood style. Really, like a bad movie, only it was good. It was fantastic to all of us."

The success of *Breathless* was so great that Jean left for Hollywood and *Let No Man Write My Epitaph* (1960), as a convincing rich girl caught up with James Darren and his drug-addicted mother, Shelley Winters. While in California, she read for Joshua Logan's new play, "There Was a Little Girl." Jane Fonda, who recently completed her first film, *Tall Story*, was Logan's god-daughter and won the part. It was at a party at the French Consulate that Jean first met novelist/diplomat Romain Gary, then acting as Charles de Gaulle's consul general in Los Angeles. The Moreuils relations had begun to deteriorate and Jean obtained an American divorce in September, 1960. It was now common knowledge that Jean and Gary were living together.

Jean returned to France and was directed by husband (just prior to their divorce) Moreuil in *Playtime* (*La Récréation*, 1961), as an American girl who is encouraged to have an affair with Christian Marquand by his mistress, Francoise Prevost. It was based on a Francoise Sagan short story. In *Time Out for Love* (*Les Grandes Personnes*, 1961) she was a carefree American girl, sharing auto-racer Maurice Ronet with a much older Micheline Presle; *The Five Day Lover* (*L'Amant de Cinq Jours*, 1961) found Jean and Jean-Pierre Cassel in a frothy and enjoyable romantic comedy about a neglected Parisian housewife and a hustler. When the comedy was first released it was thought by many critics that director Philippe de Broca had inherited the mantle of Ernst Lubitsch and Rene Clair. Jean starred with Gabrielle Ferzetti in *Congo Vivo* (1961). In this political drama, filmed in the Belgian Congo, Jean played a suicidal wife raped by a native.

On October 16, 1963, Jean, 25, and the celebrated novelist Romain Gary, 50, were married in the Corsican Village of Sarrola-Carcopino on the Mediterranean. A year before, in July, 1962, Jean gave birth to a son, Alexander Diego Gary, by Caesarean section, in an obscure Spanish village.

In The French Style (1963), was based on two stories by Irwin Shaw and directed by Hollywood exile Robert Parrish. Jean was a young painter who comes to Paris and drifts from a series of passionate, brief affairs until she meets foreign correspondent Stanley Baker.

Jean next reported to Long Island, New York to film *Lilith* (1964), a well-mounted cinematization of the J.R. Salamanca book, co-starring Warren Beatty. Until *Lilith*, her own feelings about her career remained insecure. "I didn't have the sense of really being a professional actress, I don't think, until 1964 when I did *Lilith* for Robert Rossen," Jean admitted later. "I got terribly engrossed in that. We spent a couple of weeks before shooting at a very luxurious mental home outside of Washington, D.C. And Warren and I did a couple of psycho-dramas with the patients." Jean played a nymphomaniac schizophrenic whom therapist Beatty tries to help in a study of life in a mental institution. She won the part over Sarah Miles, Samantha Eggar and Romy Schneider. The Washington *Post* commended her for "her beautiful grasp and projection of the role." The movie has acquired a reputation as the late director Robert Rossen's neglected masterpiece. Jean often stated in interviews that it was her favorite role.

Jean was working at a fast pace, establishing herself as an international star. She was directed once again by Jean-Luc Godard in *Le Grand Escroc*, a sketch from *Les Plus Belles Escroqueries du Monde* (1964). Shot in Morocco, it was omitted from the film, but was released separately as a short. Jean teamed with Jean-Paul Belmondo once again for director Jean Becker in *Backfire* (*Echappement Libre*, 1964), a routine drama with Jean as a photojournalist falling for smuggler Belmondo. For director Nicholas Gessner, she was a jewel thief with Claude Rich in *Diamonds Are Brittle* (*Un Milliard Dans Un Billard*, 1965). Claude Chabrol's *The Line of Demarcation* (*La Ligne de Démarcation*, 1966) was an espionage drama of resistance efforts filmed in Vichy, France, with Jean as Maurice Ronet's English wife, who helps spies escape the Germans. In the spy thriller *Revolt of the Caribbean* (*Estouffade a la Caraibe*, 1966) with Frederick Stafford, Jean was a mobster's daughter joining Stafford in overthrowing a South American dictator.

On her return to Hollywood for Universal, Jean appeared in the uneventful *Moment to Moment* (1966), the last film to be directed by Mervyn LeRoy. The company began shooting in the South of France and completed principal filming on the studio's backlot. The soap opera didn't offer much, but it gave Jean a Yves St. Laurent wardrobe and she was exquisitely photographed by Harry Stradling. Matters weren't helped by the relatively weak acting by young Sean Garrison, in his first and last major role. *The New York Times* said: "If only it had Alfred

Hitchcock instead of LeRoy as director. The bait is all there, but don't expect to be hooked." At Warner Brothers, Jean had better luck in a screwball comedy, *A Fine Madness* (1966), as a bored psychiatrist's wife who's attracted to a radical poet, Sean Connery.

Once again, Claude Charbrol directed Jean with Maurice Ronet and Christian Marquand in *The Road to Corinth* (*La Route de Corinthe*, 1967), a James Bond-type thriller, filmed in Athens, Greece. She was caught up with the pursuit of her husband's killers, with the assistance from a special agent, Ronet. Her husband Romain Gary directed Jean in *Birds of Peru* (*Les Oiseaux Vont Mourir au Perou*, 1968), based upon one of his short stories. Jean was a haunted nymphomaniac involved in murder and a series of sexual encounters. In the United States, the film received an X rating. The high-style cast included Danielle Darrieux, Pierre Brasseur and Maurice Ronet.

Commenting on their marriage, Gary would say: "To understand Jean, you have to understand the Midwest. She emerged from it intelligent, talented, beautiful, but with the naïvete of a child. She has the kind of goodwill that to me is infuriating—persistent, totally unrealistic idealism. It has made her totally defenseless. In the end, it came between us."

In March, 1968, while in Hollywood preparing to start Columbia Pictures' *Pendulum* (1969) with George Peppard, she flew to Marshalltown for the funeral of her 18-year-old brother, David, killed in an automobile accident. *Pendulum* was TV directed George Schaefer's first motion picture and raised some stimulating questions about civil liberties. Perhaps it was this aspect that interested Jean in the Stanley Niss script. A police captain decides to defend himself after his lawyer is unable to prove he didn't kill his wife and her lover. Jean had begun to take an active interest in liberal causes.

The Lerner and Loewe stage hit of 1951, *Paint Your Wagon* (1969), was turned into an expensive epic musical film by Paddy Chayevsky that ultimately went sour at the box-office. It took place in No-Name City, California, where gold-rush prospectors Lee Marvin and Clint Eastwood share one wife, Jean, bought from a Mormon at an auction. The boom town saga was directed by Josh Logan, who turned an already costly film into the third most expensive one ever made up until that time.

The budget, originally set at $14,000,000, skyrocketed to $20,000,000. The only trained singer in the large cast was Harve Presnell, who sang "They Call the Wind Maria." Said *Time*: "Seberg's dubbed voice is as thin as the plot." *Newsweek* wrote: "Miss Seberg, living in a ménage-à-trois with Marvin and Eastwood, occasionally betrays interesting nasty, depths to her character, but they stay submerged for the most part. While she cultivates her conventional, shallow surface." And *Women's Wear Daily* reported: "Though it is overproduced and sometimes a little weird, the movie is pretty interesting, especially once you get past the slow first half." Reportedly, during the five-month filming of Paint Your Wagon, Jean became involved in an impassioned affair with Clint Eastwood. When asked, in an interview Jean gave in 1969, what she thought of Clint Eastwood, Jean replied, "He is one of the most direct men I've ever known. I like him very much and he's attractive, too."

Ross Hunter's commercially colossal *Airport* (1970), a star-studded *Grand Hotel* plot formula, was the first of the *Airport* epics. Jean was touching as the airline agent eager to become the mistress of Burt Lancaster, the manager of a huge metropolitan airport. Director George Seaton wrote the script from Arthur Hailey's novel. Helen Hayes won an Oscar for her memorable stowaway character. After *Airport*, Jean never made another film in the United States.

Her marriage to Romain Gary was rapidly breaking up (they would divorce in 1970). Gary's short story about a dog trained by bigots to attack blacks originally appeared in *Life* magazine, entitled *White Dog* (*Chien Blanc*). It later became a book-length memoir, also dealing with Gary's marriage to Jean and the black power movement of the late 1960s. Kristy McNichol, Paul Winfield and Burl Ives starred in Paramount's *White Dog* (1982), the first picture directed in Hollywood by the late Samuel Fuller in 18 years. Except for the dog and two of the main characters, it has virtually nothing to do with Romain Gary's original work.

Gary always believed that Jean was used by various black organizations, such as the Malcolm X Foundation and the Black Panthers. It's reported that she contributed thousands of dollars to their causes. Gary felt she intentionally allowed herself to be taken because of her "double feeling of guilt, her guilt, her guilt as a movie star, and her old Lutheran guilt with its inbred poison."

Gary would also say that the FBI destroyed Jean's life. "In 1970, when we were in the process of getting a divorce, the agency (J. Edgar Hoover was still in charge) apparently gave columnist Joyce Haber of *The Los Angeles Times* information indicating Jean was pregnant with a child whose father was a leader in the Black Panthers." It's believed the story referred to Allen Donaldson (Hakim Abdullah Jamal). The blind item ran as the lead in her column on May 19, 1970. It read: "Let us call her Miss A. . . . She is beautiful and she is blonde. . . . Recently she burst forth as the star of a multimillion-dollar musical. And now, according to all those really 'in' international sources, Topic A is the baby Miss A is expecting. Papa's said to be a rather prominent Black Panther." Joyce Haber has never admitted to her source of information. According to Gary, he was the baby's father and Jean, six months pregnant at the time, was so distressed by the cruel rumors she read in *Newsweek*, which picked up the story, that she attempted to kill herself in Majorca by taking a massive dose of pills. She was found unconscious on the beach. Upon recovering, Romain Gary had her placed in a clinic in the Swiss resort village of Zermatt. She went into labor two months prematurely.

The baby, named Nina Hart Gary, a white girl, was born by Caesarean section in Geneva, Switzerland, and died two days later (August 28, 1970). "After that," Gary would say later, "every year on the anniversary of this stillbirth, she tried to take her own life." When Jean returned to Marshalltown for the burial, she made sure the painful experience took place with an open casket, for all to see that the child was white. Some one hundred and eighty photographs of the casket were taken. During this visit she purchased basketball uniforms for the Indian School at nearby Tama and bought a home for black students at the Marshalltown Community College.

In April, 1971, Jean and Romain Gary brought libel suits against *Newsweek*, the *French Weekly Minute* and *American Weekly*, a former Hearst newspaper supplement, all of which picked up the story. She was awarded an equivalent of $8,333 in damages and Gary received $2,777 from *Newsweek*. The memory of the traumatic experienced stayed with her throughout her life. Later, when Hakim Jamal was brutally murdered, Jean, now heavily into drugs and alcohol, wrote a letter to the leftist Paris newspaper *Liberation*: "Hakim Jamal, cousin of Malcolm X, ex-user, convict, Black Muslin, the most beautiful man who ever walked the earth in our time; he's dead, my Jamal—eight slugs in the belly, seated in a rocking chair, surrounded by his family. Three junkies from Vietnam did it. O.K. (extenuating circumstances) but you killed my Jamal."

Miserable and unable to come to terms with this portion of her life, Jean underwent psychiatric treatment for serious depression. Then on March 12, 1972, Jean married Dennis Berry, the son of director John Berry, who was blacklisted in Hollywood during the McCarthy hearings, in Las Vegas, Nevada. Of this period of her mixed-up life, Jean would only say, "If you keep busy, you don't go crazy."

She continued to work in a whole rash of films testifying to her European drawing power: In *Macho Callahan* (1970), filmed in Durango, Mexico, with David Janssen and David Carradine, she drew a sour notice from Kevin Thomas in *The Los Angeles Times*: "Seberg looks poorly even before she's beaten up, acts worse and is even further hindered by a series of Barbie Doll wigs. At any rate, for whatever reason, *Macho Callahan* is a mess."

Jean's stand-in on the picture was a pretty California girl, Joan Blunden, on leave from the University of the Americas, in Mexico City. We know her today as Joan Lunden, the co-host of ABC-TV's "Good Morning America." While *Macho Callahan* was in production in 1969, it was reported that Jean was having an affair with a Mexican revolutionary, named El Gato. In *Dead of Summer* (*Ondata di Calore*, 1971), an Italian psychological suspenser, directed by Nelo Risi, she was a schizophrenic woman who murders her elderly, gay husband; in *The French Conspiracy* (*L'Attentat*, 1972), a thriller based on a Moroccan politician who vanishes in Paris, she was cast opposite Jean-Louis Trintignant and Roy Scheider. Although now divorced from Romain Gary, he directed her again in *Kill!* (1972), made in Spain with Stephen Boyd and James Mason, which ran into censorship problems. Conceived by Gary as an anti-drug film, *Kill!* was a violent story hated by critics and James Mason, who did the film as a favor to Gary. Jean played Mason's wife. In

Italy, she had a cameo role as a gangster's mistress in *La Camorra* (1972) with Fabio Testi.

In 1973, Jean starred in an ABC-TV "Suspense Movie," entitled *Mousey*, directed by Daniel Petrie. Filmed on location in Montreal and England, the mystery found theatrical release in Europe as *Cat and Mouse* (1973). Jean was a young mother who seeks protection from her psychopathic husband, Kirk Douglas, whom she fears is a murderer.

Jean's remaining films were fairly bleak and did not bring her much approval, although she was still considered a "prestige" actress in Europe. Her notices were poor in *The Corruption of Chris Miller* (*La Corruption de Chris Miller*, 1973); Jean was a fashion designer caught in a ménage-à-trois leading to murder, with Marisol and Barry Stokes. The film was unsuccessful and didn't reach New York until late 1979. For director Philippe Garrel, she appeared in *The Outer Reaches of Solitudes* (1974) in which she added a Monroesque pathos to her tragic heroine. It was a storyless black and white experimental film shot and improvised on Paris streets and Jean's apartment. The drama also featured Tina Aumont, the daughter of Maria Montez and Jean-Pierre Aumont. Jean's third husband Dennis Berry directed her in *The Great Frenzy* (*Le Grand Délire*, 1974), a leftist social farce which poked fun at bourgeoise society, with Jean as a madam presiding over a bordello, with Yves Beneyton and Isabelle Huppert. "Each time Jean made a film with one of her husbands, it was a disaster," her agent Olga Horstig-Primuz told biographer David Richards.

In Italy, Jean made the comedy *This Kind of Love* (*Questa Specie D'Amore*, 1974) for Alberto Bevilacqua. It starred the popular Italian star Ugo Tognazzi in a triple role and Jean as his society wife. Also in Rome, she appeared in *White Horses of Summer* (*Bianchi Cavalli d'Agosto*, 1974) with Frederick Stafford. In this, a bickering American couple are vacationing in Sicily when their son runs away and is seriously injured in an accident.

Jean starred in, co-authored, produced and directed the short *Ballad for the Kid*, which was shown at the 1975 London Film Festival. Terribly overweight, she made her last completed screen appearance in the Ibsen classic *The Wild Duck* (1977) as the wife of a happy-go-lucky photographer. It was filmed in Vienna for a German company. Her drinking which

in the past had always been social and now become a dangerous pastime, "I'm not an alcoholic," Jean said. "I just have a
drinking problem." In a 1974 *New York Times* interview with
Bart Mills, Jean explained her way of life, "I'm feeling around.
If you want to know what I'll be doing ten years from now, I
couldn't say. It's like asking a woman whether she will be
graceful at 45. Who knows what life will do to you?"

While married to Dennis Berry (1972-78), Jean kept busy by
playing patroness to young would-be film directors, radical
leftists and other assorted artists in their apartment just off St.
Germain on Paris's Left Bank. She also attempted to write
poetry and to paint. Romain Gary lived in a separate wing of
their apartment. After Jean separated from Berry, her mental
decline was swift, drifting into numerous affairs, amid persistent rumors of chronic alcoholism. Many of her friends believed she had become a hopeless nymphomaniac. "She suffered most from losing her self-respect," said Yves Boissert,
who directed Jean in *The French Conspiracy*. Romain Gary tried
to help, "For me, Jean is so important I would do anything to
save her," he told close friends. "I can bear it that she left me
and went to another man, but I don't think I could survive if
she died."

The pressures of trying to cope had gotten to Jean, calling
forth the hostility towards a world that had done her wrong.
The realization that all her ideals had brought her much pain
proved to be too much. Twelve days before her death, she attempted suicide by throwing herself onto the tracks of a train
station after a roaring quarrel with her last lover, 20-year-old
Ahmed Hasni, but was rescued as the train approached.

Jean Seberg finally succeeded in her try at suicide. Her na-
ked, decomposed body was found on September 8, 1979, in the
back seat of her small white Renault, parked just around the
corner from her apartment. It was a most melodramatic end.
She was last seen on August 30th by her Algerian live-in
boyfriend, Hasni (who claimed they were married, but police
say they were not and that Jean used the name of Berry
officially), who said that she left their apartment at 125 Rue de
Longchamps, wearing only a blanket and carrying a bottle of
barbiturates. The bottle and an empty container of mineral
water was found in the car with the body, and the French au-

thorities estimated that she may have died the same night she disappeared. The medical examiners said she died from a combination of alcohol and pills.

Romain Gary struggled through the trauma of Jean's death. On December 2, 1980, Gary, 66, committed suicide in his Left Bank apartment by placing a gun in his mouth and firing a single bullet.

Jean left a crumpled note for her 17-year-old son, Alexandre Diego Gary, her only child. "Diego, my dear son, forgive me, I can't live any longer," the note said. "I can't deal with a world that beats the weak, puts down the blacks and women, and massacres infants. Understand me, I know that you can, and you know that I love you. Be strong. Your mother who loves you, Jean."

SUSAN PETERS

Fawnlike Susan Peters' face had the perfection of a fragile porcelain doll. Once she had established her symbol of youthful innocence, she made considerable headway with that image. Fully primed, and splashily stunning, in the MGM classic *Random Harvest*, she was nominated for an Academy Award for her work opposite Ronald Colman. Then sadness caused by a hunting tragedy robbed her of the eventual public recognition towards which she was moving. A rifle Susan was carrying accidentally exploded, shattering her spine and paralyzing her. But she wasn't about to let a disability diminish her lust for life. "I believe you've got to have hope but I also think you've got to think the way you are," she said. "I'm planning my life as though I'll never get out of this wheelchair. Then whatever happens for the good is a birthday present." Susan Peters tasted fame briefly, until her confrontation with the disabling accident eventually led to anorexia nervosa—the emotional illness that causes starvation. Her personal fight to regain her life and career touched all of Hollywood.

Suzanne Carnahan was born in Spokane, Washington, on July 3, 1921, the oldest child of Robert and Abby James Carnahan. Her brother, Robert Jr., was two years younger. Her mother was a grandniece of Robert E. Lee and a granddaughter of the Civil War general J.T. Carnahan. The Carnahans were of French and Irish descent. Shortly after Suzanne's birth, her father, a civil engineer, moved the family to Portland, Oregon. Then in 1928 (some sources say 1933) her father was killed in an automobile accident and the family moved to Los Angeles to live with their French-born grandmother, Madame Maria Patteneaude, a well-known dermatologist. Suzanne never recovered from her father's death. She once recalled, "Young as I was, I knew then the meaning of tragedy." Suzanne's mother first took a job in a dress shop and later managed an apartment building. "My mother's life was not easy but she never complained," Suzanne said. "We were poor but we managed, and had fun." With her younger brother, Bob, Suzanne grew up outdoors. She rode horseback so well that at fourteen she became a "pro," earning money for breaking and showing other people's horses. From childhood she swam superbly and played excellent tennis.

She was educated at the Laird Hall School for Girls, the LaRue School in Azusa, Flintridge Sacred Heart and Hollywood High School. Suzanne held part-time jobs during summer vacations as an elevator operator and a package wrapper at Roos Brothers Department Store. "I never once thought of acting at this time," she said. "I planned to be a doctor." According to a popular version of her "discovery," she was first spotted by talent scout Lee Sholem in a school play. She would remember: "The very next day I had my first disappointment. Mr. Sholem took me to see producer Sol Lesser about a role in Thornton Wilder's *Our Town*." The role went to Martha Scott, who repeated her stage success as the tragic Emily opposite William Holden. "During my senior year at Hollywood High I took a drama course instead of cooking because I thought it was easier," she said. "Acting meant money, and the Carnahans always needed money. So I signed with an agent."

Suzanne's first real opportunity came after graduation from Hollywood High School. In her graduation class in June, 1939, were Jason Robards, Jr., Sheila Ryan, Dorothy Morris and Lois Ranson. Writer Salka Viertel, a friend of the family and Greta Garbo's confidante-adviser, introduced Suzanne to the distinguished director George Cukor while they were having lunch in the Metro-Goldwyn-Mayer commissary. The director was preparing the Rachel Crothers' Broadway hit *Susan and God* (1940). Suzanne and Gloria DeHaven read for minor roles in the Joan Crawford vehicle and were assigned parts as ingenue lead Rita Quigley's classmates.

George Cukor, a hard taskmaster, sent Suzanne to study with dramatic coach Gertrude Vogler. Suzanne's classes at Miss Vogler's Beverly Hills home followed that of another Cukor recommendation, Rita Hayworth, also in *Susan and God*.

Although George Cukor was favorably impressed with the fledging actress, he told her, "You'll be all right, if you only don't talk through your nose. Your voice doesn't flow. It squeals." Years later, Cukor said, "Susan was an enchanting looking creature. Reminded me of a young Katharine Hepburn. Not as aggressive as Kate, but that same finishing-school appearance and drive." Salka Viertel, a former actress with Max Reinhardt, arranged for Suzanne to attend the Max Reinhardt School of Dramatic Arts on a scholarship. While she was performing in a showcase production of Philip Barry's *Holiday*, Solly Baiano of Warner Brothers' talent department "rediscovered" her. He was instrumental in the development of many Warner Brothers stars. Director Vincent Sherman tested Suzanne in scenes from *So Red the Rose* and the death bed scene from *Our Town*.

In 1940, Warner Brothers put Suzanne under contract and Jack L. Warner suggested she change her name to Sharon O'Keefe; she hated the name and soon reverted back to Suzanne Carnahan. She gave herself three years to make good and told an interviewer, "If I don't take it too seriously or allow myself to be hurt by failure, I will at least save enough money to go to medical school." Her first Warner Brothers feature was a walk-on in *River's End* (1940), followed by unbilled roles in *The Man Who Talked Too Much* (1940) and *Money and the Woman* (1940). She appeared in two "Broadway Brevities" shorts, the first was *Young America Flies* (1940), which treated new flying school methods used in college aviation courses; she appeared as Bill Orr's girlfriend. In the second short, *Sockaroo* (1940), she played a college co-ed. Warner Brothers assigned Suzanne to *Santa Fe Trail* (1940), a large-scale Western with Errol Flynn and Olivia de Havilland, an elaborate adventure of six U.S. Army officers and their fight against John Brown's abolitionists in pre-Civil War Kansas. Suzanne was the blonde-wigged Charlotte Davis, a Boston college visitor in love with William Lundigan. With an array of actors, including Errol Flynn, Rita Hayworth, Allan Jones, Irene Hervey, Jean Parker, Martha O'Driscoll, William Lundigan, Nancy Carroll, Brenda Marshall, William Orr, May Robson, Wanda McKay, George Tobias, Natalie Draper and Reginald Gardiner, Suzanne boarded the Santa Fe Special junket to Santa Fe, New Mexico, for the world premiere in December, 1940. "Those junkets they ran before the war," she remembered, "I'll never forget the one for *Santa Fe Trail*. The stock players were each assigned to a press agent. I wasn't a good sport; I locked myself in my compartment during most of the trip."

Suzanne had a variety of minor roles: *The Strawberry Blonde* (1941), *Meet John Doe* (1941) found her as an autograph seeker, and *Here Comes Happiness* (1941) as one of Mildred Coles' debutante colleagues. During the casting of *King's Row*, producer Hal Wallis told biographer Charles Higham in *Star Maker*: "We began shooting in late summer. We still had no Cassie, and Jack Warner made some ridiculous suggestions, among them Joan Leslie, Susan Peters, and that buxom example of normal middle-class, healthy womanhood, Priscilla Lane." Hal Wallis eventually cast Betty Field. Suzanne tested for roles in *One Foot in Heaven* and lost *Sergeant York*, opposite Gary Cooper, to Joan Leslie after everybody at Warners raved about her test. Suzanne believed the part to be hers, until she read in Louella Parsons' column that 16-year-old Joan Leslie had won the star-making role as Cooper's young bride.

Warner Brothers finally convinced her to change her name from Suzanne Carnahan to Susan Peters just prior to RKO Studios' borrowing her for *Scattergood Pulls the Strings* (1941). It was the second film in the Scattergood Baines series with Guy Kibbee impersonating the small-town sage who plays counselor and benefactor to the community. *The Hollywood Reporter* wrote: "The freshness of Susan Peters in her part of the romance marks this young Warner contractee a most promising newcomer." At the time, Susan was sharing a Laurel Canyon house with two other Warner Brothers starlets, Ann Edmonds and Jean Ames. The three actresses spent many hours in the photogallery, posing for glamour and pin-up photos in various settings.

Back at Warner Brothers, Susan was the ingenue lead in *Three Sons o'Guns* (1941), a comedy about three sons, Wayne Morris, Tom Brown and William T. Orr, who keep their household in a constant state of turmoil. Orr would soon leave the acting profession to marry Jack L. Warner's step-daughter, Joy Ann Page, and become a Warner Brothers executive and producer. In *The Big Shot* (1942), Susan's career took a fortunate turn; she played the girl friend of convict Richard Travis, an associate of gangster Humphrey Bogart. She had a memorable bedside scene at Bogart's demise. However, Warner Brothers did not renew her contract. They seemed at a loss as to how to handle her career.

Elisabeth Fraser was also under contract to Warner Brothers, and played Fredric March's daughter in *One Foot in Heaven*, a role for which Susan had tested. "She was always serious and very dedicated to becoming a good actress," Fraser recalls. "I ran into her on Hollywood Boulevard, soon after the studio let her go. She was discouraged and said if nothing happened within the next six months, she was leaving the business for good and entering pre-med school." Elisabeth Fraser added, "She was a warmhearted person, so sad what happened to her."

Just before the six-month period was up, a call came from Susan's agent. Director S. Sylvan Simon at Metro-Goldwyn-Mayer wanted her for a part in a Marjorie Main starrer, *Tish* (1942). It was very loosely adapted from the Mary Roberts Rinehart stories about three eccentric old maids, Marjorie Main, Aline MacMahon and ZaSu Pitts. Susan portrayed the ill-fated wife of Richard Quine who dies giving birth after she learns he's been killed in the war. She gave her part more intensity than the banal script warranted. The tear-jerker brought Susan a Metro-Goldwyn-Mayer contract. She was a Wainwright College charmer in *Andy Hardy's Double Life* (1942), the thirteenth in the Mickey Rooney series. Much of the footage served to introduce newcomer Esther Williams. In *Dr. Gillespie's New Assistant* (1942), doctor Lionel Barrymore is assigned three new interns, Van Johnson, Richard Quine and Stephen McNally. Susan was the wife of McNally. During the filming, Susan and Richard Quine became engaged. They had met in director S. Sylvan Simon's office during preproduction conferences on *Tish*, and a romance soon blossomed.

Director Mervyn LeRoy viewed her Warner Brothers test for *King's Row* and decided to cast Susan as the young English aristocrat Kitty in *Random Harvest* (1942). The Ronald Colman and Greer Garson World War I romanticism cost over two million dollars and looked every bit of it, receiving all the glossy, full-strength production mounting Metro-Goldwyn-Mayer was capable of. The film owed its extraordinary taste to producer Sidney Franklin, and the James Hilton tale achieved renowned popularity. Ronald Colman tells Susan, "My dear, you look adorable"; and Susan answers, "Well, adore me. I can bear it!" According to Doug McClelland in James Robert Parish's *The MGM Stock Company*, Ann Richards almost won the role because of her resemblance to the film's star, Greer Garson: "She (Richards) recalls producer Sidney Franklin saying, ' "You would have been so right for the part, because the girl is supposed to remind Ronald Colman of his earlier love, Greer Garson.' " Ann Richards was then assigned a role as one of Colman's relatives.

Susan's role in *Random Harvest* was that of Colman's youthful fiancée who is haunted by what might have happened during the three years he cannot recall. In her big scene she releases him from the engagement when she recognizes his dilemma. *The Hollywood Reporter* reviewer thought: "It is this scene that Susan Peters plays so superbly, one of the notable moments in a picture filled with dramatic intensity." The lush *Random Harvest*, one of the 25 top money-making movies of 1942, had a record engagement at the Radio City Music Hall in New York, where it opened on December 17, 1942. Susan's shaded, tender performance nabbed her a supporting nomination for an Oscar. She was in good company, others nominated were Gladys Cooper, Agnes Moorehead, Dame May Whitty and Teresa Wright (the winner for *Mrs. Miniver*).

Assignment in Brittany (1943) cast her as the loyal French peasant girl who loves resistance fighter Jean-Pierre Aumont, ordered by British Intelligence to impersonate a renegade Frenchman he closely resembles. This improbable drama was beautifully photographed by Charles Rosher and also marked the Hollywood debut of Aumont. The actor was compared to a younger Jean Gabin. The chemistry was right between the two co-stars as the star-crossed lovers in this three-hanky weeper. The film which followed, Jules Dassin's *Young Ideas* (1943), was a minor but pleasant madcap comedy in which writer Mary Astor weds Herbert Marshall, who is highly unsuitable in the eyes of their children, Susan and Elliot Reid.

Then Susan was cast opposite Robert Taylor in the controversial *Song of Russia* (1943), in which Taylor plays a symphony conductor who tours Russia where he falls in love with Susan. The role was said to have been originally planned for Greta Garbo, until her last picture, *Two-Faced Woman*, fizzled and she retired at 36. Again *The Hollywood Reporter* was impressed with Susan: "She has gained immeasurably in histrionic stature . . . and now earns consideration as a dramatic actress of the first rank." Author Lawrence J. Quirk reflected on *Song of Russia* in *The Films of Robert Taylor*: "Whatever praise for the acting there was went to young Susan Peters, who was radiant and fresh as the young Russian musician. Susceptible as always to the charms of his feminine co-stars, Taylor did register more spark in the more intimate scenes vis-à-vis Miss Peters, who, surprisingly, outacted her far more experienced co-star." *Song of Russia* was saved by Harry Stradling's photography and Tschaikovsky's music. In 1947, Robert Taylor testified before the House Un-American Activities Committee that he was reluctant to do *Song of Russia* and argued with Louis B. Mayer about repercussions. The film was made, according to Nora Sayre, author of *Films of the Cold War*, "In order to pay tribute to the Russian resistance, just as *Mrs. Miniver* had exalted the heroism of our British allies. . . . The two Communist screenwriters expected to make a deeply serious film about the Russians destroying their crops and villages in order to deny any sustenance to the invading troops. But the movie was produced by Joe Pasternak, whose specialty was Deanna Durbin musicals."

On November 7, 1943, Susan became Mrs. Richard Quine (then in the U.S. Coast Guard) at the Westwood Community Church in West Los Angeles, with a huge gathering of friends, fans, and press. She wore her great-grandmother's wedding dress. Their close friend, Cesar Romero, also in the Coast Guard, was best man. They were Hollywood's young magic couple. Susan said, "I'll work for two more years and then I want to start raising a family."

With a happy new marriage and a booming career, Susan's popularity grew considerably. With Quine she lived in a palatial Beverly Hills home, raised racing horses and continued her enthusiasm for outdoor life. On December 6, 1943, she took over the Teresa Wright role on the "Lux Radio Theatre" presentation of *Mrs. Miniver* with Greer Garson and Walter Pidgeon repeating their screen roles. Assigned to *Gentle Annie*, she was replaced by Donna Reed, due to complications following a miscarriage. At the time it was feared Susan wouldn't pull through and she was off the screen for nearly a year.

The glossy *Keep Your Powder Dry* (1945) found Lana Turner, Laraine Day and Susan joining the Women's Army Corps. As the wife of Captain Michael Kirby, her motives were all love and patriotism. Reviews were generally mixed, with the *Motion Picture Herald* stating: "The three lovely stars don khaki for this first full-scale screen treatment of the WACS. Their importance to a nation at war, however, is not made clear in the film. . . . Susan Peters, the constant peacemaker, gives an effective if not always believable characterization." By the time *Keep Your Powder Dry* was released in March, 1945, Susan had already suffered the tragic accident that was to cut short her young life.

On New Year's Day, 1945, with Richard Quine, his cousin Tom Quine and his wife Mary Lou, Susan embarked on a duck hunting sojourn to the Cuyamaca Mountains near San Diego, when she accidentally discharged her 22-caliber rifle, which went off as she picked it up from the ground. The bullet lodged in her spine, paralyzing her from the waist down. She was rushed to Mercy Hospital, some 65 miles away, where an emergency operation was performed. "I was always into sports— the hard, make-it-through-anything type," Susan said. "And when I was in the hospital, I told myself I was going to come through this accident. I was going to walk again." Lana Turner told Louella Parsons' readers that she and Turhan Bey had planned to go with Susan and Quine on the hunting trip when Bey was suddenly taken ill over the holidays.

Metro-Goldwyn-Mayer paid all of her hospital bills and kept Susan on a $100 weekly salary for an indefinite period, but her career was stymied, as naturally her roles were henceforth limited. She had expressed interest in doing the story of pop singer Connee Boswell, and the life of Nellie Revell, the newspaperwoman who continued her career even when bedridden, but the projects fell through. Susan's mother, Mrs. Abby Carnahan, died of a heart attack, at 52, on December 4, 1945, and Susan went to pieces. Susan's life seemed to be falling in ruins around her and then on April 17, 1946, she and Quine adopted a baby boy, Timothy Richard Quine.

Radio offers began pouring in. She guested as the doomed Diane on "Lux Radio Theatre's" *Seventh Heaven* with Van Johnson. "I was pretty scared to face that audience in a wheelchair," Susan admitted, "And my hands were shaking so hard I could scarcely hold the script. But I did it!" Van Johnson once recalled, "I liked her very much, a spiritual, dreamy kind of girl." On the "Screen Directors Guild" theatre dramatization of *Love Affair*, she played Terry McKay, the role originated by Irene Dunne. Susan scoffed at doctors who told her that she would probably never walk again. "I fooled 'em three months ago by taking a few steps," she said. "I'll be in front of the cameras again before very long, too. They can tell me I'll never walk again if they want to, but I know better." The producer-director team of Joe Pasternak and Henry Koster wanted Susan for *The Unfinished Dance*, the remake of Jean Benoit-Levy's French classic, *Ballerina*. She would play a famous ballerina who suffers a spinal injury, when moppet Margaret O'Brien accidentally pulls the wrong switch during a performance of *Swan Lake*. Susan rejected the idea. Pasternak's protégée Karin Booth was given the role of the ill-fated ballerina.

Susan would later say, "Metro-Goldwyn-Mayer kept sending me Pollyanna scripts about crippled girls who were sweetness and light, which I kept turning down. Two years after my accident, I gave up and broke my contract. I won't trade on my handicap."

Just prior to the accident, Susan had begun filming *The Outward Room*. After her accident there was some talk of resuming the production and collapsing a balcony with doubles and reshooting the finish with Susan in her wheelchair, but the idea was soon shelved. Susan and Richard Quine made their first public appearance after the accident with Lucille Ball at the opening of Desi Arnaz and His Orchestra at Ciro's. Friends such as Lucille and Desi encouraged Susan to return to work. It was Charles Bickford who brought to Susan's attention a novel he had just read, *Sign of the Ram*, by Margaret Ferguson. The leading character was a paralyzed woman who wrecked her family by possessive domination and murder. Susan discussed the novel with her agent, Frank Orsatti, who in turn interested the producer-director Irving Cummings and a deal was set with Columbia Studios.

In July, 1947, a "new" Susan began work on *Sign of the Ram* (1948) and was greeted on the set by such other Columbia players as Glenn Ford, Evelyn Keyes, Larry Parks, Cornel Wilde, Ginger Rogers and co-stars Alexander Knox and Peggy Ann Garner. "What Susan needed mostly was self-confidence," said husband Richard Quine. The uneven picture unfortunately is high gloss soap opera, with Susan pulling all the stops out as the invalid wife who rules her family with an iron hand. "I have never played someone with the emotional range that this character has, it was a real challenge," she said. "People were staying away from me, and perhaps they had good reason." John Sturges' direction extracted whatever drama the novel contained. "I know people will come in to see how I look in a wheelchair," Susan said. "If I can send them out thinking I'm an actress, I'll be satisfied. This is my great opportunity." Bosley Crowther said in *The New York Times*: "The actress is worthy of a more substantial token of respect than this. Plainly the story is clap-trap."

Production on the mediocre *Sign of the Ram* was far from easy on Susan. She had to have Quine or her aunt, Mary Carnahan, a trained nurse, with her throughout the filming. In an interview, Susan said, "I find that I do pretty well running our home from a wheelchair. There is a phone at my elbow most of the time from which I conduct domestic affairs. There is nothing dull about life, if one fills the hours constructively." She continued, "I have Dick, my baby Timothy, my home and a career. A pretty wonderful combination for any girl." Less than a year after the interview appeared, Susan asked Richard Quine for a divorce and no one was able to talk her out of it. "Dick and I probably could live together for seven or eight years but our marriage isn't going well," said Susan. "I think we should end it while we both are young enough to find new lives and before our adopted child is old enough to be hurt by the separation." She continued, "Our temperaments were different. Our discussions always ended in arguments. We didn't agree on anything."

"Susan had said again and again that she is much happier alone," Quine said at the time. "People put us both on a pedestal and we couldn't live up to this ideal." One of Quine's fears was that people would think he had walked out on Susan, he told Louella Parsons. "I certainly would never do that," he said. "This divorce is her idea. I had hoped that I would get a part with a Chicago company in *John Loves Mary* and being away it might help. I'm not going to say this is a trial separation because I'm afraid that Susan means she wants to be alone, so there is nothing I can do." They were divorced in September, 1948. Today, Richard Quine admits he still suffers tremendous pain when he thinks of Susan. "She was like a delicate fawn," he said. "Life was a glorious adventure to Susan, she was a compassionate girl who loved the outdoors. After the accident, she never wanted sympathy. We had her car specially equipped with hand controls that she successfully mastered."

In 1949, Susan opened at Hollywood's Ivar Theatre in Tennessee Williams' *The Glass Menagerie*, as the crippled Laura, living in a world of her own dominated by a collection of miniature glass animals. "I never would have had the guts to go on the stage if I hadn't been paralyzed," she said. "But I knew I had to find new ways of earning a living—or starve." She received a spontaneous standing ovation, led by Richard Quine. "The ovation completely took me by surprise," Susan said. "It's enormously satisfying." Hollywood always did love a comeback story. Susan then took the play on tour of East Coast summer theaters, including Cape Cod. The following year, she starred in Rudolph Besier's romantic comedy *The Barretts of Wimpole Street*, as the Victorian poetess Elizabeth Barrett Browning, in Princeton, Cincinnati and Philadelphia. Of her performance, the Philadelphia *Evening Bulletin* said: "Susan Peters demonstrated conclusively last night that the hunting accident which deprived her of the use of her legs five years ago has not lessened by one carat the sparkle of her acting. She acquits herself with distinction in a play which deftly minimizes her physical handicaps." Susan said, "We hope to bring it into New York. And that is very exciting." But Susan found the show extremely taxing and plans for the Broadway revival were cancelled. Tom Poston, Brooks West and Natalie Norwick were also in the cast. Susan's brother, Bob Carnahan, and his wife, accompanied Susan on the tour.

"I want to appear in more plays," she said. "But so far the ones that have been offered me are so terribly melodramatic that I have turned them down. The last one was about a love affair with a blind man who rushes up a mountain to rescue me in a fire and the experience is such a shock that he regains his sight."

In March, 1951, Susan signed with NBC-TV to star in a Philadelphia-based daytime soap opera, "Miss Susan," playing a lawyer confined to a wheelchair who works out the problems of those about her. The 15-minute teleseries also included Katherine Grill, Natalie Priest, Robert McQueeny and John Lormer. "It's tough doing live TV five times a week. But, I needed to act again," she said. In December of that year, she suffered a relapse. Friends blamed it on the Philadelphia winter weather. She was forced to abandoned the series and enter a private sanitarium.

Susan and Army Colonel Robert Clark (not the actor) became engaged and announced their plans to marry. But the wedding plans were called off, shattering Susan's efforts to conquer her medical problems. The more she worried about her health, the more she brooded over Clark. An ailing Susan returned to California, bypassing Hollywood and going directly to her brother Bob's cattle ranch in Lemon Grove, near the town of Visalia. Bob knew she was suffering and felt powerless to help. Thereafter, Susan became a reclusive figure, living in virtual seclusion. She was sicker than she'd let anyone know and her health had steadily worsened.

There was another extended period at an Exeter, California, hospital for a delicate skin graft. When Susan was released, she went back into seclusion. In September, 1952, she was feeling well again and making plans to return to the stage in another tour of *The Barretts of Wimpole Street*. "She was trying to pull her weight up to return to work," a friend recalls. "Susan was just too weak and often complained of being exhausted." But it was already too late for Susan. The damage had already taken its toll on her heart. She became very frail, and psychologically scattered, and developed anorexia nervosa as well. Very little was known about the debilitating eating disorder in the 1950s.

Susan Peters had a fatalistic sense about her life being doomed and began preparing for the final curtain, which arrived on October 23, 1952. Two months before she died, she told her physician, Dr. Manchester, "I'm getting awfully tired. I think it would be better if I did die." He added that she had been brought to the hospital in a "terminal stage of illness." The doctor gave the primary cause of death as chronic kidney ailment and bronchial pneumonia, but those who knew her all agreed with him more when he added, "I felt she had lost the will to live."

MARIE McDONALD

Marie McDonald's drive to gain success seemed so frantic at times that ambition must have been ingrained in her personality as a child. She had no idea how much the realization of that dream would cost. The sexy Marie possessed full, pouty lips, satin skin and, most often, blond tresses. The careers of many stereotyped bombshells have been launched by the exhibition and exploitation of their figures and the hoopla surrounding them. Clara Bow, Ann Sheridan and Carole Landis became "The It Girl," "The Oomph Girl," and "The Ping Girl" respectively. So it was that Marie, in an effort to publicize *Guest in the House*, became "The Body"—a label she came to regard with something very close to contempt. Though the news media portrayed Marie with more sensationalism than film accomplishments, she moved quickly from showgirl to golden glamour girl until excessive despondency exploded into a fluttering tailspin.

Cora Marie Frye was born in Burgin, Kentucky, on July 6, 1923, to Mr. and Mrs. Everett Frye. Available information on her early years is imperfect. Interviews and articles differ to such a degree that a *Collier's* magazine interview, dated September, 1944, states the proper spelling of her name as Froenu and her birthplace as Vienna, Austria. Settling in Burgin, Kentucky, when Marie was eight months old, the family anglicized its name from Froenu to Frye. Her grandmother, Marie Mouliner, was reported to be a singer on the operatic stage and her mother, as Marie McDonald, a former showgirl with Florenz Ziegfeld.

In 1929, when her parents divorced, Marie's father became a warden in Leavenworth, Kansas, at the Federal Penitentiary. Marie with her mother went to live with her grandparents in

Westchester, New York, where she attended St. Anne's Elementary School. When her mother remarried, the family moved to Yonkers, where her stepfather, Mr. Tuboni, operated a bar and grill. Marie continued her studies as P.S. 52 and Roosevelt High School, excelling in piano and the ukulele. She was so good at writing articles for the school paper that the Columbia University School of Journalism offered her a scholarship. Marie bylined her column on fashions "By Ken-Tuck," punning on the Southern drawl she couldn't shake.

Marie's physical appearance developed spectacularly. Her mother eagerly began pushing the mischievous teenager into a show business direction with dancing and singing classes. She entered numerous beauty contests, becoming "Miss Yonkers," "Miss Loew's Paradise" and "The Queen of Coney Island." The first national contest the blossoming Marie ever won was the jitterbug contest at the Harvest Moon Ball at Madison Square Garden in 1938. At 15, she left high school to become a model for John Robert Powers and lied about her age to appear in the Paradise Restaurant Club Review. When the show closed, Marie took a job as a cigarette girl at the Central Club while still modeling teen fashions for John Robert Powers. Marie was crowned Miss New York of 1939 in the annual Miss America competition. Nils T. Granlund, who was in charge of the contest, recalled in his book, *Blondes, Brunettes, and Bullets*: "She didn't win the title in Atlantic City, but she had so much class and beauty that I felt she would surely click on the stage. I brought her to George White, who had been one of the judges in the New York contest. 'Look, George,' I said. 'If I were you, I'd put this girl in your *Scandals*! White agreed.' "

George White's Scandals of 1939 opened at the Alvin Theatre on August 28, 1939 to enthusiastic reviews. Its stars were the Three Stooges, Eugene and Willie Howard, Ella Logan, Ben Blue, Ann Miller (in her first Broadway show), Collette Lyons and Ray Middleton. It was the thirteen edition and the final one in the Scandals series.

At the beginning of Marie's career, Mrs. Frye was the prototype of the stage mother, determined her daughter was going to be a star. Marie was her golden opportunity. But she lost control once Marie went on the road with *Scandals*; Marie decided not to stay with the show at the conclusion of the

Biltmore Theater engagement in Los Angeles. In Hollywood, she modeled for the prize-winning illustrator Alex Raymond as Dale Arden in the "Flash Gordon" comic strip and also for the figure of Princess Aura.

Appearing in the chorus at Earl Carroll's Theater Restaurant, Marie, along with Yvonne De Carlo, was fired without the usual two weeks' notice; Marie, for pulling several pranks backstage, and De Carlo for gaining excess poundage and not wearing the white body makeup that was required of all Carroll Girls. Carroll's formula for success was to dazzle the public with his slogan *Through These Portals Pass The Most Beautiful Girls in the World*. His opulent, flamboyant image was his own clever creation and his extravagant reviews captivated audiences in the great Ziegfeld tradition. A former Carroll Girl, Judith Woodbury remembers a night while waiting for their entrance cue for the "Tree of Jewels" number. "Marie fell asleep on one of the long backstage wooden benches and I had to wake her just in time for our entrance." On another occasion, Marie convinced bandleader Manny Strand that the guest star, singer Ella Logan, had a very bad cold and would be unable to do the radio broadcast that emanated from the popular nightspot. Marie went on in her place! "She was always getting into mischief," recalls Judith. Impresario Earl Carroll was extremely strict about life backstage and was so aggravated by Marie's continuing bad habits on-and off stage that he banished her between shows.

Marie and Yvonne De Carlo next joined the chorus of N. T. Granlund's Florentine Gardens, in a review headlining Sugar Geise. The pay was $35 a week and Dave Gould was in charge of the choreography. Important specialties included a young Gwen Verdon, with her flaming red hair, as the spectacular "Girl in Gold," her entire body painted a shimmering gold. The club also featured established performers like Sophie Tucker, the Mills Brothers, Betty and Jane Kean, and Harry Richman. The chorus line included Jean Wallace, Carol Haney, Peggy Satterlee, Marie Van Shaak (Lili St. Cyr), and her siblings, Dardy and Barbara Moffett.

"I knew Marie would become a success in show business," Sugar Geise said. "The audiences at the club responded to her sexuality and superb body. She never took herself too seriously and was always fainting backstage." Sugar Geise recalls, "Years later, I was working on one of her pictures at MGM and we were talking about the old days, when the assistant director called her back to the set. Marie shouted back, 'Just a minute, I'm talking to my girl friend.' " While appearing at N.T.G.'s club, the increasingly restless Marie eloped with roguish playboy Richard Allord, a hell-raising pal of Errol Flynn. The young couple moved into the Hollywood Plaza Hotel. Shortly after her marriage, Marie called Sugar. "She was crying and said her wedding ring was a fake diamond and she was leaving him." The union was annulled three weeks later. Allord once shared a bachelor pad with Errol Flynn and David Niven, and often figured in Flynn's wild, womanizing escapades. Dick Allord later married Marie's chum, Diana Mumby, a willowy blond Goldwyn Girl (*Up in Arms*).

Choreographer Busby Berkeley hired Marie for MGM's *Ziegfeld Girl* (1941) to add to his eye-filling spectacle staging. But just before filming got underway, she dropped out and accepted an offer to sing with Tommy Dorsey's Orchestra in New York. She met Dorsey between shows on Halloween night, October 31, 1940, while visiting with Virginia Cruzon and Judith Woodbury. Adding their vocal talents to Dorsey's music were the Pied Pipers, headed by Jo Stafford, Connie Haines, and a skinny young New Jersey singer, Frank Sinatra. Marie auditioned for Dorsey and soon joined his weekly radio show, "Fame and Fortune," as the newest Pied Piper addition. In December, 1940, she tested for a 20th Century-Fox contract in New York but the studio felt she didn't photograph well and the option was never exercised. After departing the Tommy Dorsey band, Marie obtained a singing engagement at the popular Leon & Eddie's on Manhattan's "Swing Street," a block of West 52nd Street just off Fifth Avenue dominated by a cluster of nightclubs that featured swing music. At brief intervals, Marie also sang with the Charlie Barnet, Johnny Long and Richard Himber Orchestras.

The English theatrical entrepreneur Sir Charles Frederick Bernard began courting the enigmatic beauty in grand style and encouraged her to press on toward a film career. He became Marie's mentor and a pillar of strength. With the wealthy Bernard's help she met important people who would help promote her career. He was unquestionably the most powerful man in Marie's young life at the time. Bernard paid for dental work to correct the space between her front teeth. They became inseparable friends and, most people who remember them together agree, probably more than that.

Marie returned to California and the enterprising Bernard introduced her to agent Louis Shurr. In 1941 Shurr, through Universal executive Dan Kelley, secured a stock contract for the leggy 18-year-old starlet at $75 a week. Like most new contractees of that day, Marie underwent an extensive redesigning process. Universal Pictures dropped the name Frye and she took her mother's theatrical name, Marie McDonald. She also changed from brunette to a more flattering blond. At first, she was kept busy posing for cheesecake art, in tight-clinging sweaters and fashion stills rather than making movies. Marie was finally given the ingenue lead opposite Robert Paige in *Melody Lane* (1941), one of the studio's mini musicals. On the first day of filming, director Charles Lamont found the new actress too inexperienced. Lamont bluntly informed the studio brass that Marie wouldn't do. Production was halted and a hurried call went out for Anne Gwynne to fill the role.

Universal then assigned Marie a series of one-line parts in such films as *It Started with Eve* (1941), as a cigarette girl, *You're Telling Me* (1941), *Keep 'Em Flying* (1941) and *Appointment For Love* (1941). In one of Abbott and Costello's better vehicles, *Pardon My Sarong* (1942), Marie replaced Marie Montez as a sarong-clad seductress attracted to Lou Costello. The Universal regime had moved Montez on to star status in *Arabian Nights*, co-starring Jon Hall. In 1942, Marie joined the Hollywood Victory Caravan, with James Cagney, Joan Blondell, Cary Grant, Groucho Marx, Frances Gifford, Rise Stevens, Pat O'Brien, Frances Langford, Bing Crosby, Frank McHugh, Stan Laurel, Fay McKenzie, Juanita Stark, and many others, on a bond-raising tour. *Life* magazine covered the event, focusing much attention on the sensationally built Marie.

Marie's first studio-arranged publicity date was with Forrest Tucker and her first serious romance was with square-jawed Bruce Cabot. The budding sex symbol and the dashing Cabot became regulars at the Mocambo, Trocadero and Ciro's. At 18,

Marie was a nightclub favorite. She and Bruce Cabot made good magazine copy and they became popular with photographers. Cabot would later recall: "What ultimately made Marie so attractive and lovable was that behind the dazzling face and figure, you could find a rare softness and sincerity." The well-publicized affair eventually cooled, but not before Universal dropped her option, thinking she was more interested in getting into the gossip columns than working.

Marie's new agent, Vic Orsatti, obtained a contract for her with Paramount Pictures starting at $100 a week. Her first assignment was an auspicious one, *Lucky Jordan* (1942), starring Alan Ladd as an AWOL soldier who inadvertently becomes a hero by depleting a gang of Nazi agents. Director Frank Tuttle was very skillful at such material, especially when directing his pal Ladd. Marie's footage as a luscious secretary was small, but no one could deny she generated mass appeal. "We'd had a lot of trouble casting the role. She was just a kid, but I remember this magnetism about her," recalled the late director. "There was an interesting chemistry between Marie and Ladd, even though they only had a few scenes together. She worked hard and had enormous promise. A few years later, I wanted her for *The Great John L.*, but we couldn't negotiate a deal, I believe it was with Hunt Stromberg?" The role went to Linda Darnell.

As one of Hollywood's new ranking beauties, Marie wed Vic Orsatti on January 10, 1943. He was known for his good looks, personality and irresistible charm. Orsatti was from San Francisco, where his father acted as the West Coast representative for an international steamship company. The oldest brother Frank formed the Orsatti Theatrical Talent Agency with his two brothers, Vic and Al, as assistants. They represented many of Movieland's biggest names, including Sonja Henie and many MGM contract players. Vic was credited with negotiating Henie's contract with 20th Century-Fox after her championship performance in the 1936 Olympics and once was engaged to the figure skater. Orsatti was married two other times, first to Fox star June Lang and later to Dolores Donlon. Both ended in divorce. Orsatti believed there was no limit to Marie's star potential and began shaping and molding her career. "I was a child at the time, emotionally speaking, and completely in awe of Vic," she admitted later.

Marie's pictures immediately following her marriage had little effect on developing her career. Republic borrowed her for a dreary mystery, *A Scream in the Dark* (1943), opposite Robert Lowery. Back at Paramount, she appeared in a succession of ordinary films. *Riding High* (1943) was an unmemorable Dorothy Lamour and Dick Powell musical, and *Tornado* (1943) a forgotten "B" with Marie as the pretty socialite sister of Morgan Conway, who becomes the object of murderous intrigue. In *I Love a Soldier* (1944), she was the shipyard welder friend of Paulette Goddard, Mary Treen and Ann Doran. *Our Hearts Were Young and Gay* (1944), the nostalgic comedy of Cornelia Otis Skinner and Emily Kimbrough, found Marie a voyage passenger. She played another sexy secretary in *Standing Room Only* (1944) in an appealing scene with Fred MacMurray.

After two years at Paramount, Marie found her ambitions had outrun her opportunities, and she was restless for a change. In 1944, she signed with independent producer Hunt Stromberg who cast her as Miriam in *Guest in the House* (1944), an offbeat upper-class drama based on the stage hit *Dear Evelyn*, which starred Mary Anderson. In the movie version, Anne Baxter was the seemingly sweet girl who attempts to infect a household with her malice. From the beginning, the film was beset by problems. Marie's casting was over the objections of director Lewis Milestone, who wanted Peggy Knudsen. Milestone was known to run a very tight ship. He later left the production and it was completed by John Brahm.

Marie lamented to Louella Parsons: "I had the feeling that the director chosen for *Guest in the House* never wanted me. He had seen a girl in New York (Peggy Knudsen) he thought was just right for the part, in fact, he made it so obvious that I cried my heart out every night when I went home. I prayed something would happen. It did and then Mr. Brahm took over." Critics enjoyed her raw earthiness in *Guest in the House*. Said *The Hollywood Reporter*: "It is Marie McDonald who comes close to walking away with the picture. Her zestful and keenly understanding portrayal of the artist's model is a brilliant and well-nigh flawless performance which, coupled with her loveliness, makes her the standout of the picture." United Artists' publicity department found Marie a willing and promotable subject. Unfortunately for her, the publicity forces named her

"The Body" to help sell the pathological drama. It received worldwide attention, earned her immediate recognition, and was a tag that would haunt her the rest of her life. Marie lived up to the myth—and the myth eventually shut her out of the Hollywood mainstream. She would later say of "The Body" label, "If I ever get hold of that press agent . . ." Marie blazed. "Not that I wasn't highly flattered at first. Then I ran into casting trouble and realized what a big bubble of nothing it was."

In Earl Wilson's book *The Show Business Nobody Knows*, he reminisces: "Without the title, 'The Body,' Marie wouldn't have received as much attention as she did because her acting talent remained undiscovered until her death. However, she did have a knack of getting publicity and being inventive." Plans for Hunt Stromberg to elevate Marie to star status in his Technicolor project *Glamour Girl* were unexplainably shelved. Commenting on her marriage to agent husband Vic Orsatti, Marie said, "I still pay him the regular 10 percent. But he uses it to pay the rent. And, if there's any left over, I get a present. My whole paycheck goes into the bank."

International Pictures *It's a Pleasure* (1945) was released through RKO, and starred Sonja Henie in her first film away from 20th Century-Fox. Michael O'Shea's philandering with a gold-digging charmer, Marie, brings trouble to his romance with skating star Sonja Henie. Because of Henie's "no other blondes" contract clause, Marie appeared most fetchingly flame-haired. "It's getting so people don't recognize me anymore," said Marie. Producer Hunt Stromberg announced Marie would have a major role in *Young Widow*, to star Ida Lupino and her husband, Louis Hayward. Soon thereafter, Lupino suffered a nervous breakdown (when her marriage broke up) and was replaced by Jane Russell in the wartime tearjerker. Marie's role was suddenly switched to Marie Wilson. Hunt Stromberg next loaned Marie to United Artists for the stage chestnut *Getting Gertie's Garter* (1945), directed by Allan Dwan with his usually good grace for such material. It was a remake of a Marie Prevost farce (1927), with Dennis O'Keefe trying to retrieve a diamond garter from his wife (Marie) that would get him in trouble with an old flame, Sheila Ryan. Marie received favorable comments for her comedic talents and the always dependable Dennis O'Keefe was used to good advantage. She broke off her contract with producer Hunt Stromberg in 1946, charging in Superior Court "that Stromberg had not promoted her career as thoroughly and rapidly as he had agreed." The judge ordered Stromberg to pay for an outfit she had purchased to wear on a publicity tour and $19.67 for fare home from San Francisco, where the tour ended. Darryl F. Zanuck considered her for the Tyrone Power drama *Nightmare Alley*, about life among carnival's riff-raff, but director Edmund Goulding decided on 20th Century-Fox contractee Coleen Gray.

Through husband Vic Orsatti's shrewd management and his brother Frank's close personal friendship with Louis B. Mayer, Marie was signed with Metro-Goldwyn-Mayer to star in Gregory La Cava's *Living in a Big Way* (1947), co-starring Gene Kelly. The comedy revolved around a hasty wartime marriage and a veteran's housing project. Marie and Kelly dance in an Astaire-Rogers fashion to "It Had to Be You," staged by Gene Kelly and Stanley Donen. By the time the music stops, the couple have convinced the audience that it is indeed possible for two people who have just met to do something as absurd as marry on the spur of the moment. It was Kelly's first picture after being discharged from the Army, and was to launch Marie as another Lana Turner. Said Marie, soon after *Living in a Big Way* went into release, "Nobody saw that picture except my husband and mother. It was a great script we had. Then it was torn in half and thrown out the window by a genius at Metro."

Gene Kelly didn't want to do the film until Benny Thau, the veteran MGM executive, urged him to accept the role if only for the sake of their new star, Marie McDonald. "You were once given a chance with Judy Garland (*For Me and My Gal*)," Thau reminded him, "so why not do the same for someone else?" An unhappy Marie would claim, "They would hand me a piece of paper on the set and every day it was a different girl I was playing. I danced with Gene Kelly but the camera was so far away from me that my fans thought I was my own double. I worked for months on a Russian ballet number and it ended up on the cutting room floor." When quizzed as to why the number was cut, "A certain star," growled Marie. "The certain star wasn't in the scene, that's why."

When the production was finally completed. Louis B. Mayer

brought second lead Phyllis Thaxter back for added scenes with Gene Kelly. It was meant to establish some sort of romance between Thaxter and Kelly. She looks noticeably different in their close-ups than in other scenes. With all the problems *Living in a Big Way* presented, there is an ingratiating energy in the interplay between Marie and Gene Kelly. Marie, the last of director La Cava's spoiled rich girls, is in top form, although most critics were still suspicious of her talent. Bosley Crowther's review of *Living in a Big Way* in *The New York Times* found Marie to have: "Every opportunity to display her natural gifts and very little else." Even with the traditional MGM polish, it was heavily panned by most critics as a box-office iceberg. It was to be director Gregory La Cava's last film. Viewed today, it is not the catastrophe it was labeled at the time, but rather a final mediation on La Cava's deepest concerns—dreams, the stability of an extended family, giddy elation and the morning after. More than a little dissatisfied with how MGM had trimmed her role, Marie bought back her contract at a reported cost of $14,000. She later accused Mayer of instigating a conspiracy against her at other major studios. These unsettling conditions were combined with the tension caused by Marie's disintegrating marriage to Vic Orsatti.

In 1947, Marie and Orsatti split up after almost five years of marriage. "I tried to make the marriage work, but Vic Orsatti turned out to be a completely different person from the one I married. And it made the relationship impossible in the end," Marie said. After selling his agency, following the deaths of his brothers Frank and Al, Orsatti partnered briefly with Ray Stark and Nat Goldstone, and in 1950 set up an independent company, Sabre Productions. Orsatti subsequently formed Ror-Vic Productions with Rory Calhoun, and he was executive producer of several television series, including "The Texan." He died in June, 1984, at the age of 79.

In May, 1947, while in Reno to divorce Orsatti, Marie had a brief affair with Bugsy Siegel, the reputed West Coast head of the Mafia, who liked to hobnob with the movie set. Marie fell somewhere between Wendy Barrie and Virginia Hill in the infamous Siegel's affections. During Heldorado Days, an annual event celebrating the founding of Reno's pioneer days, Siegel asked Marie to ride in the parade as Queen of the Flamingo Hotel float. Siegel's elaborate and expensive float took first prize. But eventually the syndicate boss grew disenchanted with Marie's apparent inability to get anywhere on time. Bugsy Siegel, who turned Las Vegas into a plush gambler's paradise, was murdered a month later in gangland fashion in the Beverly Hills home of Virginia Hill.

Shortly after the Vic Orsatti divorce, Marie became the wife of tycoon Harry Karl, the multi-millionaire shoe magnate, who would later marry Joan Perry Cohn, and then Debbie Reynolds. Marie told the press, "This is forever." A very private person, Karl was an orphan who had inherited his adoptive father's shoe stores. Without the influential Orsatti to guide her career, and the traumatic experience at MGM, Marie was concerned about her future in Hollywood.

Harry Karl's oldest daughter, Judy Karl Anderson (by Karl's first marriage), has these recollections, "Marie was one of the nicest, sweetest, most endearing women I have ever known, and she had a terrific sense of humor." Judy continued, "I lived in Chicago, and spent summers with Dad and Marie at their lovely California home. I never felt she was self-centered; if you had a problem she always had time to stop and listen, no matter what she was doing at the time. She could be outrageous at times, and at the same time very fragile, very down-to-earth."

With no motion pictures scheduled, Marie took to the road for personal appearances, starting at the Golden Gate Theater in San Francisco and concluding at the Roxy Theatre in New York, sharing the bill with Danny Thomas. Columbia boss Harry Cohn bought *Born Yesterday* for his most important star, Rita Hayworth. Once Hayworth had defected from the studio to marry Aly Khan, Cohn began scouting for another "Billie Dawn." Some of the many tested were Marie Wilson, Jean Hagen, Jan Sterling, Cara Williams, Gloria Grahame, Barbara Hale and Marie. She always maintained Harry Cohn promised her the Broadway comedy. Marie's version of the story goes that Harry Cohn promised her the part even though she told him, "It's Judy Holliday's part and Judy should play it." Marie continued, "I turned down *One Touch of Venus* and dozens of other roles. Then Judy was signed for the picture and Columbia handed me a role in *Tell It to the Judge* to make up for losing *Born Yesterday*."

Harry Cohn cast Marie in a secondary role with Rosalind Russell in the fanciful comedy *Tell It to the Judge* (1949). Marie turns up as a key witness in a case that lawyer Robert Cummings is working on. Each time he woos back his divorced wife Rosalind Russell, Marie pops up showing lots of decolletage and throws a monkey wrench into the proceedings. She was scheduled to begin work on another Columbia comedy, *The Good Humor Man* with Jack Carson, until she battled over differences with Harry Cohn and the role went to Jean Wallace. Marie felt no greater affection for Harry Cohn than she had for Louis B. Mayer. Thereafter Marie's movie career drastically went into a slump.

Marie next struggled through *Hit Parade of 1951* (1950), one of Republic Studio's manufactured entries in the "Hit Parade" series, opposite John Carroll. He was a carefree Las Vegas gambler-singer, caught up in a banal mistaken identity story. Marie was the crooner's dissatisfied girlfriend. John Carroll was Republic chief Herbert J. Yates's answer to MGM's Clark Gable. Marie and Carroll displayed their respective musical wares on several occasions. She warbled two ballads, "You Don't Know the Other Side of Me" and "A Very Happy Character Am I," in an appropriately torchy style.

Marie had now reached an impasse in her career. In the hope that success on the stage would change the course of her fading career, Marie finally got to play in *Born Yesterday* at the El Capitan Theatre in November, 1950, in Hollywood, As the comically ignorant chorine who becomes a mistress of junk tycoon William Bendix, Marie gave a brilliant performance and proved she was a deft comedienne. Author Garson Kanin had originally written the play for Jean Arthur before Judy Holliday took over. Marie won the most favorable reviews of her career for *Born Yesterday*. *Daily Variety* reported: "Marie McDonald stepped into the Billie Dawn role with only four days' rehearsals, replacing Pamela Britton. She was hampered by leg injuries suffered the preceding night at the dress rehearsal. Despite these obstacles, she turned in a fine performance, winning attention as she punched over the Kanin dialogue." Edwin Schallert in *The Los Angeles Times* wrote: "Marie McDonald takes over the role of Billie Dawn and makes it quite her own. Miss McDonald has physical attributes that are ideal for this part of the ex-chorus girl. Her portrayal grew admirably and interestingly through the three acts, with resultant rise to genuine dramatic heights in the climax."

Marie managed a less flashy role in *Once a Thief* (1950), as the sympathetic roommate of shoplifter June Havoc. It was quite unlike anything she had yet tackled. The independently produced low-budget film was a shining example of early 1950s film noir. Said the faithful *Hollywood Reporter*: "Marie McDonald manages the most legitimate acting moments." She would be off the screen for the next seven years.

During 1951-54, Marie lost several babies prematurely and then adopted two children, Denise and Harrison. In 1954, Marie was charged with driving under the influence of drugs and hit-and-run driving. Karl was charged with felonious assault when he tried to run down two news cameramen with his car outside the courthouse. Harry Karl paid a $250 fine for reckless driving and Marie a $50 fine for a misdemeanor hit-and-run. She then had one illness after another. Karl claimed he spent a quarter million dollars trying to improve Marie's health. She told friends she was sick only when Karl was around and obtained a Nevada divorce in 1954, testifying she was allergic to him. When there was talk of a reconciliation, Marie was quoted as saying, "You can't heat up yesterday's mashed potatoes." Immediately following the divorce, however, the Karls sailed for Europe. They tried unsuccessfully to remarry in Paris, London, Tangiers, Zurich and Liechtenstein. Finally they returned to the United States and had the knot retied in Yuma, Arizona. It didn't last long. They separated again in 1955, and Marie claimed that Karl beat her when she was four months pregnant. The district attorney's office refused to issue a complaint. The brief reconciliation produced a daughter, Tina Marie, born September 12, 1956.

After another attempted reconciliation with Harry Karl, Marie figured in a kidnapping that would receive sensational publicity when she disappeared from her Encino home in January, 1957. She turned up 24 hours later about 40 miles away in Indio, when a truck driver found her wandering along the highway. During the lengthy investigations that followed, Marie said, "I was kidnapped, beaten and robbed by two men who spirited me away and then tossed me into the desert."

When found, Marie was wearing pajamas and a house coat. While missing, police found in her home the novel *The Fuzzy Pink Nightgown*, which described a pair of abductors who kidnap a movie star. It was later filmed, starring Jane Russell as the "kidnapped" star. The Los Angeles police chief called attention to striking similarities between the book and Marie's lurid accusations, but said it didn't prove anything.

A kidnap note found in Marie's mail box was made of words clipped from newspapers. Both newspapers were found in her fireplace. However, a physician at Coachella Valley Hospital said that "two teeth were broken apparently from a punch in the face." There was another bruise high on the left cheek. She also had a black eye. A grand jury ultimately listened to Marie's emotional testimony but declined to act, and the case gradually evaporated from lack of evidence. A year later, Marie charged that Karl had hired the kidnappers. He denied it and passed a lie detector test. Disturbed and distraught, Marie admitted months later that she had made up the story because Karl had been suing her for divorce, and she was angry with him. In March, 1958, after years of stormy domestic battles, Marie was sued for divorce by Harry Karl, claiming "irreconcilable differences." Marie was awarded over a million dollar settlement.

She had an effective role in a Jerry Lewis comedy, Paramount's *The Geisha Boy* (1958). Lewis is an inept out-of-work magician who tries to entertain the troops in Japan and Korea. Marie plays a temperamental movie star on tour of the Far East, whose dignity is upset by madcap Lewis. In 1958, Marie returned as the star headliner at Frank Sennes' Moulin Rouge (the renamed Earl Carroll's Theater-Restaurant) where she had last paraded as a showgirl. It was a triumphant return to the club she was once fired from. Marie was enthusiastic. The reviews were excellent. Despite the split with Marie, Harry Karl attended the opening with his mother, who remained very friendly with her ex-daughter-in-law. Karl overwhelmed Marie with eleven baskets of red roses at the close of her cabaret act, plus a $10,000 mink coat and a Cartier watch as a dressing room surprise. "It's the happiest night of my life," she said.

As a result of the publicity generated by her kidnapping escapade and front page emotional troubles, she was in demand on the nitery circuit, going through a series of engagements during 1958-59. But Marie continued to be plagued with bizarre occurrences during the tour. In Las Vegas, while appearing at the Desert Inn Hotel, she underwent treatment for an accidental overdose of sleeping pills. "But really it was an accident. I reached for an aspirin and took six sleeping pills by mistake," Marie said, reported *Celebrity Register.* She filed a law suit against San Francisco's Fairmont Hotel for damages from a fall from the Venetian Room stage; she was treated in a Sydney, Australia, psychiatric clinic while on a concert tour; and was convicted for forging two prescriptions to obtain the painkiller, Percodan.

For RCA Records, Marie recorded an album, "The Body Sings," which sold modestly. There were whirlwind involvements that ended in marriage to William Morris agent Louis Bass (1959-60) and to Edward Callahan (1962-63), a Los Angeles lawyer and banker. Marie was frequently seen at nightclubs and parties in the company of British actor Michael Wilding. Their affair continued until Wilding had to leave for London to replace John Gielgud in Noel Coward's play *Nude With a Violin.*

"It was hell for me," Marie told Sheilah Graham, "but I made him go back to England. They've been begging him for years to come back to the London stage, but what could he do? He was married to Elizabeth Taylor and wouldn't leave her or the children. He has tremendous loyalty and he wouldn't have left me either if I hadn't made him go. Michael asked me to marry him. If I marry anyone, it will be Michael." Marie seriously considered marrying the sophisticated and witty actor, but eventually realized it would never work.

Marie was now in her early forties, an age when most glamour girls faced the prospect of diminishing offers. She was content to stay in retirement until she replaced Mamie Van Doren in the dismal *Promises, Promises* (1963), with Jayne Mansfield and Tommy Noonan. It was one of Noonan's sex-propelled contrivances and an early venture into the nude genre featuring semi big names. In this, Marie's last film, she was the wife of Mickey Hargitay and sang "Fairy Tales," looking somewhat haggard. The emotional binges over the years had taken their toll on her looks. Raymond Strait would report on-set squabbles between Marie and Jayne Mansfield in his *The Tragic Secret Life of Jayne Mansfield*: "Marie McDonald was demanding special concessions and getting them, Jayne was told. Marie was dating Don Taylor, the co-producer, and somehow it was planted in Jayne's fertile mind that Marie was upstaging her. 'She wouldn't rate that treatment if she wasn't balling the producer,' Jayne told me [Strait] during lunch on the set one day. Marie added her own particular brand of spice to the off-camera activity with cutting remarks about Debbie Reynolds who had recently married Marie's former husband, Harry Karl." Because American audiences in 1963 still hadn't been exposed to nudity on the screen, the wan comedy was banned in many states. It was tasteless and consistently unamusing as the two female stars mugged outrageously. Life was closing in on Marie—and so was death.

She was fiercely trying to rid herself of taking too many prescription pills, which caused numerous mood swings. She was also suffering from acute insomnia. In 1964, Marie's heart stopped beating for a while on the operating table for ulcer surgery in a Florida hospital. On October 21, 1965, her sixth husband, Donald F. Taylor, who produced *Promises, Promises,* found her dead at her dressing table in their Calabasas Hidden Hills ranch home in the San Fernando Valley. Friends said that despite changes in Marie's personality, she was "more relaxed and seemed happier than she'd been in years." They found no notes. On the day Marie was found dead, she had been enthusiastic and was negotiating to merchandise a chain of cosmetics and jewelry. Marie's death was tragically unexpected, although she had recently spent two weeks in Cedars of Lebanon Hospital, under an assumed name, where she underwent yet another intestinal operation. Marie's three grieving children, Denise, Harrison and Tina Marie, went to live with their father Harry Karl and his fourth wife, Debbie Reynolds. The children, now grown, have remained maternally close to Reynolds.

Marie's husband, Donald Taylor, scoffed at the possibility of suicide. "She was very happy," he told the press. "Marie finally had a firm grasp on her life, and knew what she wanted to do." The staggering blow of Marie's tragic death became too much for him. Taylor never stopped grieving over her death. In January, 1966, at the age of 47, the broken widower, shocked and in agonizing pain, took his own life with an overdose of pills. Harry Karl, divorced from Debbie Reynolds* in 1973, would die in August, 1982, following open heart surgery at 68. Debbie Reynolds later commented about her 13-year marriage, "He was able to confuse my entire life by losing all my money and his. He just didn't run his business well and he made bad investments and gambled . . . a lot of things. It took me eleven years to get out of debt."

Marie McDonald, with all her theatrical flash, could never distinguish fame from notoriety. She was always a pleasure to watch and to know, whether she was playing Movie Star for her public or just being her dizzy, beautiful, erratic self. "I'm happy with who I am. I'm myself—Marie McDonald."

GIA SCALA

Stardom is often found by those who, unable to face reality, enter into the make-believe world of motion pictures. In the case of Gia Scala this unreal world turned into a nightmare in which the star compulsively drove herself toward self-destruction. Gia was a girl filled with paradoxes. Many found her to be shy, reserved and often uncommunicative. But an uncommon combination of gentleness and mischievousness lay within her. The gentleness would always be a part of her personality, although in the last lonely years of her life, her mischievous nature would increase. It manifested in the form of rebellion from the sad loss of her young mother, a broken marriage, and her unfulfilled desire to have a child. "It's awful to be alone and not to be able to think for somebody," she said. "You must do things for somebody to be happier." Gia Scala never really had a chance.

Gia was born Giovanna Scoglio on March 3, 1934, in Liverpool, England, to Baron Pietro and Eileen Sullivan Scoglio. The aristocratic Italian family moved to the large seaport city of Messina, Sicily, when Gia was only three months old. Her father, a Sicilian import-export businessman, met and fell in love with his Irish wife in Liverpool, where she operated an art gallery. They lived in a villa near the beach. For many, many years the Scoglios lavished all their attention upon their only child, Gia. Then the close-knit family union of Gia and her parents were to have an addition. Sister Tina was to complete this giving and loving family.

Gia was an incredibly sensitive child. Years later she would say whenever she was frightened and would cry, her mother would soothe her with the promise, "Don't cry, Gia, tomorrow I'll take you to America." As Giovanna grew older in Messina, the bells chiming by one of the world's largest astronomical clocks in the ancient Duomo, her thoughts would turn to the United States. It was decided eventually that Gia's further education was to be continued in New York. So it was a natural arrangement for her to join Mr. Scoglio's sister, Agata Scoglio Pulise, and her husband Angelo in Long Island, New York.

"I knew I had to leave Italy when I was 14," Gia told an interviewer for *The Los Angeles Times*: "Otherwise, I would have married at 18 and settled down to being a housewife. I knew over here there would be opportunity and excitement," she added, "but I almost didn't make it. I came to the United States by way of Halifax, where immigration officials weren't going to let me get off the ship because I was using an Italian passport. I argued that while I was using an Italian passport, I was traveling to the United States under a British quota number. Anyway, in all the confusion, they let me in."

Tall for her age (5'8"), self-conscious Gia always had dramatic ambitions in the back of her mind. For the next three years, she studied drama while attending Bayside (Queens) High School. Gia spoke adequate English and had no trouble with her classes. Upon graduation in 1952, Gia had a brief fling as a file clerk for an insurance company, then set out to conquer Manhattan and the magical world of acting to which she knew she belonged. Her mother came from Europe to stay with her. In later years, she often remarked that those early years (1952-54) in New York had been the happiest of her life. They took an apartment on East 55th Street. Gia worked as a reservations clerk for Scandinavian Airlines during the day and studied with Stella Adler and the Actors Studio at night.

Gia's one serious romance in New York was with an ex-Marine, Steve McQueen. They met in class at the Actors Studio and were soon observed holding hands in class. Steve was handsome, brimful of personality, and exuded charm and an exuberance Gia found hard to withstand. Gia's mother, alas, disapproved of the relationship and worried that the couple were getting serious. Reportedly, Steve McQueen wanted to marry Gia. Her mother grew more and more concerned that they might elope. When McQueen snared a summer stock tour opposite Margaret O'Brien in *Peg O' My Heart*, he proposed marriage to Gia, but, confused and not wishing to make her mother unhappy, she declined. Two years after the couple split, McQueen replaced Ben Gazzara on Broadway in *A Hatful of Rain* and met dancer Neile Adams, then appearing in *Pajama Game*. They married in November, 1956. Gia confided to her sister Tina, "I almost married Steve McQueen, I was so desperately in love with him, but somehow I felt we had no future."

It was during this time Gia and her mother agreed she should shorten her name to be more euphonious and look better on a marquee. So, her nickname "Gia" became her first name, and a distant relative on her father's side, who had the easy-to-pronounce-and-remember name of Scala, provided the second name. Gia briefly worked in the office of society columnist Cholly Knickerbocker, the pen name of Igor Cassini.

Gia became a professional "quiz kid." "It was all accidental, how I started my television career," Gia told *Photoplay* magazine. "I was sitting in the audience on the Arlene Francis show, and she was interviewing me about fashions and Italian clothes. I first won a waffle-iron. Then I went on to "Name That Tune," "Stop the Music," and other television shows. I won $350 one night, then $450 and $250 another time, sometimes it was a bad night."

On one such program, Gia was seen by an agent aware of the global talent search in progress by Universal-International. For four months the studio had searched for likely candidates for the role of Mary Magdalene in *The Galileans*, which in the end was never produced. The agent notified Maurice Bergman, a New York talent executive for U-I.

Bergman was impressed and chose Gia (although she was now residing in New York) to represent Italy; Nicole Maurey of France and Miriam Verbeek of Belgium were also to go to Hollywood for screen tests. When the contest had served its exploitation purpose, the contestants were sent their separate ways. Nicole had already appeared with Bing Crosby in *Little Boy Lost* and later would make *The Bold and the Brave* and *Secret of the Incas*. Miriam returned to her job as a model in her native Belgium. And Gia Scala was placed under contract to Universal-International in the winter of 1954.

Gia sent for her mother and they took an apartment, just a seven-minute walk from the studio. "We had just one room when I started. No furniture of our own. No nothing," Gia said later. "It was a small cubbyhole of an apartment near Universal." Her mother adjusted to Hollywood. "She liked it for my sake. She never did really feel at home here. I think it's hard for people who just live here to feel at home. There is no life really. You're looking for parts, or trying to get a good part instead of a wrong one." She didn't have an automobile so walking both ways was part of her exercise program. Under the studio's aegis, she was getting language instruction (her Italian accent was still heavy, stemming from her innate shyness) and dance and dramatic coaching. Gia always had difficulty meeting people for the first time.

Some of her Universal classmates found her to be "remote and uncommunicative." Betty Jane Howarth (Jane Howard) was also under contract to Universal and befriended Gia. "I remember her as a complex girl who didn't have many friends. She was hard to get to know, but if she liked you, you were a friend for life." Years later, when Betty Jane was hospitalized over the break-up of her long-time affair with comedian Jimmy Durante, it was Gia who visited the hospital, sent flowers and offered encouragement. "I'll never forget what she did for me," says Betty Jane Howarth.

Gia's first two assignments were inauspicious; she appeared in two Rock Hudson vehicles, as the alluring daughter of Mediterranean fisherman Nestor Paiva in *All That Heaven Allows* (1955), and as the showgirl who shares a dressing-room with co-star Cornell Borchers in *Never Say Goodbye* (1956). The latter film was based on Luigi Pirandello's play, *Come Prima, Meglio Di Prima*, and was a updated remake of *This Love of Ours*, which had starred Merle Oberon and Charles Korvin in 1945.

In her first featured role, Gia turned up fourth-billed, as the daughter of a hit-and-run victim killed by Merle Oberon in *Price of Fear* (1956). The studio heads now deemed their Italian discovery was destined for a bright future. *Four Girls in Town* (1956) was an absorbing account of four contrasting would-be stars coming to Hollywood seeking the feminine lead in *The Story of Esther*. It starred Julie Adams, Marianne Cook, Elsa Martinelli and Gia as the four girls. The finish finds none getting the part when the original star, Helene Stanton, changes her mind. Gia's character was based loosely on her own emergence as an actress. The reviews singled her out as a talent worth watching.

Gia next went on loan-out to United Artists, for *The Big Boodle* (1957). Gia and Rossana Rory battled over gambler Errol Flynn's faded charms in this travelogue of pre-Castro Havana, filmed among that city's seedy nightclubs and gambling dens. Gia later admitted that she "had such a crush on Errol Flynn while growing up in Italy and was shocked at how tired and dispirited he'd become. Errol drank the whole time we were in Havana. A very unhappy and lonely man."

In October, 1956, Columbia Studios and Metro-Goldwyn-Mayer, realizing the immensity of Gia's potential, negotiated with Universal to buy up most of Gia's contract. For the next few years, she would alternate almost exclusively between the two studios.

The Garment Jungle (1957), her first Columbia film, was directed by Warner Brother veteran Vincent Sherman. The disquieting and intense story contains one of Gia's most affecting performances as labor organizer Kerwin Mathews' love interest. Together they help fight racketeers, preying on his father Lee J. Cobb's clothing factory. It was based on a series of articles by Lester Velie.

Under Richard Thorpe's heavy-handed direction, Gia moved over to Metro-Goldwyn-Mayer for *Tip on a Dead Jockey* (1957), which was based on an Irwin Shaw story in *The New Yorker*. The reviewers were puzzled by this Robert Taylor and Dorothy Malone triangle set in Madrid, but filmed on the backlot of MGM. Taylor gets involved with a narcotics smuggling ring that includes Gia and her husband, Jack Lord. *Tip on a Dead Jockey* lumbers along painfully.

Gia had become friendly with director Charles Walters on the Metro-Goldwyn-Mayer lot. When Glenn Ford and Anna Kashfi clashed at the start of *Don't Go Near the Water* (1957), Waters requested that Gia replace Kashfi. Although the new prospects seemed bright, the climate between Glenn Ford and Gia wasn't much better. The film was based on William Brinkley's spoof on navy public relations in the South Pacific. Observed *Variety*: "Ford and Gia Scala, an exotic looker on hand as the European-schoolteacher daughter of a local citizen, team up nicely to the inevitable happy conclusion."

In the days of "studio arranged dates," Gia was seen publicly at premieres and parties in the company of George Nader, Russ Tamblyn, Grant Williams, Earl Holliman and Floyd Simmons. Her career was now in full bloom, with critics comparing her to a young Ingrid Bergman, projecting the same spiritual spark. During the filming of *Don't Go Near the Water*, Gia's mother had developed a bad, irritating cough that wouldn't go away. A concerned Gia persuaded her to have a routine checkup, and X-rays were taken.

Gia had to leave for New York and an appearance on "The Steve Allen Show," to air "live" on NBC-TV on Mother's Day, promoting *The Garment Jungle*. A nationwide television audience saw her walk out on the stage, blink up at the studio lights and nod incoherently to Allen's first questions. Allen put his arm around her to steady her and she then began to cry. Newspaper accounts of what happened said Gia apparently suffered from "mike fright." She later related to *Photoplay*, "I don't know what happened. I was terribly worried. I'd kept trying to call my mother all day, with no answer. And that day," Gia added slowly, "Mother was found by a friend, lying on the floor, and in great pain."

Gia returned from New York to begin filming *Ride a Crooked Trail* (1958), a conventional Audie Murphy sagebrusher for Universal. Following a battery of tests, her mother underwent lung surgery at the Hollywood Presbyterian Hospital. The doctor was faced with the sad task of telling Gia that her mother's cancer was inoperable. Knowing how close she and her mother were, the doctor invited Gia to meet him at the Los Feliz Brown Derby, a short distance from the hospital. That night Gia had to accept the fact that her mother had only three months to live. The next morning, Gia was to make the first of many heartbreaking headlines.

En route home, Gia was involved in a minor traffic accident and charged with drunk driving. The charges were later dismissed.

On completion of *Ride a Crooked Trail*, Gia took her mother for a Hawaiian holiday. "She was a very strong woman, a wonderful woman, with a great heart. But mother had really five days out of the whole trip that were any good. She was quite ill there," she wrote in *Photoplay*. Gia had always told her mother she had pneumonia. "I said that from the first." But later, she was to learn that a priest in Honolulu, believing one of her faith should know the truth, told Gia's mother what she had probably suspected all along. "But she always knew what she had in a way—and she fought until the end." Members of her family came from Europe to help Gia care for her mother, while she prepared to start a new picture at Metro-Goldwyn-Mayer. She turned down several offers that would have taken her away from her mother. When her mother died after lapsing into a coma, Gia said, "My mother helped me so much. In a sense she was me."

Gia Scala was never to recover from her mother's death. Since her mother had been Gia's anchor throughout her life, the tragedy tore into her. For Gia it was the beginning of the end.

She should have passed up Metro-Goldwyn-Mayer's *Tunnel of Love* (1958), one of Doris Day's weakest films. Gia contributed little as an attractive young woman sent by an adoption agency to investigate Doris Day and her husband, Richard Widmark. Gene Kelly's direction did little to brighten up the tarnished material. The same year (1958), Gia became an American citizen.

Back at Columbia, she made an unpretentious programmer, *Battle of the Coral Sea* (1959) with Cliff Robertson. He's a submarine officer who is captured by the Japanese and manages to escape with the aid of Gia, a would-be Japanese agent. The supporting actors, including Teru Shimada, Rian Garrick and Tom Laughlin, struggled valiantly with the low-budget suspense thriller, but to no avail.

Gia left for Athens, Greece, for director Robert Aldrich's *The Angry Hills* (1959), based on a Leon Uris novel. This tale concerns the Greek resistance work during World War II and the various people who became involved. Gia had a strong dramatic role as the Greek mountain girl who nurses Robert Mitchum back to health and whose family sacrifices their son to save him. Mitchum later learns she's been murdered by the Nazis. Robert Aldrich and his wife, Sybil, had a strong influence on Gia and treated her like their own daughter.

After a brief rest, Gia continued to England to film an atmospheric spy yarn with Jack Hawkins in Columbia's *The Two-Headed Spy* (1959). They were a couple of British agents working inside the German lines. It had an elaborate climax with an exciting chase sequence. Gia began suffering severe bouts of depression and was becoming increasingly distraught. In the middle of production, Gia threw herself over Waterloo Bridge and tried to drown in the Thames. She was pulled to safety by a passing cab driver. It was particularly reminiscent of the memorable Vivien Leigh sequence in the classic film *Waterloo Bridge*. After a brief stay in a hospital she was released. Gia scoffed at hints that the suicide attempt was a publicity stunt. "It's something I'd like to forget," she said. "People will think what they want." Unable to come to terms with her traumatic life, Gia began to seek refuge more frequently in alcohol.

Immediately upon Gia's return to Hollywood, she resumed her relationship with actor Don Burnett. They had been romantically linked together for two years. On August 21, 1959, Gia married Don Burnett. He was the young star of the MGM-Television series, "Northwest Passage" co-starring Buddy Ebsen and Keith Larsen. Former actor and agent John Darrow and Sybil Aldrich acted as witnesses in a simple wedding ceremony, attended by a few friends of the bride and groom. The couple met three years before on the set of *Don't Go Near the Water*. They moved into his home in Malibu Beach on the Pacific Coast for a brief time, then bought a beautiful Cape Cod style home at 7944 Woodrow Wilson Drive in the Hollywood Hills. Gia and Don spent a great deal of time with his ex-neighbor Rock Hudson in Newport Beach, about 65 miles down the coast from Los Angeles. There on Hudson's 40-foot ketch *Khairuzan* (Arabic for good luck), Gia and Don relaxed on weekends, sailing to Catalina Island with friends Claire Trevor and her husband, Milton Bren, Marilyn Maxwell and publicists Lynn Bowers and Pat Fitzgerald.

Gia was directed by J. Lee Thompson in *I Aim at the Stars* (1960), a fictional history of Nazi missile scientist Wernher Von Braun (Curt Jurgens), adjusting to life in the United States after his close association with the Nazis during World War II. It was filmed in Germany. Jurgens was masterful in the lead role. Although being directed by her good friend Thompson, Gia's scenes were too few and resulted in an unfortunate waste of her talent. Gia realized she needed to be in a hit film. "It has nothing to do with your work at all," she said. "You can be ter-

rible, but it doesn't matter if the film is a hit." Her farewell to
her home studio, *The Guns of Navarone* (1961), was one of Columbia's all-time record grossers up until that time. Gia's vivid,
fascinating role of Anna, the Greek resistance fighter, would be
the apex of her floundering career. As a torture victim of the
Germans and mute as the result, she was in high company
with Gregory Peck, David Niven, Anthony Quinn and Irene
Papas. They were on location on the Island of Rhodes in Greece
for several months.

It seems incredible that Gia's performance in *The Guns of
Navarone* failed to gain her even so much as a nomination for a
supporting Academy Award. The Carl Foreman film holds together quite well now despite a few flaws. A wax figure of Gia
and Gregory Peck from her crucial scene in the film is recreated
at the Movieland Wax Museum in Buena Park, California. Gia's
impeccable work in the film is reminiscent to many of Ingrid
Bergman's Maria in *For Whom the Bell Tolls*.

In 1962, Gia and Don journeyed to Czechoslovakia to film
Triumph of Robin Hood (1962), the adventure tale for children of
all ages. The amateurishly directed adventure yarn left much to
be desired. In Italy, Don Burnett co-starred with Guy Williams
in Metro-Goldwyn-Mayer's *Damon and Pythias*. Gia was originally set for the role of Nerissa, but was replaced by Ilaria
Occhini. It was directed by Curtis Bernhardt, then in the twilight years of his film career.

Gia soon limited her professional activities to an occasional
television role, such as three CBS-TV "Alfred Hitchcock Theatre" episodes, "Mother, May I Go Out to Swim," "Deathmate"
and "A Sign of Satan"; "Hong Kong", and "The Islanders,"
On "G.E. Theatre," Gia co-starred with Ray Milland in "A
London Affair," about a woman who tries to steal a wallet. In
1966, Gia was offered a film in Madrid, Spain, opposite Rory
Calhoun in *Operation Delilah* (1966). The picture was not put
into general theatre release in the United States, but reportedly
was later sold direct to cable television.

Thereafter, she busied herself by decorating her home and
painting, and became so skilled at playing tennis that she entered several amateur tournaments. "I'd rather act from the
neck up," Gia said. "I feel very sorry for those who try to get by
on beauty only because when the beauty is gone, what will

they have left to build a career upon?" She and Don wanted children. Gia once remarked, "All I ever wanted was to get married and have babies." Her sister, actress Tina Scala, remembers a special trip back home to Messina, Italy, to consult with their cousin, Dr. Peter Scoglio, the noted Italian gynecologist. Here was a woman who wanted children terribly, but Gia's quest to have a baby proved unavailing.

In September, 1970, after several separations and reconciliations, Gia and Burnett were divorced. She was awarded $103,800 in alimony, payable over a ten-year period, and the Hollywood Hills home. The divorce was granted on the standard grounds of "incompatibility." The following year, Burnett obtained a court order restraining Gia from "molesting, striking and harassing him." Her drinking scenes were becoming terrifying nightmares during those years after the divorce.

In a *Hollywood Studio Magazine* interview, Tina Scala told writer Gloria Davis: "Actually, Gia became obsessed with thinking about her ex-husband so much that she wrote unmailed poems about him." Seriously, she went on to say, "Gia thought perhaps some traveling and a change of scene would help to alter her viewpoint and give her a more positive outlook on life. Reminders of her broken marriage to Don Burnett were everywhere in the house. So, she leased her house to Sally Kellerman and traveled through Italy and France visiting relatives and friends. In Paris, she stayed at her good friend Henry Miller's apartment, located in a select part of the city. During her visit, she attended the Cordon Bleu Cooking School and went to art classes. Her friendship with Miller had started several years earlier when he was a nearby neighbor of hers in Hollywood." An oil painting that Miller once did of Gia holds a place of honor in Tina's living room.

When Gia decided to return to California, she settled into the Sunset Marquis Hotel-Apartments until she could move back into her own home, when the lease to actress Sally Kellerman expired.

Then, on April 20, 1971, Gia accompanied by 21-year-old Larry Langston, was arrested over a dispute with a downtown Los Angeles parking lot attendant. She had refused to pay an additional fifty cents overtime charge and an ensuing fist fight between the three occurred. Passersby alerted the police and the arrest of Gia and her companion resulted. Both pleaded "no contest" to the charge and were given two years probation. Again, Gia was to receive another barrage of unflattering press. Depressed over the last escapade, she continued to slide downhill at an alarming pace.

On May 19th, Gia was ordered to undergo psychiatric observation at a hospital in Ventura County, shortly after she had reportedly collapsed in a courtroom in Ventura, where she had been charged with driving while intoxicated. Anna Kashfi, whom Gia had succeeded in *Don't Go Near the Water* some five years earlier, visited the hospital, known for patients with nervous disorders, and had Gia released in her custody. For two months, Gia stayed with Anna and her son by Marlon Brando, Devi, in a tiny West Hollywood apartment. But it wasn't all rest and recuperation within the Kashfi household. Following endless squabbles, Gia moved out.

A Los Angeles probation officer who investigated Gia's case history reported to the judge that she was suicide-prone. A few months earlier, Gia had taken roach poison and "came so close to death that she was given the last rites of the Catholic Church." The officer also stated, "Her nature appears to have been bizarre for quite some time. However, when her ex-husband recently remarried, she began to drink heavily." It was a tremendous blow to Gia when Don Burnett, now a successful stock broker, married wealthy Barbara Anderson. As police woman Eve Whitfield, his new bride appeared on the NBC-Teleseries, "Ironside" (1971-1975) with Raymond Burr as the wheelchair detective.

Gia was only 37, but looked ten years older. The once magnificent Ingrid Bergman-like looks that had helped forge her screen persona had weathered. In July, 1971, Gia was injured when her sports car overturned on a winding canyon road. In the harrowing accident, she lost part of an index finger and received multiple bruises, cuts and a neck injury. Weakened, she seemed unable to put the pieces of her life back together, as she had in the past.

Gia, finally ensconced back in her house, and with Tina Scala living nearby, would often meet her for lunch and a game of tennis. "But the time together would usually end with me getting angry because Gia would start in on her marriage to Don breaking up and it made her too distraught to think of anything else," Tina said. "Her general change of behavior upset me no end. I just couldn't understand this change of personality, she wasn't herself. She seemed to have no control over her emotions."

Metro-Goldwyn-Mayer publicist Dore Freeman was a dominant influence in Gia's exasperating life. Freeman is well-known as the world's largest collector of Joan Crawford photographs and memorabilia. With Gia's health revived, platonic friend Freeman would escort her to industry functions, one of the last being the grand opening night ceremonies of the restored Robert Aldrich Studios. She was a frequent guest at intimate dinner parties with Freeman in the West Hollywood community. Actor Robert Cotney remembers the Gia of this time as "being very positive with varied interests, seemingly renewed with a new lease on life." With sincere intentions, Gia began taking medication to stop drinking and signed with new management to govern her career. But despite all this, the handwriting was on the wall.

In an unexplainable turn of events, Gia Scala was to make headlines for the last time. On April 30, 1972, paramedics were called to her Hollywood Hills home by Larry Langston. There, in her bedroom on the second level, was the dead body of Gia Scala. Langston and some assorted "friends" had last seen her alive at 6 a.m. when she came downstairs for a few minutes and then returned to her bedroom. They claimed Gia had been drinking and taking pills to try to sleep. When the group returned around 8 p.m., they found the actress unconscious. Several bottles of medication and empty liquor bottles were found about the cluttered bedroom. There was no evidence of foul play. The police listed her death as a "possible accidental liquor and drug overdose." It was well-known amongst her friends that Gia had been despondent over her divorce from Burnett, misdemeanor charges and other profound hurts.

The recitation of the rosary and a requiem mass were held at the small St. Victor's Chapel. It was a sad and simple service. Dore Freeman held on to a stunned Tina Scala, and other members of Gia's family sat paralyzed with grief. Friends, many from Universal, sobbed quietly, among them Elaine Stewart, Betty Jane Howarth, Tina Louise, Norma Eberhardt, Guy

Williams, and Robert and Sybil Aldrich. They came to say their final goodbye. The man Gia so dearly loved, Don Burnett, with his parents, went conspicuously unnoticed in the last row and fled before photographers knew he was even in attendance. Gia is buried with her mother at the Holy Cross Cemetery.

Dr. Thomas Noguchi personally called Tina Scala to inform her of the autopsy report which uncovered the fact that Gia had early stages of arteriosclerosis. This resulted in her brain getting hardly any oxygen, which is a rare occurrence when it happens to anyone that young. In retrospect, these findings would explain her emotionally unbalanced behavior and turmoil of mind the last two years of her life. Gia's traumatic personality change was not that of an "identity crisis," which many of her close friends believed, but of medically substantial conclusions over which Gia really had no control.

Gia Scala was gifted, vulnerable and scarred far too brutally in the Hollywood jungle. "The saddest thing is that there were still many things Gia wanted to accomplish but never got the chance," said Tina Scala. In paying homage to her sister, Tina founded the Gia Scala Repertory Company in Santa Monica.

JAYNE MANSFIELD

Jayne Mansfield with her glistening platinum blond hair and spectacular figure, was endowed with an I.Q. of 163 plus an insatiable lust for publicity. Her frustration stemmed from an inability to establish herself as anything more than a voluptuous sex-symbol. For three fleeting years, she reigned as the next golden symbol to compete for the unattainable heights of Marilyn Monroe. The Mansfield fantasy was quickly cemented into place, carried on by her private life, the wild extravagances of the posh Pink Palace mansion and the publicity stunts which became obvious and in bad taste. In the final years, the pathetic figure of Jayne became the target of much adverse criticism. There appeared to be a shadow hovering over her spirit like a premonition of the eventual tragic occurrence. Although her career had collapsed into little more than self-parody, Jayne Mansfield still had the intelligence to avoid the suicidal syndrome of some of her contemporaries. But fate intervened, creating a more hideous demise.

Vera Jayne Palmer was born on April 19, 1933, in Bryn Mawr, Pennsylvania, on the Philadelphia "main line." Her father, lawyer Herbert Palmer, died of a heart attack when Jayne was three. Jayne told columnist May Mann: "My father wanted a son to carry on the family name and tradition, because Daddy always said he was going to be President some day. He was brilliant and he had that kind of determination and strength. I have inherited this determination and drive from him." Her mother, Vera Jeffrey Palmer, an elementary school teacher, returned to teaching and put the child in the care of a housekeeper friend, Sally Rice. In 1939, Vera married Harry "Tex" Peers, a sales manager who moved the family from Phillipsburg, Pennsylvania to Dallas, Texas.

Jayne attended University Park Grammar School and was considered a violin prodigy and also played the viola, piano, and bass fiddle. Like many a stagestruck child, Jayne took dancing classes from the Louise Finley Studios. Her school chum Barbara Keeling was president of the Dale Evans Fan Club; Jayne became a member and joined other fan clubs. She became fascinated with the idea of being a movie star and even after reaching star status at 20th Century-Fox, never lost her starry-eyed feeling about Hollywood. Jayne read movie magazines and covered her bedroom wall with photos of Hedy Lamarr, Gene Tierney and Johnny Weismuller. She soon had other interests. "I suddenly changed when I became twelve. I changed overnight from the skinny little girl to one with curves popping out all over," Jayne remembered later.

At Highland Park High, Jayne became friendly with Ann Wedgeworth, who also wanted to become an actress. Ann would go on to win a Tony Award for her work in *Chapter Two* on Broadway. In Martha Saxton's *Jayne Mansfield and the American*, Ann commented that, "She was very friendly. Jayne was very sweet and we neither of us had a lot of friends. It was a very cliquey school. Jaynie was very goodhearted." In 1949, Jayne met Paul Mansfield, who attended nearby Sunset High School in Oak Cliff. A cheerleader and president of his class, he sang and was a member of "The Sunset Quartet." They fell in love and were secretly married on January 28, 1950, by a Baptist minister in Fort Worth, Texas. Jayne and Paul made elaborate plans to keep their marriage a secret. She was concerned what the Peers would say, and she wanted to graduate from Highland Park High that June. The newlyweds rented a small place, but Jayne continued to live with her parents. When she became pregnant a few months later, she told her mother and stepfather. They decided to have a second ceremony on May 10, 1950, and Jayne Marie was born on November 8th. While Paul attended the University of Texas in Austin, Jayne took a job behind the front desk at Gregg Scott's Dance Studio. She also joined the Austin Civic Theatre and made her first stage appearance in *Ten Nights in a Bar-Room* at the Playhouse.

When Paul was recalled to active reserve duty to an Army camp at Augusta, Georgia, Jayne saw her opportunity to leave for California and the UCLA campus. Mrs. Peers took care of little Jayne Marie. While attending school at UCLA, she kept her marriage and child a secret, and entered the "Miss California" contest. "I realized this was an opportunity, so I agreed. I was so excited when I was chosen in the local final twenty. I made the mistake of telling Paul, and he demanded that I either drop out or else! So I had to resign. I never knew whether I would have won or not," she said. After one semester, Jayne reluctantly returned to Dallas and family life.

In 1951, with the Korean War on, Paul was called to active duty as a second lieutenant in the army and stationed at Camp Gordon, Georgia, for a year. It was at the Army post that Jayne next appeared on the stage, in *Anything Goes*. When Paul was shipped to Korea, she returned to Dallas and enrolled at Southern Methodist University, where she was able to take her infant child along to classes. Ann Wedgeworth would also tell Martha Saxton that at SMU, Jayne had dyed her hair black. "It looked great on her," Ann went on. "She had always wanted to be a movie star. But then she had a lot more confidence in herself. She had really gotten into the idea of going to Hollywood." During 1952-53, Jayne studied chemistry, abnormal psychology and drama. She went from door to door selling baby picture albums and joined the Baruch Lumet (Sidney's father) classes at the Dallas Institute of the Performing Arts. Her first stage appearance for Lumet was in *Death of a Salesman*, on October 22, 1953. She had a number of small parts on a local television station and was crowned "Miss Photoflash of 1952."

In April, 1954, Paul Mansfield returned from Korea and they soon took off in a red used Buick convertible with Jayne Marie and a menagerie of pets, referred to as "Noah's Ark," and headed for Hollywood and the big dream. "When Paul came back I was already packed to go before he even set foot in the house," Jayne said. "He thought I might have changed my mind about Hollywood by then. But he was stuck with his promises." In North Hollywood, they found an apartment at Fulton and Van Nuys Boulevard. Paul got a job with a small East Lost Angeles newspaper and Jayne found a job at the Wilshire Wiltern Theatre, selling popcorn and candy. Later, Jayne worked as a photographer's assistant at Esther Williams and Ben Gage's restaurant, The Trails.

With determination and a blunt manner, Jayne phoned Paramount Studios and asked for Milton Lewis, head of new talent. "This is Jayne Mansfield," she said. "I have won several beauty contests and I have studied drama and I want to be a movie star. I thought I might as well give Paramount first right of refusal!" Unbelievably, Mr. Lewis' secretary set up an appointment. Jayne did a scene from *St. Joan*. Lewis recalled, "That pretty kid from Texas." When Lewis viewed the audition, he said, "With your looks you should be doing comedy." He gave her a test scene from George Axelrod's *The Seven Year Itch*. Paramount was enthusiastic and first offered $75 a week, and then, for some unknown reason, the deal fell through. Jayne would never work for Paramount. She signed up with Marilyn Monroe's first modeling agent, Emmeline Snively of the Blue Book Model Agency, who sent her to Gene Lester, the photographer for the Earl Carroll Girls. Her first job was for General Electric with several other models around a swimming pool.

She acquired an agent, Robert Schwartz, who took one look and said, "Okay. Let's do the hair blond." There was a test at Warner Brothers, but they didn't bite. Jayne finally got on television on the live "Lux Video Theatre" in October, 1954. "I received $300 for sitting at a piano and speaking ten lines of dialogue in "An Angel Went AWOL," she said. It took care of two car payments for her new shocking pink Jaguar. The next month Jayne made her film debut, opposite Lawrence Tierney and John Carradine in *Female Jungle* (1956), a low-budget thriller. Jayne would remember, "It was a quick picture, made in ten days. But I loved every minute of it, even when I had to lay on the hot sidewalk playing my own dead body. The budget didn't allow stand-ins." The film was also released as *Hangover*. The Mansfields soon decided to separate and Paul returned to Texas. "When I married you, you had brown hair and you weighed 138 pounds. That's the way I married you, and that's the way I loved you," was Paul Mansfield's philosophy.

The week before Christmas, 1954, Jayne met James Byron, who was a press agent for Marilyn Maxwell, Terry Moore and Linda Darnell. It was Byron who started Jayne on her never ending publicity treadmill. In Raymond Strait's biography, *The Tragic Secret Life of Jayne Mansfield*, Byron fondly recalled, "'Jayne had a star quality. She was very much like a raw gem.

Until it is polished it is not recognized by the untrained eye. With his highly trained eye, Jim Byron recognized what the public would buy. He knew Jayne Mansfield would sell because she was an original—the genuine article. He would see to it that her attributes were properly handled.'" Byron introduced Jayne to agent William Schiffrin and celebrity attorney Greg Bautzer.

Much has been written about circumstances surrounding how Jayne joined the *Underwater* press junket. The facts are that in January, 1955, Byron, with the help of columnist James Bacon arranged for Jayne to join RKO Studios' contingent departing for Silver Springs, Florida, on behalf of the world premiere of *Underwater*, starring Jane Russell and Richard Egan. On the plane, she sat next to Joseph Schoenfeld, then editor of *Daily Variety*. Schoenfeld and Jayne soon became fast friends. She stole the proceedings away from Jane Russell, Lori Nelson, Debbie Reynolds and Mala Powers. This Jayne did solely by means of her personal activities plus one prop—a bright red bathing suit apparently a size or two too small for her. "I wanted to be a movie star since I was three," Jayne told reporters. "They told me I'd be another Shirley Temple, but I guess I outgrew it." Photos of her in the swim suit began to cascade all around the country. In February of that year, Jayne would cause quite a stir as the centerfold in *Playboy*, helping to push publisher Hugh Hefner's circulation ahead a few notches. All the controversy resulted in a six-month Warner Brothers contract after studio executives viewed her previous test.

Jayne was hoodlum Albert Dekker's mistress in *Illegal* (1955). *The New York Times* noticed: "*Illegal* tries to blue-print *The Asphalt Jungle*'s Marilyn Monroe. . . . Jayne Mansfield plays precisely the same role." She then was a cigarette girl in producer-director's Jack Webb's *Pete Kelly's Blues* (1955) and Perry Lopez's cheap moll in *Hell on Frisco Bay* (1956). Jayne came into an inheritance around this time, from her Grandmother Palmer's estate, and bought a house on Wanda Park Drive in Benedict Canyon, high in the hills. Director Nicholas Ray tested Jayne for the ingenue lead opposite James Dean in *Rebel Without a Cause* and Warners announced Jayne would appear in Liberace's *Sincerely Yours*. When that dud finally went into production, Lori Nelson had the part. Warner Brothers decided to loan her out for an independent production, *The Burglar* (1957), to be filmed in Philadelphia. She projected the necessary aura of come-hither sex as jewel thief Dan Duryea's hard gunmoll.

Marilyn Maxwell had turned down the play *Will Success Spoil Rock Hunter?* William Schiffrin sent the script to Jayne in Philadelphia with the message, "It's lousy. I don't see how it can run more than six weeks. But you'll be great in it and it will save five years in your career." Jayne wasn't too happy about it; she wanted to be a movie star. But she had also been notified that Warner Brothers planned to terminate her contract. Other actresses, besides Marilyn Maxwell, being considered for *Will Success Spoil Rock Hunter?* were Mamie Van Doren, Sheree North and Roxanne Arlen. Jayne decided to give it a try. "They had never heard of me," said Jayne. "But there were two points in my favor. One, I was only 90 miles from New York and I could be there in a short time from Philadelphia. And, most important, I was playing the feminine lead in a picture. Also, as the icing, I had a scrapbook filled with publicity on just the kind of girl they were presumably looking for."

When producer Jule Styne and writer-director George Axelrod saw her walk into their office, they whispered to each other, "If this one can read, she's got the part." She could. And she did. The curtain rose at the Broadhurst Theater on October 12, 1955, with Jayne lying on her stomach, on a massage table, partially covered by a towel. She was sensational! Miraculously, box-office grosses continued to increase. Instead of six weeks, *Will Success Spoil Rock Hunter?* ran a year and some 452 performances. Also in the cast were Walter Matthau, Orson Bean and Tina Louise. Jayne played a satirical characterization of a Marilyn Monroe-type actress who captivates a milquetoast screenwriter. The public loved her and New York City just couldn't get enough of Jayne Mansfield. In his column, Walter Winchell wrote: "Jayne Mansfield is as beautiful as Marilyn Monroe in every department and effortlessly delivers the most devastating impression in years." She couldn't venture out without drawing mobs of enthusiastic fans and became a favorite celebrity at supermarket openings with appearances touching off cheers and applause. As the play gained increasing stature, Jayne grabbed appearances on "Person to Person," "The

Ed Sullivan Show," two television specials and the cover of *Life* as their cover story, "Broadway's Smartest Dumb Blonde."

Jayne's name was linked with director Nick Ray, Greg Bautzer, designer Oleg Cassini, pilot Robby Robertson, Richard Egan and Steve Cochran, until she met square-cut, handsome Mickey Hargitay at New York's Latin Quarter in May, 1956, while he was appearing in Mae West's unique nightclub act, which included nine muscle men and Louise Beavers. Jayne was at a ringside table with Jule Styne and his date, Ruth Dubonet. "Who's that beautiful hunk of man?" Jayne wanted to know. Following the midnight show, Mickey Hargitay joined their table. A few days later, when photographs (taken at the Cherry Blossom Festival) made the New York *Daily Mirror*, Mickey had a phone call from Mae West. "Stay off the floor," Mae warned, "and on the stage or I'll reverse your position." Hargitay was a Budapest-born body builder who emigrated from Hungary in 1947, worked in a Brooklyn fruit market and as an upholsterer before forming an adagio act and then winning the title Mr. Universe of 1955 at London's Palladium Theatre. Hargitay was ambitious, and he had an estranged wife and a young daughter in Indianapolis. Jayne, meanwhile, was living at the Gorham Hotel with Jayne Marie, a maid, and the usual complement of animals—four cats and three dogs. Mickey Hargitay soon departed Mae West's act and joined the Jayne Mansfield bandwagon.

It was Buddy Adler at 20th Century-Fox who sensed Jayne's movie potential when he and wife Anita Louise saw the play. Jayne was tested in a scene from John Steinbeck's *The Wayward Bus*, filmed at Fox's New York City headquarters on West 54th Street. Buddy Adler bought *Will Success Spoil Rock Hunter?* for $125,000 merely to get Jayne released from her contract. Jayne was to receive $2,500 a week. Fox's publicity director Harry Brand said, "Jayne Mansfield, alone, accounted for more than 450 performances of *Rock Hunter* and that's an enviable mark for any Broadway new star!"

Jayne returned to Hollywood in triumph, launched as the star of *The Girl Can't Help It* (1956), by far the best of the 1950s rock 'n' roll musicals. She was the girl-friend of retired mobster Edmond O'Brien, who is determined to turn her into a rock queen. With the help of alcoholic agent Tom Ewell, she hits the top of the charts in short order. The film features a classic sequence with Little Richard singing the title song while Jayne prances. *The New York Times'* Bosley Crowther wrote: "Her range at this stage appears restricted to a weak imitation of Marilyn Monroe. A hint to her limitations is given in the plot, which comes to the hopeless conclusion that she can do nothing more than make weird sounds." The *Los Angeles Reader* said: ". . . The cutting in a nightclub scene between Little Richard's lamentations and La Mansfield's undulations is alone worth the price of admission." It was based on a Garson Kanin story and directed by the comic genius Frank Tashlin, known for his solid craftsmanship, particularly with comedies. Director Tashlin once told Jayne, "Why do you want to be a star? It's a life of no privacy, heartaches and frustrations." She answered, "I like the minks and the Jaguars."

Then came John Steinbeck's *The Wayward Bus* (1957), with Jayne as a wistful bubble-dancer involved with traveling salesman Dan Dailey. They meet during a character-revealing journey in bad weather and near disaster. The trip also enables others (including Joan Collins and Rick Jason) to sort their priorities and make decisions. "It was said that 20th hired me as a threat to Marilyn Monroe, but when I brought up the subject everyone denied it," Jayne was quoted as saying. "Marilyn wasn't very happy about it because she thought we were the same type. But I believe Marilyn's a very talented actress and I've said so often. To the best of my knowledge, I never took, or for that matter was offered, a part Marilyn had turned down."

Jayne reprised her Broadway role of zany Rita Marlowe, opposite Tony Randall, in *Will Success Spoil Rock Hunter?* (1957), helmed again by Frank Tashlin, who kept only the title of George Axelrod's hit play for his screen adaptation. In their two features together, Mansfield responds beautifully to Tashlin's technique of double-entendre suggestiveness. The Tashlin films were not big money makers when first released but are now recognized cult classics of the 1950s. The *Los Angeles Reader* observed: "Jayne Mansfield, in an outrageously funny parody of herself (yes, it is possible), co-stars in a film about greed, lust, power, and all the other wonderful things that make life worth living." *Will Success Spoil Rock Hunter?* is very possibly the definitive Mansfield movie. When asked which of his pictures he liked best, Frank Tashlin would reply, "I'm most satisfied with *Will Success Spoil Rock Hunter?* They had to buy the play to get Mansfield. I tried to get out of using the play and then decided to reverse it and make it into something else entirely. I only kept maybe one or two speeches from the play. I wrote the script of *Rock Hunter* in 13 days."

Jayne was advised by Frank Tashlin and her agent not to take on *Kiss Them for Me* (1957), starring Cary Grant, about three Navy pilots' (Grant, Ray Walston, Larry Blyden) romantic misalliances over a four-day leave at a Nob Hill hotel in San Francisco. "Don't play second fiddle to Suzy Parker," said Tashlin. "I pointed to the fact that Suzy gets Grant in the end. But Jayne wanted to work with Cary Grant." Model Suzy Parker was the object of Grant's affections, with Jayne more animated than usual as a dumb blonde playgirl. Some reviewers found Jayne's work "more grotesque than funny." and Stanley Donen's uneven direction didn't help.

Agent William Schiffrin would later say, "Like most stars, Jayne could sometimes be difficult. One minute, you'd be ready to kill her, the next moment she was an angel. She was one of the most compassionate women I have ever known." Jayne once said, "I like to live each day as if it were the last but I also want to have the foresight to provide for the future." In January, 1958, now divorced from Paul Mansfield, Jayne married Mickey Hargitay, by whom she would have three children, Miklos, Zoltan and Mariska. The wedding was attended primarily by a small army of press at a charming glass A-frame church, the Wayfarer's Chapel in Palos Verdes Estates, overlooking Portuguese Bend and the Pacific Ocean.

In Las Vegas, the new Tropicana Hotel offered Jayne $25,000 per week for four weeks. *Variety* said, "She's a curiosity piece, something of the order of Marlene Dietrich, and as such should draw business. Basically, she's merely doing walk-ons in the show disguised as comedy bits." Included in this Monte Prosser "Tropicana Holiday" revue were Hargitay, Cathy Crosby (Bob's daughter), George Chakiris and Sean Garrison. Jayne drew standing-room-only crowds, including Sophia Loren and husband Carlo Ponti. The show was held over for three additional weeks. She subsequently worked at the Dunes Hotel with her "House of Love" act, and at the downtown Fremont Hotel as her salary and popularity declined.

Twentieth Century-Fox sent Jayne to England to play a saloon keeper in *The Sheriff of Fractured Jaw* (1959), opposite Kenneth More. She told the press, "It's fabulous. It's got cowboys and Indians and everything. It's a British western shot in Spain. I play a completely different type of girl. This girl runs the town while she runs a saloon." While in England, Jayne also filmed two potboilers, *The Challenge* (1961) with Anthony Quayle, as a brainy floozy who masterminds a robbery, and the tedious *Too Hot to Handle* (1962) with Leo Genn. In the latter, she was a hard-edged Soho stripper, employed at the Pink Flamingo Club. Jayne performed a strip number which ran into much censorship problems. *Variety* thought Jayne's "Acting tepid and, at times, ludicrous."

Every move Jayne made was calculated to attract more attention to herself. She bought a luxurious thirty-five room, three-story, Spanish-style pink mansion that once belonged to singer Rudy Vallee, located at 10100 Sunset Boulevard in Beverly Hills. Jayne and Mickey happily splashed for movie magazine layouts in the heart-shaped pool. You can still see the two-foot-high tile letters on the bottom of the pool that read: "I love you, Jaynie." Fans who were invited to visit Jayne at the Pink Mansion were shocked to find that her love for animals didn't include house-training. Mickey Hargitay was actually a mild-mannered, shy guy who liked the simple home life. The couple made colorful copy at the beginning of the turbulent 1960s.

In Italy, Jayne did her twinkling cutie act with Mickey in *The Loves of Hercules* (1960), which is shown often on television. Hercules (Hargitay) falls in love with Jayne, who's been promised to another. When his competition is murdered, Hercules is suspected. Twentieth Century-Fox loaned Jayne out again for Allied Artists' *The George Raft Story* (1961), with Ray Danton, which had very little to do with Raft's actual past. In Greece, she played an actress in 20th's *It Happened in Athens* (1962) with newcomer Trax Colton. It was an absurd tale that proved her last feature under contract to Fox and ended Colton's brief career. A small headline in the New York *Daily News*, July 4, 1962, summed up Jayne's exit from 20th: "Jayne Mansfield dropped by Fox." It was rumored that Jayne stubbornly refused to listen to friends' advice to cool her actions and offended many important 20th Century-Fox executives. In *Jayne Mansfield and the*

American Fifties, Martha Saxton wrote: "[Her agent] feels that she never understood that sex and business were separate. When one of her advisers did something successful for her, she would often offer sex as a reward."

Just prior to leaving Fox, Jayne made her "dramatic television debut" in a 20th Century-Fox segment of "Follow the Sun," entitled "The Dumbest Blonde" opposite Brian Keith and Barry Coe. She spoke in her normal speaking voice and not the breathy manner she had adopted. On "Kraft Mystery Theatre," Jayne appeared with Richard Anderson and John Ericson in "House on the Rue Riviera." Jayne totaled three Christmas trips with the Bob Hope troupe, entertaining American servicemen abroad. She talked about doing a television series with Mickey, which she described in the press as half situation comedy and half body-building. And the publicity machine continued. In Italy, she was involved in a hair-pulling fracas over an Italian producer. While attending the Mardi Gras in Rio de Janiero, Jayne was stripped to the waist by excited fans. She and Mickey were lost at sea for thirty-six hours in the Caribbean. *The Los Angeles Times* reported: "Film Star Jayne Mansfield is feared drowned off Nassau." Broken straps and falling bras became a way of life, a life she sadly loved. All the adverse publicity had been putting a terrible strain on her marriage.

Jayne slipped off to Mexico to divorce Mickey. However, Jayne found herself pregnant and too emotionally drained to go through with it. Hargitay was deeply upset at Jayne's flagrant marital infidelity. They soon reconciled, even though their marriage was a sad shambles. Soon after their daughter Mariska was born their reconciliation plans failed and they divorced.

Producer-actor Tommy Noonan hired Jayne for *Promises, Promises* (1963), an early eroticism sexploitation epic, which featured Jayne in the raw. When *Playboy* magazine asked her to pose nude again, she agreed, since she owned ten percent of the film. The best thing about *Promises, Promises* is that it had a messy eroticism that kept it watchable. Otherwise, it was humdrum. Other cast members Noonan, Marie McDonald and Mickey Hargitay worked hard but the film received few "art house" (as they were known then) bookings.

It all began falling apart for Jayne as the many widely publicized stunts appeared more in desperation than fun. There
were only film offers from Europe, and with her usual desper-
ate intensity, Jayne flew off for Italy and *Panic Button* (1964), in
which she and Maurice Chevalier filmed a Romeo and Juliet
parody for a TV pilot. In *Chevalier*, by Gene Ringgold and
DeWitt Bodeen, Maurice Chevalier was asked about working
with Jayne: "It was most enjoyable. Some smart producer
should exploit her comedy potential because she really has a
flair for *outre* humor. There's nothing phony about it either.
When we were rehearsing a dance scene where we do the
Twist—now that's a dance that's ruined people half my age—
her bra broke. She stopped to make adjustments, looked
around, and said to me, 'Things like this happen to me all the
time. And always at rehearsals—damn it.' "

Going at a tremendous speed, Jayne filmed *Homesick for St.
Paul* (1964) with a German rock star, Freddy Quinn, the
German-Italian *Dog Eat Dog* (1965), with Cameron Mitchell,
and *Primitive Love* (1965), with ex-husband Mickey Hargitay.
The latter film was a travelogue with Jayne and Mickey visiting
nightclubs, judging beauty contests and going to a massage
parlor. After her death, *The Wild, Wild World of Jayne Mansfield*
used some of the same footage. These mediocre films occasionally dip into the area of the barely watchable. Jayne's publicist
told biographer Martha Saxton, "She made a lot of pictures that
weren't successful so she got to thinking she wasn't going to
make it on talent. She tried to do it the other way. Agents lost
respect for her."

Back in the United States, Jayne toured with Mickey in *Bus
Stop* and *Gentlemen Prefer Blondes*, two renowned Marilyn
Monroe films. The cast of *Bus Stop* included Ann B. Davis,
Stephen Brooks and Elizabeth Hartman. It was directed by
Matt Cimber, who would subsequently become Jayne's third
husband in 1964. Soon after marrying Cimber, Jayne gave birth
to a third son, Antonio. Her dependency on alcohol worsened.
And then yet another front page story! Jayne, Hargitay and
Cimber staged a fight on New York's upper East Side, which
just happened to have two photographers close at hand. It was
an emotionally exhausting encounter. Jayne and Mickey battled their way through a constant tug-of-war over the custody

of their children, with Hargitay accusing Jayne of being an unfit mother and of neglecting her family for her career. "It wasn't easy for either of us," said Hargitay.

Husband Matt Cimber now took full control of Jayne's career. A proposed weekly television series, "The Jayne Mansfield Show" never happened and Cimber rejected the "Gilligan's Island" TV series, which revived Tina Louise's career. Jayne toured Canada in *Nature's Way* by Herman Wouk and hoped for a return to Broadway in *The Rabbit Habit*, but the show closed during its summer tryout. In January, 1966, audiences were still flocking to get another look at Jayne at New York's Latin Quarter. It must have held some strange memories for her, as it was almost ten years before that she had met Mickey at the same nightspot.

Jayne continued to make some dreadful films, mostly filmed on a minuscule budget, like *The Fat Spy* (1966) starring Jack E. Leonard and Phyllis Diller. *Variety* said, "*The Fat Spy* is from dudsville. . . . The story erodes around a Florida island but someone must have lost the script." She also appeared in *Las Vegas Hillbillys* (1966); *Spree* (1967); a cameo in *A Guide for the Married Man* (1967); and *The Loved One* (1965), with her scene as a travel receptionist with Robert Morse deleted. They became painful to view. In 1966, Matt Cimber directed Jayne in the unfinished *Single Room Furnished* (1968). While it had a mediocre script and, at times, an eerie quality, Jayne is totally convincing as she moves from a crippled teenager to an over-the-hill prostitute. It contains a poetic, almost magical quality, but these moments are too few to compensate for the sluggish story. Rumors abounded that she was drinking recklessly during production. In one of her last interviews, Jayne said: "My career is moving in a sensitive direction. I'm going to do a movie in which I portray three parts—a prostitute, a cripple and a pregnant unmarried. . . . I want to make a big indentation on the world." It was completed posthumously, and rushed into theaters and then quietly disappeared. The ad line read: "Jayne Mansfield, a legend in her time, has left us a legendary character. . . . In her last and finest performance," said her loyal friend, Walter Winchell.

While Jayne was taking publicity pictures at Jungleland in Thousand Oaks, a lion attacked and mauled her young son,

Zoltan. The boy was given a fifty-fifty chance to live and under-went three major operations, including removal of his spleen. The emotional binge took its toll on Jayne. News reports showed her looking bloated and overweight. The Matt Cimber marriage was over (1966) and she was now linked with a San Francisco trial attorney, Sam Brody, who had assisted Melvin Belli in the Jack Ruby case. "It's been so turbulent, my life," Jayne said. "Some people are born like that. With turbulence. That's my destiny." Sam Brody now became a willing accom-plice in Jayne's never-ending quest for headlines.

Despite Jayne's private traumas, she showed up at the 1966 San Francisco Film Festival. The Festival chairman told the press, "She was not invited. She came by herself. She's not welcome. I finally approached her and said, 'Madame, I don't know how much a pound you are charging, but what ever it is I will pay it if you leave.' I suppose it would be nice to have some sexy starlets at the Festival as they do at Cannes. In my opin-ion, Jayne Mansfield does not meet the standard." The sad irony was, Jayne did have an invitation, but was making such a spectacle of herself, with another wave of outrageous behavior, that the Festival people wanted no part of her. While in the Bay City, Jayne paid a visit to the high priest of the Church of Sa-tan.

On the last downslopes of her nightclub career, Jayne was working the honky-tonk circuit in England, Ireland and Stockholm with her new companion, Sam Brody, whose es-tranged wife, Beverly, disabled with multiple sclerosis, sued for divorce and accused Jayne of committing adultery with her husband. The Brody relationship was a series of drunken fights, jealousy and shattering rages. The tour was a catastro-phe. She was asked to leave the Rose of Tralee Festival in Ireland after the Bishop of Tralee learned she was a practicing Satanist. Jayne and Sam Brody got into a fight with a patron at the Afroskandia Club in Stockholm, and she wound up sprawled on the nightclub floor. Returning from the ill-fated European tour, there was yet another blow. Her oldest daugh-ter, Jayne Marie, now sixteen, walked into a West Los Angeles police station in tears, with welts and bruises on her body. She told the authorities that the explosive-tempered Sam Brody had inflicted them with a leather strap. The family doctor said Jayne had spanked her daughter, "Like any good parent." While an investigation was begun, Jayne Marie was placed in protective custody.

The charges were still pending when Jayne left with Brody and her three younger children for Biloxi, Mississippi, to appear at Gus Stevens' Supper Club. She first stopped at the Keesler Air Force Base (in Biloxi) to entertain GIs. In February, 1967, she had toured Vietnam. Jayne's show at Gus Stevens' club was a tawdry song-and-dance act. Still, when it was over, she told the club manager, "I've never been happier in my life." Shortly after midnight, on June 29, 1967, Gus Stevens loaded Jayne into his Buick hardtop and even provided her with a driver, Ron Harrison, so she could get to New Orleans in time to keep a noon television interview over local station WDSU-TV. When the party left Biloxi, the car carried sons Miklos, Zoltan and daughter Mariska, as well as Sam Brody, Harrison and four Chihuahua dogs. The route to New Orleans was on US Highway 90, a two-lane route known as the Old Spanish Trail. Twenty miles out of New Orleans, on a narrow, winding stretch of the highway there came the sudden grinding sound of breaking glass and crunching metal. The car in which Jayne and the others were riding plowed into the rear of a trailer truck which had stopped behind a city mosquito control truck that was spraying the swamps. The impact was so fierce the top of the sedan was sheared off as it ripped into the sharp edge of the trailer. The European press falsely reported that Jayne had been decapitated, but gruesome police file photos show that she was scalped, and it was actually her blond wig that appears on the dash in the photos, and is the source of the persistent decapitation story.

Jayne, Brody and Harrison never had a chance in the front seat. They were killed instantly. The three children, thrown to the floor in the back seat, escaped major injury. The truck driver hailed a passing motorist who rushed the children to a hospital. Zoltan suffered a minor concussion but the other children were unharmed.

Jayne's bizarre death had plunged her family and friends into an abyss of grief and remorse. Mickey Hargitay was devastated, as he took control of the funeral arrangements. He decided that Jayne should be buried in Pen Argyl, Pennsylvania, beside her father, Herbert Palmer, in the family plot in the Pen Argyl Cemetery. Her copper casket was draped with five hundred pink roses, with a large heart in the center. Hargitay, as he struggled to maintain his composure, said that "Nobody really understood her. Nobody knew the real Jayne." That week in Beverly Hills, a memorial service was held for her in the All Saints Church, organized by columnist friend May Mann and 20th Century-Fox. Just prior to her death, Jayne was offered a London stage production of *The Memoirs of Fanny Hill* that she wanted very much to do.

The engagement at Gus Stevens' Supper Club was a last minute booking; Jayne was stepping in for Mamie Van Doren. Once asked if she knew Jayne Mansfield or Marilyn Monroe, Van Doren responded, "Sure, I knew Jayne and Marilyn. We were called 'The Three M-s.' I did a picture with Jayne called *Las Vegas Hillbillys*. It was a stupid movie. The very job which killed her," she said, "she took over from me down in New Orleans. What they didn't have is what I have. I've lived to tell the story (*Playing the Field*) that getting older isn't all that bad." Despite her image as a 1950s sex symbol, Mamie Van Doren is objective about her survival in Hollywood, "I'm really blessed— and I'm lucky I'm still here."

In 1978, Jayne's five children were awarded only $1,700 apiece from their mother's estate, once valued at about a half-million dollars. The bulk of the estate went to creditors and lawyer fees. The same year, singer Englebert Humperdinck bought the fabled Pink Palace. Loni Anderson and Arnold Schwarzenegger portrayed Jayne and Mickey in a distorted CBS-TV drama, "The Jayne Mansfield Story" in 1980. Anderson characterized Jayne as an actress who put her career over her personal life. "But there she lay, dead at 34, already a has-been," she said. "And look at Marilyn Monroe and Jean Harlow! All of them died too young to appreciate and enjoy that whole other part of life that has nothing in the world to do with celebrity." On viewing the television drama, Hargitay said, "People never understood the full image of Jayne. The story gives people the essence, the quality and mystique of Jayne Mansfield."

In the late 1960s, Mickey Hargitay starred in several spaghetti actioners, including *Stranger in Sacramento*, *The Sheriff*

Won't Shoot and *The Crimson Executioner*. Married to his third wife, Ellen, a TWA flight attendant, Hargitay now operates an interior plant center, Mickey Hargitay Plants, in Hollywood. A strongly liberated and independent young woman, Mariska Hargitay attended UCLA and majored in drama, and showed a down-to-earth naturalness in *Road Trip, Welcome to 18* and *Jocks*. Undeniably, she bears her mother's buoyant energy and good looks. "I was sixteen before I became interested in what sort of person my mother had been," said Mariska. "The kids I grew up with didn't know who she was. And I was just a child when she died. I'm not interested in being a glamorous, big-star like my mother was. That was the aim of the 1950s, I guess. Me, I just want to become a good actress."

On June 29, 1987, the twentieth anniversary of Jayne Mansfield's death, Sabin Gray (the owner of a massive collection of Mansfield memorabilia) and members of the Jayne Mansfield Memorial Fan Club supplied a pink marker at the Hollywood Memorial Park Cemetery.

At her peak, Jayne Mansfield had a theory about her success. "Shock," she explained. "It was shocking things that got me where I am today. That's why I am a star. No one wants to see, or read about, a dull subject. I don't consider myself a dull subject." Dull she certainly wasn't.

MARILYN MONROE

As present-day audiences watch Marilyn Monroe films, they see an actress whose grasp of her skills may vary from film to film, but undeniably possesses in full measure that ill-defined gift of star quality. Marilyn represented the ultimate embodiment of erotic womanhood. She added her own ineffable electricity, an enchanting amalgam of girlish helplessness and womanly self-possession, wide-eyed naïveté and sly self-parody. But whatever Marilyn's screen persona, from versatile actress to especially gifted comedienne, she fascinated the public. Her glamour was a pure product of her will. As with practically every major film actress, Marilyn's great popularity was based on the fact that the fans loved her, not really the roles she filled. When her self-discipline, never really strong, started to dissolve, she lived in a detached world of rapid deterioration. She became haunted by her unhappy childhood, hounded by self-doubt and driven to prove herself more than just a sex symbol. In the end, Marilyn Monroe finally exhausted herself trying to keep her end of the bargain.

Norma Jeane Mortenson was born on June 1, 1926, in the maternity ward of the Los Angeles General Hospital, the child of Gladys Pearl Monroe Mortenson, 25, who would spend the majority of her life institutionalized and whose own mother, Della Mae Monroe Grainger, died in a mental hospital. When Gladys's first husband, John N. Baker, deserted her in 1923, he left her with two children, Berneice and Jack (sometimes referred to as Hemitt). They were taken away from Gladys by Baker's family and raised in Kentucky, where Jack reportedly died. Throughout her life, Marilyn remained unsure of the identity of her father, although she finally accepted a C. Stanley Gifford, who was the manager at Consolidated Film

Laboratories, a processing lab where Gladys assembled nega-
tives. Gifford and Gladys had dated before and during her
pregnancy.

Gladys married Martin Edward Mortenson, a Norwegian-
born mechanic, in October, 1924, and within a year they separated. Years later, Marilyn said that Mortenson had been killed
in a motorcycle accident long before she was born. Mortenson
was listed on Marilyn's birth certificate as her father. The sequence of events that happened in the next several years remains contrived, depending on whom the researcher believes.
But it is generally agreed that for the next few years, little
Norma Jeane was cared for by Albert and Ida Bolender of
Hawthorne, while her mother worked at Consolidated Film
Labs, then as a film cutter at Columbia Studios. Norma Jeane
attended Washington Street School during 1932-33 with the
Bolender's adopted son, Lester.

In October, 1933, Gladys saved up enough of her small salary
at Columbia Studios for a down payment on a white bungalow
near the Hollywood Bowl, just off Highland Avenue. It's also
believed they lived at 6012 Afton Place, across the street from
Columbia. Gladys rented the entire house to an English couple
and leased two rooms for Norma Jeane and herself. The British-
ers, when they weren't working in motion picture, would help
care for Norma Jeane. No one seems to remember their names,
but the husband was George Arliss's stand-in, his wife a
"dress-extra," and their daughter was stand-in to Madeleine
Carroll. Marilyn would later say, "You wouldn't exactly say I
had what you could call a normal childhood. They say you forget the bad things in your life and only remember the good
ones. Well, maybe for others it's that way, but not for me."

In January, 1934, when Norma Jeane returned home from
the Selma Avenue School, the Englishman gently told her,
"Your mother was taken ill today. She's gone to the hospital for
a while." Gladys had been taken to General Hospital and, after
a diagnostic study, to the Norwalk State Hospital, now known
as the Metropolitan State Hospital, where her own mother,
Della, died in 1927. Gladys's sickness was diagnosed as para-
noid schizophrenia. It had destroyed both her parents and her
brother Marion, and now it had finally caught up with her. Columbia Studios continued to pay Gladys's salary for several

months after she was hospitalized. When the English couple felt obliged to find another flat and allow the bank to take the house, Norma Jeane went to live with them. A co-worker and friend of Gladys, Grace McKee, was named legal guardian until Norma Jean turned 21. When the British family decided to return to England, neighbors of Grace McKee, the Griffens, took the child in. When the Harvey Griffens, originally from Mississippi, wanted to return there, they offered to adopt Norma Jean. So did Gladys's friends, Reginald Carroll and his wife, but Gladys couldn't bring herself to give consent.

Norma Jeane was then made a ward of the County of Los Angeles. She would be farmed out by the county welfare agency to a series of foster parents, who were paid $20 a month. None of her foster homes apparently offered her even the barest security, much less love. "I always felt insecure and in the way," she would remember, "but most of all I felt scared—I guess I wanted love more than anything in the world." At one of these "homes," Norma Jeane was seduced by an elderly boarder. She recalled in later years that he was an old man who wore a heavy golden watch over the wide expanse of his vest, and that he gave her a nickel "not to tell." When she nevertheless did tell, the woman who was her foster mother severely punished her for making up lies about the "fine old man."

On September 13, 1935, Norma Jeane was taken to the Los Angeles Orphan's Home Society. She was forcibly carried into the orphanage shouting, "I won't go in there. I'm not an orphan. I'm not. My mother isn't dead." Since legal guardian Grace McKee had married Erwin "Doc" Goddard, a bit player and stand-in for Joel McCrea, Grace thought Norma Jeane would get more proper care at the Orphan's Home Society until they were able to provide for her. Meanwhile, Grace did try to keep up a regular visiting schedule at the orphanage, promising always that soon she'd have Norma Jeane come live with her. Norma Jeane attended the Vine Street Elementary School, while living at the home. She would remain there until June 26, 1937. In 1980, a former "orphan" at the establishment granted an interview to Lisa Mitchell for *Westways* magazine: "She was a very generous person who would never say no to you if you asked her for something. I remember her sitting quietly at a piano we had there and playing for us. She always reminded me of a doe. A funny thing: In 1962, I got the feeling that I should write to her. Whether she'd remember me or not, I wanted to let her know she had a friend. I did write the letter, and a month later, she passed away." The orphanage is now known as Hollygrove for Children.

Norma Jeane was taken to live with a family in Compton and then shuttled to several temporary family "situations," including the home of Enid and Samuel Kindlecamp. In 1938, Grace rescued Norma Jeane and moved her into the Goddard's household. Norma Jeane also spent a great deal of time with Grace's elderly aunt, E. Ana Lower, a Christian Scientist widow, who lived a short distance away at 6707 Odessa Avenue in Van Nuys. Around 1939, the Goddards purchased the Odessa Avenue property when Aunt Ana moved to West Los Angeles. Over the years, Marilyn would say, "This woman was the greatest influence in my whole life. I called her Aunt Ana. The love I have today for simple and beautiful things is because of her. Bless her. She was the only person I ever really loved with such a deep love you can give only to someone so kind, so good, and so full of love for me."

Grace McKee Goddard's step-daughter, Nona Goddard, later became an actress, taking the name of Jody Lawrance. While Jody was a Columbia contract player in the early 1950s, a very low profile was kept on the two actresses' relationship, as Marilyn's career zoomed at 20th Century-Fox. This was perhaps because Columbia head Harry Cohn never quite got over the fact he once let Marilyn's contract lapse after only six months. "I'd been in two dozen foster homes myself," Jody said. "But once you've been in a couple, you've had it. You become cagey, cynical, and you know how to get the most out of people. Marilyn was always looking for a father, mother and family all rolled up into one."

Norma Jeane and Jody's older sister Bebe were the same age and both attended Van Nuys High School. "Norma Jean was such an energetic, athletic girl. That's what drew me to her early on," Bebe remembered. "She won two first place awards in track and field and high-jumping when she was eleven, while a student at the Lankershim School. She loved all sports and could outrun any girl in school. We shared a bedroom at a house on Odessa Avenue after I came out from Texas to live with my dad and Grace in 1940." The ranch house was set back from the street in the middle of dozens of beautiful pepper trees. "On weekends we sometimes attended the La Reina Theater in Sherman Oaks," Bebe said. "Norma Jean and I would get so embarrassed when Grace would pick us up at school or the theater in her 1926 Plymouth automobile."

Norma Jeane later transferred to University High School, from September, 1941, through February, 1942. She was now living with Aunt Ana, who had moved to another one of her homes on Nebraska Avenue. When Norma Jeane was just past her sixteenth birthday, Aunt Ana and Grace urged her to marry the Goddard's ex-neighbor, James Edward Dougherty, 21, a Lockheed Aircraft worker. He was a former student body president at Van Nuys High who once appeared with classmate Jane Russell in *Shirtsleeves* for the school ("Maskers") drama group. Marilyn would later say about the marriage: "My marriage brought me neither happiness nor pain. My husband and I hardly spoke to each other. This wasn't because we were angry. We had nothing to say." The marriage took place on June 19, 1942, at the home of Mr. and Mrs. Chester Howell at 432 S. Bentley Avenue in Westwood. They were close friends of the Goddard family. Norma Jean's first foster parents, the Albert Bolenders, and some of the bride's classmates from University High were there. The Goddards did not attend the ceremony, having recently moved to West Virginia where "Doc" accepted a salesman's position (they did not return to California until several years later). The wedding reception was held at the Florentine Gardens.

The young couple rented a small one-room furnished house at 4524 Vista del Monte in Van Nuys. They later moved to nearby Bessemer Street, while Dougherty worked on a metal-shaping machine at Lockheed Aircraft. In the next box was his close buddy, Robert Mitchum. Dougherty would frequently show the aspiring actor photos of his young wife. At night, Mitchum was appearing in small theater productions. On one occasion, the Doughertys, with Mitchum and his wife, Dorothy, went to hear Tommy Dorsey's Orchestra at the Hollywood Palladium. They were among the many couples to stop dancing and gather around the bandstand to listen to featured vocalist, Frank Sinatra while he sang. "I loved her," Mitchum has said. "She was very kind. That was probably one of her faults, if you can count it as a fault. She was enormously generous and deeply and desperately loyal, often to the wrong people. And, of course, people took advantage of her."

According to Dougherty, the first two years of their marriage were idyllic. "We were very much in love," he said later. "She caught everybody's eye, and sometimes I was very jealous. Once Roy Rogers noticed her in a clothing store, and asked her name. I walked up and said: 'Yes, that's my wife.' " In early 1944, Dougherty entered the United States Merchant Marine, and Norma Jeane, inheriting her mother's restless energy, took a defense plant job at actor Reginald Denny's Radio Plane Parts Company, in the San Fernando Valley, at $20 a week. Dougherty was stationed on Catalina Island as a physical training instructor. She first worked as a paint sprayer, and later on an assembly line, inspecting parachutes. An Army photographer David Conover was commissioned by his commanding officer, Ronald Reagan, to shoot a photographic essay of women in war for *Yank* magazine, the Armed Services magazine. On June 26, 1945, Conover was dispatched to the Radio Plane Parts Company, and it was there that he met Norma Jeane, who showed an instinctive response to the camera and told him she wanted to become a model. Conover also took a set of photographs in the Mojave Desert for her modeling portfolio. She promptly signed up with Emmeline Snively, head of the Blue Book Model Agency, located in the Ambassador Hotel.

The agency asked Norma Jeane to enroll in a $100 modeling course, and guaranteed her enough work to help finance it. "You're very girl-next-doorish," Snively told her. And she found her a $10-a-day job for ten days as hostess for the Holga Steel Company at the 1945 industrial show, held at the Pan-Pacific Auditorium. She took "sick leave" from her job at the defense plant, paid for the course and became a full-time model. A job for Lustre Creme Shampoo gave her a free hair straightening and blond bleaching. She quickly became one of the busiest Blue Book models. "When I was a model, I wanted to be on the cover of *The Ladies Home Journal*," she once said. "Instead, I was always on covers with names like *See, Click, Pic* and *Laff*."

In the spring of 1946, struggling actor Ken DuMain was as full
of enthusiasm and ambition as Norma Jeane. "I was just out of
the service and trying to make it as an actor. I moved into a
small apartment-hotel, The Gower Plaza Hotel, located at 1607
N. Gower Street. Across the hall lived a young model, Norma
Dougherty. I never knew her as Norma Jeane." It was a close
relationship without any romantic involvement. Then Ken recalls one particular evening. "Norma told me about this female
impersonater, Ray Bourbon, who was appearing at a Sunset
Strip nightclub. She'd heard he was terrific and asked if I
would escort her to the club. I said of course, she was always so
grateful." At the club, the performer told the young couple
from the stage, "Two people as pretty as you two should be
sitting up front!" Norma was fascinated by the risque mimic
and begged Kenny to stay for a second show.

"I didn't have enough money, but she said she knew the bar-
tender and he'd cash a check for thirty dollars. It was the same
night that I met some of her friends back at the hotel. I believe
one of them was her estranged husband, James Dougherty. He
kept reminding her that they had an important appointment
the following day with a lawyer. I moved soon afterward and
we lost track of each other," DuMain said. "Years later, I came
across a copy of *Modern Screen* magazine with some early
pin-up photos of Marilyn Monroe. Not until that moment did I
realize my friend, Norma Dougherty, was in fact Marilyn
Monroe."

Actor Ted Jordan, who played Nathan Burke on the old
"Gunsmoke" series, also befriended the young model around
the same time. "The first time I ever saw her I was a lifeguard at
the Hollywood Roosevelt Hotel and I was up on the platform
by the pool and I could see this group of models," Jordan remembers. "I went over to where she was standing and you
could pick her out because she had this gorgeous figure. I still
remember the bathing suit she was wearing. I got talking to her
and she said she was trying to get into pictures like me. So we
had something in common. We started dating—hamburgers in
a place called the Haig and swimming at the Chapman Park
Hotel Pool. We often went down to MacArthur's Park and rode
around at night in those little electric boats they had then."

Emmeline Snively took Norma Jeane to talent coach Milton

Lewis at Paramount Pictures. Lewis was enthusiastic about her reading—but Paramount wouldn't approve a test. "I was surprised the studio wasn't interested," said Lewis. "They certainly didn't have anyone like her under contract; apparently they felt she had no talent." Miss Snively, through her friend, agent Helen Ainsworth, contacted Ben Lyon, the ex-actor, now a 20th Century-Fox casting executive, and set up an interview for July 17, 1946. The mannish looking, 200-pound "Cupid" Ainsworth was in charge of the West Coast branch of National Concert Artists Corporation. Ben Lyon had Norma Jeane read a scene from *Winged Victory* (the Judy Holliday role) and arranged a silent color test to be given on the set of *Mother Wore Tights*, which was then in production with 20th's reigning queen, Betty Grable.

Fox placed her under contract at $75 a week. In *Daily Variety* on September 5, 1946, under "new contracts," 20th Century-Fox announced the signing of Norma Jeane Dougherty and Jane Ball. Within two weeks, Norma Jeane became Marilyn Monroe. Ben Lyon chose Marilyn because she reminded him of his former girl friend, Broadway star Marilyn Miller. The Monroe part came from her maternal grandmother. Ironically, Marilyn's friend Ted Jordan, through his uncle, bandleader Ted Lewis, and writer Damon Runyon, also landed a stock contract with 20th Century-Fox in the same month. Director Walter Lang later recalled, "On the set of *The Shocking Miss Pilgrim*, Marilyn had a bit part as a switchboard operator. Visiting the set one day, I heard a woman's voice repeating the word 'Hullo' over and over in various inflections. It was Marilyn, aided by her voice coach, practicing for her big moment. But when it came time, she'd completely forgotten what to say." The scene does not appear in the completed film.

On October 2, 1946, while James Dougherty was overseas, Marilyn obtained a Nevada divorce in Las Vegas. "I was married to Norma Jeane, not Marilyn Monroe," remembers Dougherty. "She was a sixteen-year-old naïve, sweet kid who needed a lot of love and security. She had a great sense of humor, and was warm and truthful." Marilyn then embarked on a regimen of acting and diction lessons and posed for endless cheesecake and publicity stills. She attended a theatre workshop on the estate of director Howard Hawks, situated in an old barn. Now an insurance company executive and president of Project Rainbow (focusing on the needs of senior gays), Robert Arthur remembers Marilyn as "a student who combined acting ability with a lively curiosity. However, I really didn't know her very well."

Finally, Marilyn could be glimpsed in *Scudda Hoo! Scudda Hay!* (1948) starring Lon McCallister and June Haver. Marilyn and Colleen Townsend can be seen rowing a boat up to a dock in the background, with most of their footage cut. After this inauspicious debut, Marilyn played a waitress in *Dangerous Years* (1947), a juvenile delinquency exploitation drama. It starred ex-Dead End Kid William Halop, who, while on trial for murder, learns he's really the D.A.'s son.

"One day I got a call from Burt Hicks, a friend at 20th (the father of Dolores Hart)," Ted Jordan recalls. "He said you had better stay away from Marilyn because the rumor was going around that we were hot and heavy and she was seeing Joe Schenck, the 20th Century-Fox mogul." Jordan, who went on to become the fifth husband of Lili St. Cyr, believes his contract was not exercised because of his relationship with Marilyn. She bragged in later years, "I was never kept, to be blunt about it. I always kept myself." Not long before Marilyn's own contract was dropped in August, 1947, Fox sent her to study at the Actors Lab, operated by Morris Carnovsky and J. Edward Bromberg, members of the Group Theatre in New York. Carnovsky's wife, actress Phoebe Brand, remembers, "I never knew what to make of her. I didn't know what she thought of the work. Frankly, I would never have predicted she'd be a success. She was extremely retiring. What I failed to see in her acting was her lovely comedic style. I was blind to it." Between modeling jobs, Marilyn won the second lead in the Florence Ryerson-Colin Clement 1940 comedy, *Glamour Preferred*, at the Bliss-Hayden Playhouse. The playhouse was run by Harry Hayden and his actress wife, Lela Bliss. Marilyn also appeared in a production of *Stage Door* at the Bliss-Hayden Playhouse.

Marilyn first met Joe Schenck at one of his lush Sunday dinner parties, attended by many starlets, at his Holmby Hills estate. Through Schenck's connections with pioneer friend Harry Cohn, Marilyn signed with Columbia Pictures on March 9, 1948. The man in charge of talent, Max Arnow, sent her to their studio drama coach, Natasha Lytess, who had been married to the German novelist, Bruno Frank, and who had been a member of the Max Reinhardt acting group in Germany in the pre-Nazi days. Natasha was to become the most influential person in Marilyn's early movie career. A little more than a week after Marilyn's signing with Columbia, her Aunt Ana Lower died.

It was Natasha Lytess who persuaded producer Harry Romm to give Marilyn the ingenue lead in the mini-musical, *Ladies of the Chorus* (1948). She played a strip-teaser who danced in the same chorus line as her mother, Adele Jergens, and falls in love with millionaire playboy, Rand Brooks. Marilyn had two numbers and was given a Rita Hayworth-style hairdo. The film was harmless fluff. The musical director on *Ladies of the Chorus* was strapping, handsome Fred Karger. While Schenck began to drift out of her life, Karger began seeing her away from the studio, impressed with Marilyn's fragility and her apparent inability to cope with people around her.

"Marilyn made it very clear that she wanted to be his wife," a close friend of Karger recalls. "But her fierce ambition terrified him. Besides, he always gravitated to beauties." Karger had been divorced and was living in a household of women, which included his sister, Mary, and her two daughters and his own small daughter, Terry. But it was his mother, Anne Karger, to whom Marilyn became deeply attached, replacing Aunt Ana. Thus began a friendship with Mrs. Karger that was to outlive her affair with Fred Karger and last throughout Marilyn's life. Up until Mrs. Karger's death, a huge oil painting of Marilyn hung in her living room in her cottage on Harper Avenue.

The end of the romance with Karger revealed, for the first time, that Marilyn was already flirting with another escort—death. After the romance failed she made her first of several attempts at suicide. Karger later became an orchestra leader at the Beverly Hilton Hotel and married Jane Wyman in November, 1952. They divorced two years later, but remarried in March, 1961, this time staying together for four years. Fred Karger died at 63 of leukemia, on the 17th anniversary of Marilyn's death, August 5, 1979.

Marilyn knew exactly what she wanted and knew of the struggle it would take to achieve it, and the countless humiliations she would be forced to endure. During her six-month stay at Columbia Studios, Marilyn moved into the Hollywood Studio Club. It was only two blocks away from the orphanage where she had once lived. The three-story Mediterranean Club was then a well managed residence branch hotel of the YWCA for studio employees only. According to Judy Joanis, who managed the club, Marilyn was not what Hollywood touted her to be.

"A Fox secretary, Marcella Knapp, phoned Florence Williams, the director of the club, and reserved room 307 for Marilyn for $12 a week on June 3, 1948," she said checking the records. "Her roommate was Clarice Evans, who was studying opera. Quiet, she would come in and spend half an hour hanging over the front desk, usually carrying books with her. She read a lot, but always came down for breakfast looking so lovely other girls perked up and looked at their appearance. When she sat down, everybody gradually gathered around her. The press always wrote that she was out on the town with a lot of men. That just was not true. Marilyn ate dinner here often and spent most of her time studying. She was quiet and very serious about her acting. If she went out, she always came in early, usually about 9:30 p.m. The club had a curfew of 11 p.m. weekdays, midnight on weekends, and girls had to sign a register if they came in after hours. Marilyn was so sweet. She didn't have much of a wardrobe, not many clothes, but what she did have were simple and pretty. I remember Marilyn used the hall pay phone numerous times each day. Some of the girls who worked as movie extras became a little irritated with her during the hours they had to call Central Casting. She spent a great deal of time washing and brushing her hair and drove a battered Ford convertible," she said.

Another file card had Marilyn moving to a single, room 334. "It is not true that she posed for the calendar photos to pay her back rent. Marilyn was gone a year when she posed for that picture." It's obvious Marilyn left her mark on Miss Joanis too. When asked if Marilyn ever returned to the club, she sighed deeply, "No."

After *Ladies of the Chorus*, Marilyn's option with Columbia was dropped in September, 1948, and the budding starlet began a free-lance interval. Kay Gorcey was Groucho Marx's wife and had been prominently featured in his *Copacabana* (1947).

Today, Kay remembers just how Marilyn came to be assigned the sexy walk-on in *Love Happy* (1949). "I was to do the bit with Groucho, although the producer, Lester Cowan, had interviewed three other girls," Kay said. "On the night before we were to shoot the scene, I had a terrible argument with Groucho and told him, 'Get someone else for the part.' Cowan was frantic, remembered Marilyn and contacted her agent (Harry Lipton)."

A seductive Marilyn was to enter the office of private detective Groucho Marx and breathlessly say, "Some men are following me." Marilyn and dancer Paul Valentine received "introducing" billing. Her classic scene is still fun to watch. During the filming, Kay remembers Marilyn was dating banker Al Hart, later head of City National Bank.

Marilyn was sent on her first personal appearance tour to promote *Love Happy* to Chicago, New York (where she had her first taste of fan adulation while installed at the Sherry Netherland Hotel), Detroit, Cleveland and Milwaukee. Tired and lonely, she deserted the promotion tour in Rockford, Illinois, and returned to Hollywood.

When Marilyn became a star, her first agent, Harry Lipton of National Concert Artists Corporation, would say: "She was so unsure of herself with that terrible background, it gave her a quality that set her apart."

Comedian Ken Murray once almost hired Marilyn. At his Beverly Hills home, Ken reminisced about the afternoon he auditioned her for his show *Blackouts* on the stage of the El Capitan Theater on Vine Street. "I was taking the show to New York and our star Marie Wilson wasn't going and we had invested thousands of dollars in a new wardrobe for her and decided no one would get the part unless she could also fill the costumes. Marilyn was sent to me by a friend, Charles Wick, who was with the William Morris office. Into my dressing room walked the most unusual girl I had ever seen. She was blond, beautiful and buxom. When she walked she had the manner of a startled bird. She read the script in a low husky voice. I seriously considered giving her the job, but she failed the last exam," Ken smiled. "The most perfect thirty-six still doesn't fit perfectly into the perfect thirty-nine. She had an accompanist, and sang two songs in a very sexy voice. In the end, I had to tell her I couldn't take her. She was terribly upset. Marilyn wanted badly to go East with us."

Photographer Tom Kelley on an occasion had advanced Marilyn five dollars for cab fare after she had crashed her car into another vehicle in front of LaRue's Restaurant on the Sunset Strip. In the summer of 1949, Marilyn appeared at his studio at 736 North Seward Street to pose for a Pabst Blue Ribbon Beer billboard ad, and was greeted by his wife. Natalie Kelley Grasko spoke about that meeting some thirty years ago in her home high above the hills of Silver Lake. "I didn't see anything in particular to distinguish Marilyn from many of the other models we had seen," Mrs. Grasko said, "Her hair was reddish-blond and worn in the style of the late 1940s, long, curly and fluffed around her face. I took her into the dressing room and had her change into a bathing suit. Tom asked her to pose holding a beach ball over her head. It was a difficult pose to hold for any length of time. Marilyn held that position for about an hour, although I'm sure she must have ached. We asked her if she wanted to rest but she said that she'd hold it until we got all the shots we wanted. Later, Tom asked if she would consider posing for artistic nude color shots for calendars. She said she didn't think so." A week later, Marilyn called Natalie Kelley. "I've thought it over. I'll do it," she said. Previously, Marilyn posed semi-nude for Earl Moran, the noted magazine illustrator who specialized in pinup art.

The appointment was made for a few evenings later. "There were just three of us in the studio that night," Natalie said. "Marilyn, Tom and myself. Tom draped red velvet on the floor, and she posed lying on it. They listened to the phonograph on which I was playing an Artie Shaw recording of "Begin the Beguine." Tom shot her from ten feet above. They worked for two hours." Natalie remembers the experience as extraordinary in its intensity. After it was over, the three went to Barney's Beanery for chili and coffee. "Marilyn told us, 'Many photographers have asked me to pose completely in the nude for them,' she said. 'I've always refused. The other day when I phoned you I needed to take the assignment because I'm flat broke. I'm way behind in my room rent and a $50 bill looks like Fort Knox.' "For the fun of it, Marilyn signed the release, dated May 27, 1949, with the pseudonym, Mona Monroe." Looking

for a buyer of his Kodachrome, Tom Kelley found Chicago li-
thographer John Baumgarth, who ran a print shop in a suburb,
Melrose Park. Baumgarth paid Kelley $300 for the color shots
and then paid $600 for the plates and complete rights for its re-
production.

In March, 1952, Alice Mosby of the United Press broke the
nude calendar story with explosive results. "Even though
Marilyn was becoming famous," Natalie said, "she still
dropped in to see us. She came by one afternoon and asked to
see the calendar. Marilyn had never seen any of the photographs she had posed for. When I showed it to her, she was
not shocked. She just looked at it as though she was studying a
stranger. She studied it carefully, then said she thought it was
very good. Marilyn was pretty proud of it." Just before she
completed *Clash by Night*, she phoned Natalie to ask if she
could have 25 calendars for the crew. "We had to get them for
her through the lithograph company." Marilyn once asked
Kelley to borrow the unused transparencies to show then-
boyfriend Joe DiMaggio and never returned them. After
Marilyn died, an attorney for the estate found them, but,
Kelley recalled shortly before his death in 1984, "They were so
faded it was like looking through a piece of glass. They were
absolutely unusable." The famed calendar is said to have sold
55 million copies. Collectors' items now, the Monroe calendars,
"Golden Dream" and "A New Wrinkle," sell for $250 to $300.
"And I don't even have one," Natalie said, regretfully. The
Monroe nudes appeared in *Playboy* magazine's premier issue,
with Marilyn on the cover, October, 1953.

In the October 10, 1949, issue of *Life*, photographer Philippe
Halsman shot a layout of aspiring starlets. The article was entitled, "Eight Girls Try Out Mixed Emotions." Marilyn, Suzanne
Dalbert, Cathy Downs, Dolores Gardner, Lois Maxwell,
Laurette Luez, Jane Nigh and Ricky Soma were seen in a
matching series of photos depicting their reactions to a variety
of situations. It was Johnny Hyde, an executive vice-president
of the William Morris Agency, who is generally credited with
first recognizing the star potential that lay ahead for Marilyn.
Hyde also played Svengali in the careers of Veronica Lake, Rita
Hayworth, Dorothy Lamour and Betty Hutton. He was 53 and
had a bad heart, and Marilyn was all of 22. Hyde fell madly in

love with her. Hyde, according to Marilyn, told her on their first meeting, "I sense something in you that masses will like." The Morris agency bought up her contract from Harry Lipton. Johnny Hyde would prove the catalyst that would enable Marilyn to move from starlet to star. "Johnny was marvelous, he really was," said Marilyn. "He believed in my talents. He listened to me when I talked, and he encouraged me." There is no denying Johnny Hyde propelled Marilyn to stardom.

Through Johnny Hyde, Marilyn landed the second feminine lead in a Mickey Rooney rollerdome epic, *The Fireball* (1950). Hairstylist Agnes Flanagan was assigned the feminine cast. Agnes remembered: "What a loveable child she was. Marilyn wanted to wear her hair in a certain way which required a fall (hairpiece) and she couldn't afford one. I felt sorry for her and ordered one from Bobby Roberts at Max Factor and charged it to the company. When her few scenes were completed, and Agnes was removing the fall, Marilyn looked in the mirror and said, 'Oh gee, I wish I really looked like that,' I asked the producer, Bert Friedlob, to let her keep it. It was a small favor to ask but Marilyn never forgot it." Agnes then took from her billfold a strip of Marilyn's hair test shots for *The Fireball* that she always carried with her until she died at the Motion Picture Hospital in 1985.

Marilyn often visited Agnes Flanagan and her husband, a studio electrician, at their home. The Flanagans had two children, and Marilyn spent a great deal of time with them, often telling Agnes that she wished she had a family of her own. Agnes later assisted Sydney Guilaroff at MGM and would remain part of Marilyn's studio entourage. "When Marilyn became successful, I had to be very careful not to admire anything in her presence because she'd see to it that a duplicate was delivered at my door the next day. Just before she died, Marilyn asked her makeup man, Whitey Snyder, and myself to make her up for a *Life* layout. While sitting in her lovely garden, I made the mistake of admiring her colorful new lawn swing. An exact duplicate was delivered to my home the very next day!"

In *A Ticket to Tomahawk* (1950), Marilyn was one of four chorines (Marion Marshall, Joyce MacKenzie and Barbara Smith) shuttling through an embattled area of Durango, Colorado, during the Indian Wars. Back at 20th Century-Fox, after five weeks of location filming, her part was so insignificant that no one there seemed to have been aware she had returned as a free-lance player.

The film that changed Marilyn's life was Metro-Goldwyn-Mayer's *The Asphalt Jungle* (1950). The bitterly realistic novel about big city crime was to be directed by John Huston and produced by Arthur Hornblow, Jr. One role remained to be filled—the crooked lawyer Louis Calhern's mistress Angela, whom the script described as an 18-year-old who could be soft yet instinctively cunning. Huston wanted Lola Albright, who had just scored a hit in *Champion* with Kirk Douglas. MGM also tested Barbara Payton, Georgia Holt (the mother of Cher), Joi Lansing and Claudia Barrett. Then Lucille Ryman, the studio's talent head, came to John Huston with Marilyn.

When Marilyn appeared for her interview in Arthur Hornblow's office, she was extremely nervous, her hands were shaking as Huston gave her the script. "Listen, kid, don't worry about this," he told her. "Just take it home and look it over, then come back when you're ready to give me a reading." Marilyn was ready three days later, aided by Natasha Lytess. Not happy with her reading, Marilyn asked if she could try again. After the second run, Huston laughed. "You didn't have to do it twice, honey. You had the part on the first reading." Producer Hornblow recalled that Marilyn arrived on the set "scared half to death" and dressed as a "cheap tart." John Huston would later say, "Within the international sex symbol that is Marilyn Monroe, is a nice, quiet young woman fighting to get out. In fact, I don't think she really cares very much about sex at all."

When *The Asphalt Jungle* went into release, Marilyn experienced the heady, potentially destructive situation of suddenly being a hot property. Everyone wanted her, and Johnny Hyde had to sift the offers, take and reject scripts and decide what direction to follow. *Photoplay* magazine wrote: ". . . This picture is packed with stand-out performances. . . . There's a beautiful blonde, too, name of Marilyn Monroe, who plays Calhern's girl friend, and makes the most of her footage." The New York *Herald Tribune* said: "It is a violent exhibition, dedicated to sluggings and large-scale jewel robberies, but John Huston has made it a taut and engrossing melodrama. . . .

Marilyn Monroe and Anthony Caruso lend a documentary effect to a lurid exposition."

Just prior to *The Asphalt Jungle*, Marilyn was unbilled as reporter Dick Powell's nightclub date in *Right Cross* (1950) and in *Hometown Story* (1951) as Jeffrey Lynn's newspaper publisher secretary (Metro-Goldwyn-Mayer bought it for distribution from General Motors). Marilyn's only commercial was for the Union Oil Company—pitching their Royal Triton Gasoline product.

Johnny Hyde separated from his wife and bought a house at 718 North Palm Drive, Beverly Hills. It is believed that Hyde felt that minor plastic surgery would be beneficial to remove a small lump from the tip of Marilyn's nose which tended to widen at the bridge when she laughed or smiled. Marilyn reportedly recuperated at the Palm Drive address while agent Hyde negotiated with writer-director Joseph Mankiewicz for her to portray Miss Casswell in his brilliant backstage drama, *All About Eve* (1950). Writer James Robert Haspiel, an authority on Marilyn's career, questions the validity of the plastic surgery story. Instead, he believes Marilyn was sent to Madame Renna's Salon in Beverly Hills by 20th Century-Fox. She was well-known for using non-surgical methods of contouring the face in shape through treatment.

Marilyn's character in *All About Eve* was an aspiring actress being kept by drama critic George Sanders. She moved easily under Mankiewicz's direction, holding her own against Bette Davis and Anne Baxter. Nominated for no less than 14 Oscars, the film won six, including best picture. The *Los Angeles Reader* wrote: "Memorable in smaller roles are Marilyn Monroe as 'a graduate of the Copacabana School for the Dramatic Arts,' and Barbara Bates as Phoebe." George Sanders would comment after filming *All About Eve*, "I lunched with Marilyn once or twice during the making of the film and found that her conversation had unexpected depths. She showed an interest in intellectual subjects, which was quite disconcerting. In her presence, it was hard to concentrate."

Studios now wanted to benefit from the public's rapidly growing interest in Marilyn. MGM, who had hesitated in signing her because of their own resident blond star, Lana Turner, saw 20th Century-Fox re-sign Marilyn in October,

1950. In December, Johnny Hyde died of a heart attack on the day that Fox began production on Marilyn's next film, *As Young As You Feel* (1951). At the funeral service, his family wouldn't allow her to sit with them. Overcome with grief over her guiding mentor's death, Marilyn cried out hysterically, "Wake up, please wake up, oh my God, Johnny, Johnny." She had to be taken away. In *As Young As You Feel*, she played Albert Dekker's provocative secretary.

With Johnny Hyde gone, Marilyn made another important friend in Spyros Skouras, the president of 20th Century-Fox. When possible, Skouras tried to persuade producers to use Marilyn. Accordingly, she was rushed into *Love Nest* (1951), a mildly amusing comedy revolving around the problems of June Haver and William Lundigan. Actors were beginning to complain about Marilyn's lateness, which had plagued her all her life. About her tardiness, she told *Life* magazine, "A lot of people can be there on time and do nothing, which I have seen them do, and you know, all sit around and sort of chit-chatting and talking trivia about their social life. Clark Gable said about me, 'When she's there, she's there. All of her is there! She's there to work." In *Let's Make It Legal* (1951), Marilyn paraded around in a bathing suit in the hopes of winning Zachary Scott and his zillions.

Barbara Bates, who was playing Claudette Colbert's daughter in *Let's Make It Legal*, had worked in *All About Eve*, in the film's climactic final scene. She first met Marilyn in the publicity department photo gallery. Barbara was married to an older man and once asked Marilyn to lunch at her apartment, just a few minutes from Fox. Possibly influenced by their perpetual search for father figures, the actresses were drawn together. Marilyn confided to Barbara that Johnny Hyde had asked her to marry him, but she knew in her heart it would never work because of the age difference. Marilyn used to kid Barbara about being the most contented girl she'd ever known. But the sad truth was Barbara's own life would fall apart and end in self-destruction. The *All About Eve* girls' career paths took different directions. Marilyn's triumphed while Barbara was caught up in a succession of "sweet young wholesome" parts.

In New York, Spyros Skouras called Darryl Zanuck and wanted to know more about Fox's future plans for Marilyn.

Zanuck, never one of her biggest admirers, felt she was limited to a Marie Wilson-type career. Skouras was furious, "But look at the tremendous publicity she's getting. Let's throw her in pictures. If the exhibitors like her, the public likes her." Skouras tried to persuade Nunnally Johnson to use her in *Phone Call From a Stranger*. But Johnson vetoed the idea, and hired Shelley Winters from Universal. RKO next borrowed Marilyn to play a Monterey cannery worker in Fritz Lang's *Clash By Night* (1952). She received equal billing alongside Barbara Stanwyck, Robert Ryan and Paul Douglas. *The New York Telegram* noted: "Perhaps we could mention the first full-length glimpse the picture gives us of Marilyn Monroe as an actress. The verdict is gratifyingly good. The girl has a refreshing exuberance, an abundance of girlish high spirits. She is a forceful actress, too, when crisis comes along."

Marilyn returned to 20th Century-Fox for director Edmund Goulding's *We're Not Married* (1952), an anthology film about several young married couples who discover that their weddings were not legitimate. She played the winner of a beauty contest for married women, improbably wed to David Wayne. RKO Studios had borrowed Marilyn for only $13,000, but when director Fritz Lang suggested her for *The Big Heat* at Columbia a few months later, the asking price was now $100,000. As her popularity grew, so did her disregard for publicity. Marilyn was late on the set, late for interviews, and late for social engagements. She was to have her first distressing failure in *Don't Bother to Knock* (1952), co-starring Richard Widmark, as a psychotic baby sitter with, ironically, a background of mental illness. Natasha Lytess blamed British director Roy Baker for Marilyn's first inept performance. "All the equipment that Miss Monroe has to handle the job are a childishly blank expression and a provokingly feeble voice," said Bosley Crowther in *The New York Times*.

There was another storm in store for the public. Columnist Erskine Johnson discovered that Marilyn's mother was alive and in a California State Hospital, Rock Haven in Verdugo Hills. The story was treated sympathetically. In previous years, Marilyn had declared that both parents were dead and that she had been raised in foster homes as an orphan.

Marilyn was more happily cast in *Monkey Business* (1952) with

Cary Grant and Ginger Rogers, as Charles Coburn's unskilled secretary. Marilyn's new boyfriend was Joe DiMaggio, the New York Yankees ex-jock. When he visited the set of *Monkey Business*, DiMaggio posed with Marilyn and Cary Grant. When the photos appeared throughout the country, Grant's face was cropped. *O. Henry's Full House* (1952) teamed Marilyn with Charles Laughton in "The Cop and the Anthem" segment as a streetwalker. It was unquestionably the best of the unrelated episodes. "Everything is so wonderful—people are so kind," she said. "But I feel as though it's all happening to someone right next to me. I'm close—I can feel it, I can hear it, but it isn't really me."

Marilyn was now a full-fledged star and was assigned to the tawdry drama *Niagara* (1953), filmed mostly in Niagara Falls. Clad in a skin-tight red satin dress most of the time, she tried to lure Richard Allen into killing her borderline psychotic husband Joseph Cotten in this Freudian field day. The film has never been sufficiently explored or acknowledged. "Marilyn Monroe and Niagara . . . a raging torrent even nature can't control," said the ads for *Niagara*.

Twentieth Century-Fox originally bought *Gentlemen Prefer Blondes* (1953) for Betty Grable, who lost out to Marilyn as the typical dumb blonde who knew that diamonds are a girl's best friend, and Jane Russell as her partner in gold-digging. This dazzling mixture of sexual ambiguity and hokum is as entertaining today as it was back in 1953, with Marilyn in the role that epitomizes her onscreen persona. She and Russell got along famously, working in unison, with neither trying to outdo the other in this opulent Technicolor blockbuster. When *Gentlemen Prefer Blondes* opened at Grauman's Chinese Theatre in, August 1953, both Marilyn and co-star Jane Russell were invited to place their footprints in cement in the forecourt of the theatre. Marilyn once said, "I used to go to Grauman's Chinese and try to fit my foot in the prints in the cement there. And I'd say, 'Oh, oh, my foot's too big, I guess, that's out.' I did have a funny feeling later when I finally put my foot down into that wet cement. I sure knew what it really meant to me—anything's possible, almost."

Marilyn finally caught up with Betty Grable and Lauren Bacall in *How to Marry a Millionaire* (1953). The first Cinema-

Scope comedy borrowed that old theme from *The Greeks Had a Word for Them*, with three gold diggers out on the town, each trying to catch a wealthy husband. Like most of director Jean Negulesco's 1950s work, it is bland and chic, featuring a large cast—mostly to fill the CinemaScope frame. "Honey," said Betty Grable. "I've had mine—go get yours." Marilyn and Alan Ladd were the recipients of *Photoplay's* Gold Medal Awards (1953), held at the magazine's annual dinner at the Beverly Hills Hotel. Joe DiMaggio was so upset by the cut of her gown that pal Sidney Skolsky had to escort her. Joan Crawford was equally upset at Marilyn's sexy attire. "Sex plays a tremendously important part in every person's life," she told the press. "People are interested in it, intrigued with it. But they don't like to see it flaunted in their faces."

It was inevitable that even Marilyn would end up in a Western, *River of No Return* (1954), with Robert Mitchum and Rory Calhoun, which is often referred to as Marilyn's worst film. Mitchum and Monroe star as a miner and a saloon singer who join forces for love and profit during California's gold rush. The two stars don't exactly strike romantic sparks, but their presence is enough. Director Otto Preminger keeps the Western action moving at a leisurely but reasonably diverting pace. Marilyn sang "I'm Going to File My Claim" and "One Silver Dollar." Preminger was constantly at odds with Marilyn, mostly due to her tardiness and his hatred for Natasha Lytess. Joe DiMaggio flew to the Banff, Canada, location to visit with Marilyn after she sprained her ankle. Years later, Preminger said he would never direct Marilyn again, "Not for a million dollars tax free."

Marilyn was put on suspension for refusing *The Girl in Pink Tights* and took off for San Francisco and Joe DiMaggio. The "storybook wedding" was held on January 14, 1954, in a civil ceremony at the City Hall, the bridal night was spent at the Clifton Motel in Paso Robles. Then the honeymooners went to Japan, where DiMaggio, the Yankee Clipper, had been a national idol. Marilyn found time to entertain the GI troops in Korea, while her bridegroom remained in Tokyo. When she returned, an exhilarated Marilyn told Joe DiMaggio, "It was so wonderful, Joe. You never heard such cheering." He answered, "Yes, I have. Don't let it go to your head. Just miss the ball once. You'll see they can boo as loud as they can cheer."

As a wedding present, 20th Century-Fox lifted its suspension and Marilyn next reported for *There's No Business Like Show Business* (1954), a roaring extravaganza. The New York *Daily News* wrote: "It is a star-studded production with an Irving Berlin score that gives the film rhythm, bounce and a pleasant nostalgic quality. . . . Marilyn stars in three specialty numbers amusingly, as she does a comic burlesque of the sexy singer of naughty songs." She was unhappy over the costume designs of Miles White and insisted that her friend, Billy Travilla, be brought in to make her wardrobe. At her insistence, Jack Cole was brought in to create the dance routines, although Robert Alton was already signed and did all the other staging for the film. Both Cole and Travilla had contributed their superior talents on *Gentlemen Prefer Blondes*. Gwen Verdon assisted Jack Cole on Marilyn's numbers. Donald O'Connor, one of the stars of *There's No Business Like Show Business* recalls, "I think she was her best P.R. For example, we were doing a scene together, and she had her hair piled high and was wearing high heels, which made her taller than I was. And the director asked me to work on an apple box, because he was afraid to ask the star herself. So I went over and asked her if she would mind taking off her shoes. She laughed and said, 'Of course!' and did the scene in bare feet."

Director Billy Wilder had collaborated on the adaptation of the George Axelrod play *The Seven Year Itch* (1955). Marilyn and DiMaggio began having troubles during the filming of the New York exteriors, and Natasha Lytess (now on the 20th Century-Fox payroll) wasn't helping matters. As the girl upstairs who innocently tempts the "summer widower" Tom Ewell downstairs, she was, wrote the New York *Daily Mirror*: "The personification of this decade's glamour—now a fine comedienne, making her one of Hollywood's top attractions." The reviews were glowing and Billy Wilder said, "Don't you forget it. Marilyn knows comedy. Her sense of timing is precise."

Fashion designer Billy Travilla worked on several Monroe films and his best-known creation is the billowing white dress she wore over a drafty Manhattan street grating during the making of *The Seven Year Itch*. "Marilyn was a combination of child and woman and I've never known another like her," Travilla once said. "Women can copy her and mimic her, but they can't beat Marilyn. She was a complex, incredible, magnificent lady. Marilyn had a gorgeous body. She had beautiful breasts, but we had a little help in those days and a few bust pads were thrown in. Marilyn was not huge—she was just right. But for the look of the clothes then, all the girls padded their bras. That was the style. I never knew when I designed that dress it would become the most famous and most publicized dress in the world. I still have it and it is insured for thousands. I wish I had Marilyn's other clothes. In 1971, I retired to Spain for a while and I threw out ten of her dresses. At home I have framed the famous Marilyn Monroe nude calendar. It is signed: 'To Billy, my love. Please dress me forever because I love you. Marilyn.' "

Marilyn's personal life was in turmoil, after only nine months of marriage the DiMaggios decided to divorce. She told the judge, "I hoped to have out of my marriage love, warmth, affection, and understanding. But the relationship turned out to be one of coldness and indifference. . . . About the question, if there was a new man in her life, Marilyn said, "There is no other man, there never has been." Interviewed in New York, DiMaggio stated, "I want to be a good friend to Marilyn. I have nothing else to say except 'no comment.' If she wants the divorce, she will get it."

She was dissatisfied with the roles that 20th Century-Fox was offering, and thus turned down *How to Be Very, Very Popular*, *The Revolt of Mamie Stover* and *The Girl in the Red Velvet Swing*. Marilyn went to New York and studied with Lee Strasberg at the Actor's Studio and moved in with Milton Greene and his wife Amy on their Connecticut farm. Greene, a photographer, would form Marilyn Monroe Productions. He had met the star when he photographed her for *Look* magazine. Marilyn said, "I formed my own corporation so I can play the better kind of roles I want to play. I didn't like a lot of my pictures. I'm tired of sex roles. I don't want to play sex roles any more." When asked what type of roles she wanted to play now, she replied, "Grushenka in a dramatization of Dostoevsky's *The Brothers Karamazov*." She now wanted to learn the Stanislavsky Method of acting. The decision marked the end of Marilyn's association with Natasha Lytess. Natasha stayed on the Fox payroll as drama coach for young talent for a short time. Then, before her health began to fail, she taught from her home. In 1964, she left Rome to enter a cancer clinic in Switzerland, where she died.

Playwright Arthur Miller became a frequent visitor to the Actors Studio, where in February, 1956, Marilyn appeared in a scene from Eugene O'Neill's *Anna Christie*. Fox and Marilyn patched things up a month later with a new contract, granting her $100,000 per picture. Also, she liked the property 20th had bought for her, *Bus Stop* (1956), the William Inge play. She chose Joshua Logan to direct. He wanted Rock Hudson, but new coach Paula Strasberg requested Albert Salmi, who originated the part of Bo, the cowboy who falls for the lonely chantoosie who yearns for bright lights. Marilyn decided on New York actor Don Murray. The reviews all agreed Marilyn had matured as an actress. Incredibly, she wasn't nominated for an Oscar. Ingrid Bergman won the Academy Award that year for *Anastasia*. There were rumors during *Bus Stop* that Marilyn had started drinking and was quite unreasonably uncooperative.

Before departing for England to film *The Prince and the Showgirl* (1957), Marilyn married Arthur Miller on June 29, 1956, at the Westchester County Court House. "We're so congenial," said Marilyn. "This is the first time I think I've been really in love. Arthur is a serious man, but he has a wonderful sense of humor. We laugh and joke a lot. I'm mad about him." The elaborate production of *The Prince and the Showgirl* was based on the play *The Sleeping Prince* in which Sir Laurence Olivier, with his wife, Vivien Leigh, as co-star, opened in London. It was especially written for them by Terence Rattigan. Sir Laurence Olivier would now direct as well as star. "It has long been my hope and dream to work with Sir Laurence," said Marilyn. As the film stumbled to completion, Olivier was becoming increasingly disenchanted with his leading lady and she with him. Not surprisingly, the comedy received lukewarm reviews. Marilyn now drank Dom Perignon champagne, and sleeping pills gave her temporary relief from her chronic insomnia, but, like a number of other movie queens, she exercised no judgment in the use of them.

When 20th Century-Fox offered Marilyn the Marlene Dietrich role in *The Blue Angel* remake, she rejected it and finally agreed to star in *Some Like It Hot* (1959) with Jack Lemmon and Tony Curtis for United Artists. Taking place during the Prohibition ara, it was easily Marilyn's most popular film. It was also the only one of her profit-sharing films that helped to pay her many debts after her death. Marilyn, appearing overweight and tired, was a ukulele-strumming singer with an all-girl orchestra; Lemmon and Curtis appeared in drag most of the time. Billy Wilder had directed Marilyn in *The Seven Year Itch* and now claimed she was more of a problem than ever. When Wilder was asked if he wanted to direct a third picture with Marilyn, he said, "I am too old and too rich to go through this again." The New York *Post* pointed out: "To get down to cases, Marilyn does herself proud, giving a performance of such intrinsic quality that you begin to believe she's only being herself and it is herself who fits into that distant period and this picture so well." After completing *Some Like It Hot*, Marilyn, in December, 1958, had a miscarriage.

In June, 1959, Marilyn underwent corrective gynecological surgery at the Lenox Hill Hospital in New York. The trouble within the Miller marriage came to the surface while Marilyn was filming *Let's Make Love* (1960), with French actor Yves Montand, the husband of Simone Signoret. George Cukor directed this show-business tale of love between an off-Broadway actress and a multi-millionaire backer. Marilyn threw a party at the 20th Century-Fox commissary for Yves Montand, and, much to the surprise of everyone, arrived on time, explaining that since she was the hostess it wouldn't be right to be late. Her affair with Yves Montand during the filming was no particular secret, and certainly had much to do with the eventual break-up with Miller. Simone Signoret often dismissed reports of the affair between her husband and Marilyn with a shrug. "A physical affair can't stand up against a relationship of moral dependence built up over ten years," she declared.

On the set of *Let's Make Love*, on Marilyn's birthday, June 1, 1960, the cast and crew gave a birthday party which included a huge cake containing 34 Marilyn Monroe look-alike dolls dressed in black tights from the "Specialization" musical number. Jack Cole's assistant choreographer, Maggie Banks, worked endlessly with Marilyn on the dance numbers. She remembers, "We worked long rehearsal hours and Marilyn wouldn't call it a day until she was absolutely positive she had the routine down pat. We had an electrician on the show whose wife was ill in the hospital. I saw Marilyn, still dressed in her white polo coat costume, hand him a roll of bills; he started to cry and Marilyn just hugged him and walked away. I believe the emotional strain of her early years was just too much for her."

Marilyn's acting coach, Paula Strasberg, haunted the production, clad in solid black, like a Stanislavskian specter. Whenever Marilyn was unavailable, it was explained that she was studying her lines with Paula. In director Nunnally Johnson's estimation, Marilyn was "an asset to the Strasbergs and that whole New York crowd. They're like most people in show business, they're not above showmanship."

The title and idea for Marilyn's next film, *The Misfits* (1961) came from a short story Arthur Miller had written years before and, on her instigation, shaped into a vehicle for his wife, with Clark Gable and Montgomery Clift, a drama of lonely people coming together in Reno, Nevada. John Huston was chosen as director for what would prove to be Marilyn and Clark Gable's final film. A number of scenes were filmed at Reno's Riverside Hotel. A certain irony was in evidence at the hotel. Appearing in the lounge was Ann-Margret Olsson, a vocalist with the Suttletones group, and ex-Northwestern University combo. The film's producer Frank Taylor had seen Ann-Margret work and invited the young performer to visit the "Dry Lakes" location site. Marilyn's stand-in, Evelyn Moriarty, recalls that just before the lunch break Marilyn spotted the teenage beauty. She turned to Evelyn and asked, "Who is that girl with the long dark hair?" Evelyn replied that she was singing in a lounge in Reno. At which point, Taylor brought the shy Ann-Margret over to meet the star. Marilyn sensed the importance of the meeting to the young singer and was gracious and offered encouragement. Just a few years later, Ann-Margret, now a star herself, would inherit Evelyn Moriarty as her own stand-in, an association that continues to this day.

In an interview, John Huston was asked about certain actors who are not terribly impressive in person, yet achieve some sort of magic through the eye of the camera. Huston replied, "I never felt, for example, Marilyn Monroe's highly publicized appeal in person. But it was obviously there on the screen. I think the camera is simply a better observer than the human eye. It sees into the soul somehow." And he added, ". . . On the screen it comes across as though incandescent lights have been thrown on." In the midst of *The Misfits* production, Marilyn would be hospitalized for overexhaustion. Only 12 days after completion, Clark Gable would die from a heart attack allegedly brought on by exertions imposed during filming. After Gable's death in November, 1960, his wife Kay Williams Gable said, "It wasn't the physical exertion that did it. It was the horrible tension, that eternal waiting, waiting, waiting."

Soon after completing *The Misfits*, Marilyn and Miller, no longer the lovebirds they once were, divorced in Juarez, Mexico, in January, 1961. She then suffered another collapse, and entered Payne Whitney Psychiatric Clinic in New York for psychiatric care. "I'm locked up with all these poor, nutty people," Marilyn wrote Lee Strasberg. "I'm sure to end up a nut if I stay in this nightmare. Please help me. This is the last place I should be. I'm on the dangerous floor. It's like a cell." Later, Marilyn was transferred to the Neurological Institute at Presbyterian Hospital.

Arthur Miller married a third time, to photographer-journalist Inge Morath. He was once asked about the continuing fascination with Marilyn years after her death. "It's just exploitative," he said. "If it weren't her, it would be somebody else. They're just making money on her." He called it "just greed" and added, "the same thing she had in her life is what she's got in her death." Marilyn's life began crumbling under the strain of living in a fishbowl. The media surrounded her like vultures, snapping her picture and barraging her with questions. Some friends were frightened that Marilyn was on the brink of taking her own life. When Marilyn was released from Presbyterian Hospital, she became the constant companion of ex-husband Joe DiMaggio, and they traveled to Florida where he was batting coach for the Yankees at their spring training camp.

Marilyn returned to Hollywood and moved into an apartment at 886 Doheny Drive until publicist Pat Newcomb, an assistant to Arthur Jacobs, found a small but comfortable one-story Spanish Colonial hacienda in Brentwood. The house was one of two built over thirty years earlier at the end of 12305 Fifth Helena Drive. Both houses had ten-foot brick walls surrounding their fronts and, because they were on a dead-end, maximum privacy. In March, 1962, Marilyn attended the Hollywood Foreign Press Association's ceremonies with Mexican film writer Jose Bolanos at the Beverly Hilton Hotel. She was awarded their Golden Globe statuette as winner of "World Film Favorite," which was presented by close friend Rock Hudson. Marilyn appeared noticeably intoxicated on the telecast.

Marilyn began filming *Something's Got to Give* and it proved a prophetic title. The costume and hair tests revealed a dramatic change since *The Misfits*. She was slim and youthful looking, leading to rumors that she had undergone plastic surgery. The film was a remake of a 1940 Irene Dunne and Cary Grant comedy, *My Favorite Wife*. She was never happy with the script and delayed the starting date until April 23, 1962. Marilyn showed up on the set only a handful of days and there was talk that she was taking too many pills and was physically and mentally ill. The late George Cukor, who directed *Let's Make Love* and the uncompleted *Something's Got to Give*, believed Marilyn was "very observant, tough-minded and appealing, but adored and trusted the wrong people." Then Cukor thought a moment, "I liked her very much. I found her extremely intelligent— inarticulate but extremely intelligent. And driven. She was a very peculiar girl. And she was absolutely lovely looking. She looked better on the screen than she did in real life. She was very pretty in real life, but not as dazzling as she was on the screen."

Because Marilyn was having difficulty concentrating on her lines, George Cukor decided to film the swimming sequences, in which Marilyn takes a swim in the pool while Dean Martin watches from a balcony above. Marilyn wore a bathing suit when she went into the pool, then took it off, and completed the sequence nude. Hair-stylist Agnes Flanagan told *Playboy* magazine: "After she made the swimming sequence, she asked me, 'Do you think it was in bad taste?' I told her there was nothing suggestive about it at all. Her figure was more beautiful than it had ever been. A perfect body like Marilyn's looks beautiful nude, and beauty is never vulgar. Her animal magnetism, though sometimes flamboyant, always had an appealing, childlike quality which seemed to be poking fun at the very quality she symbolized."

In the midst of filming, Marilyn flew off to New York to appear at President John F. Kennedy's massive birthday party at Madison Square Garden on May 19, 1962, in front of an audience of 22,000. She sang "Happy Birthday," while Peter Lawford, making a joke of her reputation for tardiness, introduced her as "the late Marilyn Monroe." Reporting back to 20th Century-Fox, the old habits began taking over again. Sometimes she didn't show up, sometimes she'd arrive late, keeping co-stars Dean Martin, Cyd Charisse, Phil Silvers and Wally Cox waiting for hours. Her faithful maid, Hazel Washington, made gallons of black coffee to help her try to shake off the effects of the pills.

On June 1, 1962, Marilyn's 36th birthday, she made her last appearance on the swimming pool set (which was a reproduction of George Cukor's Mediterranean-style villa) on Stage 14. There was a celebration at the end of the day with birthday cake and champagne. A cake glittering with several dozen sparklers was rolled in. Marilyn wept when they all exploded at once. On Monday, June 4th, she reported that she was ill and couldn't work. When she didn't show up for several days, the 20th Century-Fox executives decided to shut the production down and fire its star. An angry Marilyn said, "Tell them [Fox executives] it's time some of the studio heads realized what they're doing. If there's something wrong with Hollywood, it starts at the top." Marilyn also sent the cast and crew telegrams, "Please believe me, it was not my doing. . . . I so looked forward to working with you." George Cukor, who had always been sensitive to her moods and state of health, and Dean Martin stood by her.

Marilyn Monroe's stand-in Evelyn Moriarty has remained loyal to her former "boss." Several months before Marilyn died, she telephoned Evelyn and asked if she would accompany her to New York on the night owl flight. "I wasn't on a picture, so I said okay. Marilyn sent her chauffeur, Rudy Kautsky, to pick me up and then we drove to the Beverly Hills Hotel, where Marilyn was living at the time. We smuggled her dog, Maf, on the plane with us. She just adored that little dog. Marilyn asked if I would stay a few days in New York, but I couldn't and took the next plane back to Los Angeles. She hated doing anything alone." Evelyn remembers the last conversation they would have. "It was on a Wednesday afternoon, August 1st, when we spoke for the last time. She was happy, very happy. She was in active negotiation with Fox, the picture was going to be put back into production. 'See, Evy,' she told me, 'we'll be back to work soon, just like I promised.' We spoke about ten minutes. Marilyn figured the picture would be resumed the following week, that's how close they were to settling their differences. Poor Marilyn, she was too good to be hurt so. I like to think, though, that for all the pain she did have some happy moments on this earth and that maybe I helped a little. Things just piled up and Marilyn went to pieces."

Marilyn continued to suffer from insomnia, to lapse into deeper and deeper depressions. She saw her psychiatrist almost daily. She visited Mexico City with Pat Newcomb, housekeeper Eunice Murray and hairstylist George Masters on the prowl for furniture and decorative pieces for the new house. Marilyn also found time for interviews and fashion layouts with *Life*, *Vogue*, and *Cosmopolitan* magazine. In one of her last interviews, with *Life*, Marilyn had this to say about being famous: "Fame to me certainly is only a temporary and a partial happiness—even for a waif, and I was brought up a waif. But fame is not really for a daily diet, that's not what fulfills you. It warms you a bit but the warming is temporary. It's like good caviar, you know—it's good to have caviar but not when you have to have it every meal and every day," Marilyn said. "I was never used to being happy, so that wasn't something I ever took for granted. I did sort of think, you know, marriage did that. You see, I was brought up differently from the average American child because the average child is brought up expecting to be happy—that's it, successful, happy and on time. Yet because of fame I was able to meet and marry two of the nicest men I'd ever met up to this time."

The final 24 hours of Marilyn's life are now clouded in controversy and speculation. We first learned Marilyn spent the day beside her swimming pool with Pat Newcomb, who acted as a buffer between 20th Century-Fox and the constant demands for interviews; she was actively guarding Marilyn's privacy. Early that evening (August 4th), Marilyn talked to Peter Lawford on the telephone. Marilyn and hairdresser Julius Bengtsson, in the company of Peter and Patricia (Kennedy) Lawford, had flown to Lake Tahoe to see Frank Sinatra's show at the Cal-Neva Lodge. According to some sources, Sam Giancana (the Chicago Mafia boss) was also in the Sinatra party. Marilyn also spoke with Joe DiMaggio, Jr., the baseball star's son by his first marriage to actress Dorothy Arnold. At some point during the evening there was another phone call, or perhaps Marilyn made a call, or attempted to. One or the other event occurred. Marilyn reportedly couldn't sleep and called her psychiatrist, Dr. Ralph Greenson. He suggested a drive to the beach, but she didn't go. At around eight p.m., Marilyn closed and locked her bedroom door. She was never seen alive again. Housekeeper Eunice Murray saw the light on in Marilyn's room around midnight. This was unusual but not alarming. When the light remained on until three a.m., Murray panicked. Marilyn ignored her loud knocks on the door. Murray said she went outside the house and from the French window could see that Marilyn was clutching the telephone receiver in her hand, lying motionless across the bed. Murray summoned Dr. Greenson, who, when he arrived, broke the French window with a fireplace poker and gained entry to her bedroom. They discovered Marilyn cold and lifeless.

An empty bottle of Nembutals was found near Marilyn's body. Incredibly, though, no residue of these pills was ever found in her stomach when an autopsy was performed. The evidence pointed to all the classic features of a homicide—but that theory has never been proven. And the phone call. Who was it that Marilyn had been talking to? Many have suggested, with authority, that it was Robert Kennedy, then the Attorney General of the United States, or President John F. Kennedy. Peter Lawford maintained that the calls had nothing to do with the Kennedy family. Lawford always confessed that he felt responsible for her death. "I blame myself," he said. "Marilyn phoned around six p.m. to cancel a dinner invitation, 'Peter, I don't think I'm going to make it tonight because I just don't feel well,' said a depressed sounding Marilyn. 'Will you say goodby to Pat, and to Jack and to yourself, because you're a nice guy.' I was the very last person to speak to her, and if I had acted quickly, she would be alive today. I have lived with that ever since. I should have gone to her house. I didn't do it." Coroner Dr. Thomas Noguchi, known as "coroner to the stars," reported Marilyn's death was "probable suicide." The coroner's investigator who signed Marilyn's death certificate now claims he was forced to sign the document even though he believed the investigation of her death was incomplete.

Joe DiMaggio took charge of her funeral at the Westwood Village Funeral Chapel, and refused to allow many of the Hollywood crowd, including Peter Lawford and Frank Sinatra, to be present during the last rites. Lee Strasberg read the eulogy that he prepared. "She had a luminous quality—a combination of wistfulness, radiance, yearning—to set her apart and yet made everyone wish to be a part of it, to share in the childish naïvete which was at once so shy and yet so vibrant," Strasberg said. Walter Winchell took charge of the press. There were over two thousand fans lined up four deep surrounding the Westwood Funeral Park.

Marilyn's mother died in her sleep on March 11, 1984. She was eighty-three years old and had been living at the Gainesville Nursing Center, a convalescent hospital.

In late 1985, because of the enormous amount of publicity caused by Anthony Summers' book *Goddess: The Secret Lives of Marilyn Monroe* and two TV documentaries, the Los Angeles County grand jury was pressured to look into Marilyn's death. The issue of whether to open an investigation was under review by the grand jury's criminal justice committee, which recommended against reopening the 1962 case.

Marilyn's death was an inherent risk of the game she was playing, a game whose frivolous rules both hid and revealed a deeply serious struggle. The form that struggle took was self-destructive. Marilyn Monroe was not so much a victim as a casualty. *Something's Got To Give*, and it did.

SHATTERED DREAMS

The following actresses all went through the same Hollywood experience, presented as creatures of the cosmetic myth. First came the initial splash, the adoration of fans, and, for some, a brief moment of fame. In true fan magazine fashion, when the dream factory was at its dreamiest, they were the real-life Hollywood Cinderella Girls, who all shared a pathetic end. In some cases, the circumstances of their last hours are unclear, clouded with mystery and rumors of foul play. For others, suicide, scandal, drugs, accidents, or alcohol ended their misery. They burst from obscurity into the spotlight of the studio image makers, suggesting both independence and vulnerability. They are but a few of Hollywood's saddest and heartbreaking stories.

The death of *Thelma Todd*, 30, was a bizarre tale. The scandal was fueled by the cloak of secrecy which was wrapped around her death from the start. An ex-Miss Massachusetts, she became the perfect foil for the the Marx Brothers in *Monkey Business* (1931) and *Horse Feathers* (1932), and was known for her infectious gaiety and comic ability. Thelma had recently completed *The Bohemian Girl* (1936) when she was found dead, slumped over the wheel of her Lincoln Phaeton, by her maid, a week before Christmas, 1935. She had attended a party given in her honor by Ida Lupino at the Trocadero nightclub two nights earlier. Her chauffeur drove Thelma to her beach restaurant, Thelma Todd's Sidewalk Cafe, around four a.m. Above the club, on the second floor, she shared a home with her partner and lover, director Roland West. From the highway, Thelma climbed the 271 steps to the garage behind the cafe. Forgetting her keys (as was theorized) and unable to wake

West, she went into the twin garage and settled into her car to await morning. The ignition was switched on, but the battery was discharged. "Either she went to sleep with the motor running or was overcome before she could help herself," said the coroner. Her attorney thought it was the work of her mob connections. The case of "The Ice-Cream Blonde" remained one of the Tinseltown's most intriguing puzzles until the massive coverup by both the industry and the LAPD was unraveled in 1987. It was learned that Roland West had locked the garage "to teach her a lesson" because of her tardy return home, not thinking Thelma might asphyxiate. Due in part to Busby Berkeley's murder trail (which got underway on the day Thelma's body was found), it was felt that the true story of her death should not be revealed. Detectives believed that West's confession was meaningless "because he'd have the best lawyers," according to Thelma's boss, Hal Roach. No one was ever indicted for the death of Thelma Todd.

The most spectacular of all Hollywood suicides is perhaps that of PEG ENTWISTLE, 24, a sadly wasted talent who had just completed a role in RKO's *Thirteen Women* (1932) with Irene Dunne. Divorced from actor Robert Keith, she was a graduate of the Theatre Guild. In September, 1932, beset by the fact that there were no other offers, the emotionally charged actress climbed up the side of Mt. Lee to the top of the fifty-foot "Hollywoodland" electric sign and plunged to her death from atop the letter "H." A suicide note to her uncle was found in her purse: "I am afraid I am a coward. I am sorry for everything. If I could have done this long ago I could have saved a lot of pain."

DOROTHY DELL, 19, was climbing toward the pinnacle of success. First as Miss New Orleans, then Miss Universe of 1930 and appearances in the Ziegfield Follies, she went on to become the voluptuous nightclub singer pal of Shirley Temple in *Little Miss Marker* (1934). She was Paramount's newest "sex symbol" and their answer to Fox's Alice Faye. Returning from a party in the Altadena Hills, she and her date were killed in a car crash, in June, 1934. Their automobile went over an embankment, hit a telephone pole, and rammed into a boulder.

Dorothy was killed instantly, her escort died a few hours later. A girlhood chum of Dorothy Lamour, her last completed film was the posthumous *Shoot the Works* (1934), in which she introduced the haunting "With My Eyes Wide Open, I'm Dreaming."

Cecil B. DeMille's discovery HELEN BURGESS, 20, was emerging as a bright talent. Her film debut was in DeMille's *The Plainsman* (1936), as Buffalo Bill Cody's (James Ellison) wife. She caught a severe cold while in the midst of shooting *A Night of Mystery* (1937). It developed into pneumonia and she died in April, 1937. Paramount decided against refilming her few remaining scenes and instead used a double. A similar situation would occur two months later, when "The Blond Bombshell," *Jean Harlow*, would succumb to uremic poisoning while filming Metro-Goldwyn-Mayer's *Saratoga*.

Polish-born LYDA ROBERTI, 31, was a platinum blond comedienne and one who was destined to burn out far too quickly. Her career kept zooming at Paramount (1932 through 1935) with her sexy, language-mangling voice, singing "Mata Machree" in *Million Dollar Legs* (1932) and appearing in *The Big Broadcast of 1936*. She replaced Thelma Todd as Patsy Kelly's bosom pal in a series of Hal Roach shorts, prior to a fatal heart attack, which she suffered while bending over to tie a shoelace in March, 1938.

PEGGY SHANNON, 34, was promoted by Paramount as the successor to Clara Bow and replaced the ailing "It" girl in *The Secret Call* (1931) opposite Richard Arlen. She was paired with Spencer Tracy in Fox's *The Painted Woman* (1932) and *Society Girl* (1932), but by the late 1930s she had become a steady drinker with increasingly erratic behavior. The once-so-hot career ended with *Street of Missing Women* (1940). In May, 1941, her husband found her dead at the kitchen table, with an empty glass and burnt out cigarette near her hand, in their run-down North Hollywood apartment.

GLORIA DICKSON, 28, loved to drink and party on the Hollywood social circuit. She and another unknown from Idaho,

Lana Turner, made their auspicious starts in Warner Brothers' *They Won't Forget* (1937). But within a few years, Gloria's curious career floundered from too much liquor and pills, appearing wan and blowzy in *Lady of Burlesque* (1943) with Barbara Stanwyck. She was found burned to death in her Hollywood Hills home in April 1945. Apparently trapped on the upper level of the hilltop house, she made her way to the bathroom, where her badly charred body was found. Friends believed it was an unfortunate accident caused by a carelessly flipped cigarette.

Ethereal looking PEGGY O.'NEAL, 21, was the epitome of healthy sexiness in *Song of the Open Road* (1944) and *It's a Pleasure* (1945). Her agent Vic Orsatti had just negotiated a Paramount contract in April, 1945. On the day she was to sign the agreement, Peggy was found dead from the effect of sleeping pills. It was the climax of a violent quarrel with her screenwriter lover, after "he walked out on her," said a friend.

Impresario Earl Carroll's favorite star was BERYL WALLACE, 38. Her movie parts were unremarkable compared to her appearances in Carroll's spectacular Hollywood nightclub reviews. They were romantically linked for several years. Beryl was killed in a plane crash en route to New York City in June, 1948, along with Earl Carroll. Their ashes are entombed at Forest Lawn Memorial Park. On top of the crypt is a large replica of Carroll's own hands holding a life-sized figure symbolizing the statuesque Beryl.

Before Oona O'Neill married Charlie Chaplin, she was slated for the second lead in *Three Russian Girls* (1944) with Anna Sten. When she bowed out, MIMI FORSYTHE, 30, who never acted before, was handed the plum role. She subsequently married producer Benedict Bogeaus and retired. Beset with depression and an emotional breakdown when Bogeaus left her to marry actress Dolores Moran, Mimi took her own life in August, 1952.

Lovely ABIGAIL "TOMMYE" ADAMS, 32, had made a half-hearted attempt at a career, mostly low budget Westerns (*Colorado Serenade*, 1946). Her free-wheeling lifestyle proved frustrating. Divorced from Lyle Talbot, she had an endless stream of male conquests and a stormy ten-year involvement with George Jessel. The frivolous playgirl was found dead in a tawdry Sunset Strip apartment, dead from excessive drinking combined with drugs in February, 1955.

ONA MUNSON, 52, scored her most important success as Clark Gable's mistress in *Gone With the Wind* (1939). The role of notorious Belle Watling, the leading madam of Atlanta's red-light district, was a personal triumph. Her roles gradually diminished, with the exception of Josef von Sternberg's *The Shanghai Gesture* (1941). In 1952, Ona underwent major surgery and suffered increasingly from depression afterward. In February, 1955, she was found dead in her New York apartment by her husband, set designer Eugene Berman. She left a cryptic note, "This is the only way I know to be free again." Her last stage appearance was in a 1953 New York revival of *First Lady*.

Czech beauty MIROSLAVA, 25, had her career first catch fire in *The Brave Bulls* (1951) with Anthony Quinn, followed by a *Life* magazine cover and a co-starring role with Joel McCrea in *Stranger on Horseback* (1955). She moved to Mexico City and was emerging as one of that country's biggest stars. Despondent, she took her life in March, 1955, over the bullfighter Luis Miguel Dominguin.

A Marilyn Monroe double, PAT WILLIAMS, 24, was Marie Wilson's understudy and subsequent replacement in *Ken Murray's Blackouts* for its New York engagement. During the Hollywood run of the show, Pat was pursued by Howard Hughes, who showered her with flowers. When *Blackouts* closed, Pat held contracts with Metro-Goldwyn-Mayer and Columbia Pictures, and appeared most notably in *Sound Off* (1952) opposite Mickey Rooney. Then everything began to go sour. Unable to find any movie work, once Columbia dropped her, Pat worked as a Las Vegas showgirl. In August, 1956, she was found sitting in a chair, wearing a bright red dress and in full stage makeup—dead! Her skin was splotched with the telltale blue spots of barbiturate poisoning.

The sloe-eyed beauty MARTA TOREN, 31, came to Universal fresh from Stockholm's Royal Dramatic Theatre. She made her Hollywood debut in *Casbah* (1948), followed by *Sword in the Desert* (1949) and *Sirocco* (1951) with Humphrey Bogart. She left Hollywood to work in European films, winning awards for *Maddalena* (1954). She died suddenly while appearing in a play in her native Sweden, in February, 1957, of a brain tumor.

DOREEN WOODBURY, 27, never felt that she was cut out to be a movie star—not a really important one. Columbia's Henry Cohn thought otherwise and ordered a build-up for the ex-dancer of *Son of Sinbad* (1955). Cohn thought she had a certain potential, and launched her in *The Shadow on the Window* (1957). While in rehearsals for *Pal Joey* (1957), Doreen suddenly killed herself over a broken romance in February, 1957.

Pretty, doll-like JUDY TYLER, 24, scored on Broadway in Rodgers & Hammerstein's *Pipe Dream* in 1955. She had just completed MGM's *Jailhouse Rock* (1957) with Elvis Presley and was awaiting the results of her *Marjorie Morningstar* screentest, when she and actor husband Gregory Lafayette were killed in an automobile crash outside of Billy the Kid, Wyoming, in July, 1957. They were en route to New York, where Judy was to become a regular panelist on the popular 1950s game show "Pantomime Quiz," and then do a summer stock tour of *Desire Under the Elms* with her husband.

German-born ROSE STRADNER, 45, was one of Louis B. Mayer's European discoveries during his eventful 1937 talent search. Other talent acquired on the same trip were Greer Garson, Ilona Massey and Hedy Lamarr. Rose was introduced in *The Last Gangster* (1937) as Edward G. Robinson's wife. She interrupted her career for marriage to writer-producer Joseph L. Mankiewicz, but later revitalized her career in *The Keys of the Kingdom* (1944), as the memorable Mother Superior. Troubled and bitter, in September, 1958, she was found dead of an overdose of sleeping pills in her Mt. Kisco, New York, home.

Rebellious LYNNE BAGGETT, 42, was wed to Academy

Award winning producer Sam Spiegel, a connoisseur of beautiful women. She showed some promise in *D.O.A.* (1949) and *The Mob* (1951) with Broderick Crawford. Then it all went wrong, ending in blaring headlines, with her serving 50 days in the county jail for the hit-and-run death of a nine-year-old boy. She then ended up partially paralyzed from drug addiction and diagnosed as a chronic depressed neurotic. Lynne eventually did succeed in a suicide attempt in March, 1960. A large quantity of sleeping pills had ended her torment.

The recklessly talented DIANA BARRYMORE, 38, and alcoholism were no strangers. The daughter of John Barrymore, she was brought to Hollywood amid a hoopla of fanfare for Universal's *Eagle Squadron* (1942) as Robert Stack's sweetheart. When her next film, *Between Us Girls* (1942) was dismissed as a total botch, she began drinking. It soon became a serious problem and stumbling block toward further advancement in her movie career, and Universal eventually broke her contract. Her tawdry 1957 autobiography, *Too Much, Too Soon*, was filmed by Warner Brothers. Her excessive drinking and outrageous behavior finally exhausted her, and Diana was found dead in her New York apartment in January, 1960. The police concluded that there was no evidence of suicide or foul play. Diana's friend, the late Tennessee Williams, always claimed that she had "blood streaming out of her mouth and that there was a heavy marble ashtray shattered against the wall and other evidence of struggle and violence," none of which is recorded in police reports.

Rambunctious, wise-cracking BEVERLY WILLS, 29, was a carbon copy of her famous mother, Joan Davis. During the 1950s, Beverly lent her own comedic talents to *Skirts Ahoy* (1952), *Small Town Girl* (1953) and *Some Like It Hot* (1959). She had just completed *Son of Flubber* (1963), when in October, 1963, an early morning fire killed Beverly, her two young sons, and her grandmother. She apparently fell asleep while smoking in the bedroom of her Palm Springs home. It was the same house where her mother suffered a fatal heart attack at 53, in May, 1961.

KARYN KUPCINET, 22, was a product of the Actors Studio and the daughter of noted Chicago columnist and television host Irv Kupcinet. She made her film debut with Jerry Lewis in *The Ladies' Man* (1961) and appeared on the TV series "The Gertrude Berg Show" with Skip Ward. The vibrant young actress was found strangled during Thanksgiving week 1963, in her West Hollywood apartment, by an unknown assailant. Despite a full-scale investigation, the case was never solved. For over twenty years it has remained a lingering Hollywood mystery. In a 1976 interview, her father said, "We have a good idea who did it, but nothing we could ever prove."

Mexican-born PINA PELLICER, 24, was an extraordinarily gifted actress, giving a star caliber performance with Marlon Brando in *One-Eyed Jacks* (1961). Her passionate liaison with Brando lasted only a short time. Pina was the recipient of the San Sebastian Film Festival award for best actress for *Autumn Days* (1962). Overworked and embittered, she died by her own hand, in Mexico City, just before Christmas, 1964.

CAROLYN MITCHELL (a.k.a. Barbara Ann Thomasen), 29, was an ex-Miss Muscle Beach of Santa Monica. She had abandoned her career following a misbegotten effort, *Cry Baby Killer* (1958), opposite Jack Nicholson, to become Mickey Rooney's fifth wife. In January, 1966, while Rooney was hospitalized, she was shot to death by her lover, Milos Milocevic, a Yugoslavian chauffeur for French star Alain Delon. They were found dead in the Brentwood bedroom of the Rooney home, a murder-suicide. She had been trying to break off the affair.

Senorita ESTELITA RODRIGUEZ, 50, was a perennial favorite of mentor Herbert J. Yates. Some sources believe she was "the other woman" in his life. The Republic Pictures chief displayed Estelita's tempestuous charms in such quickies as *Cuban Fireball* (1951), *The Fabulous Senorita* (1952) and *Tropical Heat Wave* (1952). She was enthusiastic about starring in Lupe Velez's life story, when she was found dead on the kitchen floor of her North Hollywood home in March, 1966. The cause of death was never made public. "Pappy" Yates had died a month earlier, while Estelita's ex-husband, actor Grant Withers, had taken his own life in 1959.

Wholesome MARJIE MILLAR, 35, was a blond girl-next-door ingenue whom mogal Hal Wallis took an immediate personal interest in. A Stephens College graduate, she was effectively featured in Paramount's *Money From Home* (1953) and *About Mrs. Leslie* (1954). When an auto accident left her partially crippled in 1958, she returned to her hometown of Tacoma, Washington, to operate a dancing school. In April, 1966, Marjie died from the lingering aftereffects (16 leg operations) of the car accident.

HELEN WALKER, 47, fluttered in a brief blaze of fame, with Alan Ladd in *Lucky Jordan* (1942), and as a capable dramatic actress; she was the unscrupulous psychologist in *Nightmare Alley* (1947). On New Year's Eve, 1946, she was involved in an auto crash. A soldier Helen had given a ride to was killed. She suffered severe fractures and as a result lost out on *Heaven Only Knows*. Her stalled career soon disintegrated, complicated by a long siege of alcoholism. At a 1955 birthday party, Helen arrived bearing gifts wrapped in her old movie stills. "They're not good for anything else," she said bitterly. She then proceeded to get very drunk. In time, the alcohol pushed Helen toward paranoia and emotional collapse. She'd been forgotten when cancer claimed her life in March, 1968.

DOROTHY ABBOTT, 41, was spotted by Paramount while parading at Earl Carroll's nightclub. Her pretty naturalness carried her through *Night Has a Thousand Eyes* (1948), *A Connecticut Yankee* (1949) and as Jack Webb's girlfriend-secretary on TV's "Dragnet." In a shroud of depression, she took her own life in 1968, over the split-up of her marriage to Rudy Diaz, a narcotics officer turned actor.

JOAN TABOR, 35, often worked on TV as a foil for such comedians as Jerry Lewis (with whom she appeared in *The Bellboy* 1960), Bob Hope and Jack Benny. On stage she co-starred with husband Broderick Crawford in *Born Yesterday* and *Dead Pigeon*. The marriage was a stormy one. A year after they divorced, in

December, 1968, Joan was found dead from "an accidental overdose of drugs." Newspapers reported she had the flu for about a week and had been taking several kinds of drugs.

The role of exotic "Tremartini" in *The Story of Dr. Wassell* (1944) was sought after by Simone Simon, Yvonne De Carlo and Elena Verdugo. The actress finally chosen by Cecil B. DeMille was unknown CAROL THURSTON, 48. She soon found it difficult to overcome portraying innocent native girls. Her career came to a virtual halt by the mid-1950s. No longer an enticing ingenue, Carol was fighting a losing battle to find her true identity when she killed herself on New Year's Eve 1969.

SUZANNE DALBERT's, 43, Hollywood sojourn was a brief one. A Parisian sex kitten discovery of Hal Wallis, she made her bow as the vampish student in Paramount's *The Accused* (1948). When her career failed to ignite, Suzanne returned to France, where she swallowed a bottle full of sleeping pills in 1971.

The Italian import PIER ANGELI, 39, was often described as fragile but indestructible. One of MGM's most radiant young actresses, she starred with Kirk Douglas in *The Story of Three Loves* (1953) and with Paul Newman in *Somebody Up There Likes Me* (1956). When her much-publicized marriage to Vic Damone ended, she returned to Italy. In 1971, a lonely and nearly forgotten Pier returned to Hollywood at the invitation of Debbie Reynolds. She was staying at the home of drama coach Helena Sorrell, who found Pier dead by an overdose of barbituates in September, 1971.

BELLA DARVI, 44, suffered the fate of most of Darryl F. Zanuck's European imports. When her performance in *The Egyptian* (1954) and *The Racers* (1955) failed to register at the box-office, her career and affair with Zanuck fizzled out. Bella quietly returned to the Monte Carlo gambling tables, where the limelight was brighter. Her behavior became wildly impulsive and she found her safest haven in liquor and drugs. In September, 1971, Bella was found dead, one week after she had taken her life by opening the gas jets on her cooking stove.

Everything happened so quickly for PEGGIE CASTLE, 45, one of the 1950s' real Golden Girls. She snatched some important film parts, as Bette Davis' rebellious daughter in *Payment on Demand* (1951), and in two pictures based on Mickey Spillane's detective stories, *The Long Wait* (1954) and *I, the Jury* (1953), as the psychiatrist-killer. She was discharged from Camarillo State Hospital only a few months when she was found dead in a shabby apartment above Hollywood Boulevard, in August, 1973, a victim of alcoholism.

JUDITH RAWLINS, 36, was a vivacious girl, groomed by Paramount and showcased in *G.I. Blues* (1960) with Elvis Presley. The daughter of a musician, she liked to date singers such as Vic Damone, Bobby Rydell and Presley. Her career was brief and she became Damone's secretary, later his second wife. But soon after the marriage crumbled, Judith commited suicide in their Bel Air home in March, 1974.

The brutal death of BARBARA COLBY, 36, as she left a yoga class has never been solved. The ex-daughter-in-law of Ethel Merman, she was featured in *California Split* (1974) and *Memory of Us* (1975). Barbara had scored a critical success in a local Los Angeles production of *Murderous Angels*. Police still wonder, could the shooting be linked to the play, an act of vengeful execution? The robbers demanded money—but that may have been a coverup in the July, 1975, shootout mystery.

Red-haired GEORGIA DAVIS, 54, began her career as the protégée of Howard Hawks, with a small role in *Ball of Fire* (1941). MGM signed her up and immediately put her into *The Harvey Girls* (1946), as one of Angela Lansbury's dancehall girls. In 1945, she married Red Skelton and her film career stopped. After they divorced in 1971, Georgia's drinking soon escalated into chronic alcoholism. The turmoil of her personal life ended in May, 1976, when she fired a bullet into her head in her Palm Springs home. It was exactly 18 years ago to the day after her eight-year-old son, Richard Skelton, had died of leukemia.

The name of ALLISON HAYES, 47, conjures up B-movies like *The Disembodied* (1957), *Attack of the Fifty-Foot Woman* (1958) and

The Hypnotic Eye (1960). Shortly after her death from cancer in February, 1977, some macabre facts surfaced. It appears that several years prior to her death, Allison was exposed to large doses of radiation during a desert film location. The exposure ultimately cut short her life.

MAGGIE McNAMARA, 48, had a model's classically sculpted face. As a teen model, she appeared on scores of magazine covers. She was nominated for an Academy Award for the role of the naïve virgin who let herself be lured to William Holden's apartment in *The Moon is Blue* (1953). By current standards, it's an extremely trivial work. There were also worthy parts in *Three Coins in the Fountain* (1954) and *Prince of Players* (1955) opposite Richard Burton. She suffered a nervous breakdown following the breakup of her marriage to writer David Swift. When she died from an overdose of pills in February, 1978, Maggie was employed as a secretary in New York City and totally alienated from the world of show business.

Hugh Hefner once said about his *Playboy* centerfold subjects, "They marry famous people and become well-known and well-connected." But a few weren't so lucky. The girl launched as the 1970s "Queen of the B Movies," CLAUDIA JENNINGS, 29, was voted as "1970 Playmate of the Year." Boyfriend Hefner soon discovered her talents extended far beyond mere beauty; she appeared in the off-Broadway revival of *Dark of the Moon*, then specialized in sleaze and violence films, including *Truck Stop Women* (1974), *Deathsport* (1978) with David Carradine and her last, *Fast Company* (1979), opposite John Saxon. She became swept up with the Hollywood drug scene with pal VICKI MORGAN (the murdered mistress of Alfred Bloomingdale). In October, 1979, as she was driving to an interview for the remake of *The Postman Always Rings Twice*, on the Pacific Coast Highway, Claudia's Volkswagen convertible drifted across the center divider and ran head-on into a pickup truck. Claudia died while attempts were made to free her from the wreckage.

The dazzling, gorgeous face and figure of DOROTHY STRATTEN, 20, evoked memories of a young Marilyn Monroe in *They All Laughed* (1982). Her untimely death, two years earlier, in August, 1980, cut short what many predicted was sure to have become an outstanding film journey. She was found shot to death in the bedroom of her estranged husband, Paul Snider, who had then committed suicide. He had become insanely jealous of her relationship with director Peter Bogdanovich. When Snider balked at being pushed aside, he became her nemesis. It was a classical plot with contemporary embellishments. Accusations by Dorothy's lover, Bogdanovich, in his best-seller *The Killing of the Unicorn*, portray her as the victim of the *Playboy* machine. Just a few months before Dorothy died, she was crowned Hugh Hefner's reigning "1980 Playmate of the Year," just ten years after the equally tragic Claudia Jennings won the title.

Bright and bubbly, JENNY MAXWELL, 39, flunked her test for *Lolita*, but went on to saucy ingenue roles in *Blue Denim* (1959) and *Blue Hawaii* (1961) with Elvis Presley, then quit the business cold. In June, 1981, she and her husband, noted attorney "Tip" Roeder, were mysteriously shot to death outside their posh Beverly Hills condominium. The mystery surrounding the exact circumstances of their brutal murder still baffles friends and the police.

There was a constant, striking aura of sadness about BRENDA BENET, 35, who was quite successful as a soap opera villainess on NBC-TV's "Days of Our Lives." But the viewers saw only the character's evil deeds, not the real-life traumas of an actress who struggled against personal tragedies. Married to actor Bill Bixby, she put her promising film career (*Walking Tall*, 1973) on the back burner. Estranged from Bixby, she died of an apparently self-inflicted gunshot wound in April, 1973. Brenda had been deeply depressed and despondent ever since her six-year-old son had died a year earlier of a severe throat infection.

DOMINIQUE DUNNE, 22, made her film bow in *Poltergeist* (1982), as the older sister in a family troubled by ghosts in a suburban home. On Halloween Eve, October, 1982, she encountered her own real-life horror story. Her former live-in boyfriend, John Sweeney, strangled her during a quarrel outside her West Hollywood home. The young actress died six days later, without regaining consciousness. Investigators claim the argument was over Dominique's wanting to end the relationship and Sweeney wanting to move back in. She was the daughter of a literary family that includes uncle John Gregory Dunne, aunt Joan Didion, father Dominick Dunne, and brother, actor Griffin Dunne.

The gentle loveliness of SUNNY JOHNSON, 30, was quite evident as the frustrated figure-skater in *Flashdance* (1983), *National Lampoon's Animal House* (1978) and *Where the Buffalo Roam* (1980). Her career was blossoming (she had just completed the TV series "Bay City Blues") when she became seriously ill, and was found unconscious in the bathroom of her Hollywood apartment. She died a few days later, in June, 1984, having suffered a cerebral hemorrhage.

CAROL WAYNE, 42, was an old-fashioned type of movie starlet, best known as Johnny Carson's zany "Matinee Lady" on "The Tonight Show," and more impressive in *Heartbreakers* (1984). She allegedly was fighting a cocaine and alcohol dependency when she jetted off to a Mexico resort to "clear her head." In January, 1985, a fisherman discovered her lifeless body floating in Santiago Bay at Manzanillo, on Mexico's Gold Coast. The autopsy report disclosed that she had drowned.

The enchanting smile of SAMANTHA SMITH, 13, captured American and Russian hearts when she visited the Soviet Union in 1982 as a guest of then-President Yuri Andropov. But it was to be a tragically short life. She died with her father, and six others, in the fiery crash of a Bar Harbor Airlines plane in August, 1985, while returning home to Maine during a break in Robert Wagner's short-lived TV series, "Lime Street." Samantha had written a book about her experiences in Russia and hosted an interview show on the Disney Channel before landing the role of Wagner's daughter. "She touched the world, and she touched us too. We are quite simply devastated," Robert Wagner said.

SUSAN CABOT, 59, became typecast as an exotic temptress, frequently in harem attire in a string of Universal epics, *Flame of*

Araby (1951), *Tomahawk* (1951) and *Son of Ali Baba* (1952). On rare occasions, she showed surprising dramatic flare, as in *Machine Gun Kelly* (1958) opposite Charles Bronson. In 1959, she was romantically linked to Jordan's King Hussein. The two never publicly acknowledged that they were lovers, but reports that they were having an affair lasted for over a year. In later years, Susan spent her free time involved in several charitable activities, including the American Film Institute. The diminutive actress was found bludgeoned to death in her expensive hilltop (San Fernando Valley) home in December, 1986. Her dwarfed son Timothy Roman, 22, was charged with the brutal murder. She was said to have suffered recurrent mental breakdowns and to have withdrawn into a reclusive existence in her once elegant home, which was falling into disrepair.

In *A Patch of Blue* (1965), ELIZABETH HARTMAN, 43, gave a sensitive performance as the blind girl who falls in love with Sidney Poitier. It earned her an Academy Award nomination. Although important roles followed in *The Group* (1966), *You're a Big Boy Now* (1967) and *The Beguiled* (1971), her career was never to regain its full lustre. In June, 1987, she leaped to her death from a window of her fifth floor studio apartment in Pittsburgh, Pa. She had recently been an outpatient at Western Psychiatric Institute and Clinic in Pittsburgh.

The angelic moppet, HEATHER O'ROURKE, 12, was spotted by Steven Spielberg in the MGM commissary and cast in *Poltergeist* (1982). As the child tormented by evil spirits, Heather delivered the key line, "They're heeere!" She returned for the sequels, *Poltergeist II* (1986) and had just completed *Poltergeist III* (1988), when she died during complications from a congenital intestinal obstruction in San Diego, California, in February, 1988. She was the second actress from the original *Poltergeist* to die unexpectedly.